For Nonconformism:
Max Horkheimer and Friedrich Pollock

Historical Materialism Book Series

The Historical Materialism Book Series is a major publishing initiative of the radical left. The capitalist crisis of the twenty-first century has been met by a resurgence of interest in critical Marxist theory. At the same time, the publishing institutions committed to Marxism have contracted markedly since the high point of the 1970s. The Historical Materialism Book Series is dedicated to addressing this situation by making available important works of Marxist theory. The aim of the series is to publish important theoretical contributions as the basis for vigorous intellectual debate and exchange on the left.

The peer-reviewed series publishes original monographs, translated texts, and reprints of classics across the bounds of academic disciplinary agendas and across the divisions of the left. The series is particularly concerned to encourage the internationalization of Marxist debate and aims to translate significant studies from beyond the English-speaking world.

For a full list of titles in the Historical Materialism Book Series available in paperback from Haymarket Books, visit: www.haymarketbooks.org/series_collections/1-historical-materialism.

For Nonconformism: Max Horkheimer and Friedrich Pollock

The Other Frankfurt School

Nicola Emery

Translated by
Karen Whittle

Haymarket Books
Chicago, IL

First published in 2022 by Brill Academic Publishers, The Netherlands
© 2022 Koninklijke Brill NV, Leiden, The Netherlands

Published in paperback in 2023 by
Haymarket Books
P.O. Box 180165
Chicago, IL 60618
773-583-7884
www.haymarketbooks.org

ISBN: 978-1-64259-997-8

Distributed to the trade in the US through Consortium Book Sales and Distribution (www.cbsd.com) and internationally through Ingram Publisher Services International (www.ingramcontent.com).

This book was published with the generous support of Lannan Foundation, Wallace Action Fund, and the Marguerite Casey Foundation.

Special discounts are available for bulk purchases by organizations and institutions. Please call 773-583-7884 or email info@haymarketbooks.org for more information.

Cover art and design by David Mabb. Cover art is a detail of *Construct 16, John Henry Dearle for Morris & Co, Compton / Kasimir Malevich, First Suprematist Textile Design*, paint and wallpaper mounted on linen (2005). Collection of the Barts Health NHS Trust.

Printed in the United States.

10 9 8 7 6 5 4 3 2 1

Library of Congress Cataloging-in-Publication data is available.

Contents

Preface VII
Acknowledgements IX
List of Figures X
Translator's Note XI

1 **For Nonconformism** 1
   1.1 Transgression, Autobiography, Philosophy 1
   1.2 Forms of Life 20
   1.3 Psyche and History 32
   1.4 Biopower and the Hidden Faculties of Existence (Eroticism, Friendship, Art) 47

2 **The Era of State Capitalism: Morphology and Genesis Starting from Friedrich Pollock** 77
   2.1 Friedrich Pollock's Ideal Type 77
   2.2 Between Domination and Welfare 98

3 **Expatriation, Disorientation, Islands** 117
   3.1 Leaving Germany (Eichmann Trial, Israel and the Atlantic Pact) 117
   3.2 Free from the Coercion of the Reality Principle (Switzerland, Little Utopia) 128
   3.3 Beyond Instrumental Architecture (the Houses in Montagnola) 148

4 **Automation and the Eclipse of Democracy** 171
   4.1 Era of Automation and Crisis: Pollock's Prognosis 171
   4.2 Is Critical Theory Antiquated? 179

5 **Critical Theory and Longing for the Other** 197
   5.1 The Absent Alterity 197
   5.2 Critique of Instrumental Reason and Religion 210
   5.3 Critical Judaism (beyond Identity, beyond Sovereignty, beyond Zionism) 215

Appendix: Figures 227
Bibliography 242
Index 250

Preface

Subject of a great many interpretations and much research, the vicissitudes of the famous Frankfurt Institute for Social Research nevertheless still reserve some little-known pages which have strangely fallen almost into oblivion or were perhaps never investigated. Occupying a fundamental place among these are those which concern the existential relationship and reciprocal intellectual influence that for over 50 years bound philosopher Max Horkheimer and economist Friedrich Pollock, protagonists of two parallel lives, one inconceivable without the other, in certain aspects *one almost the mirror of the other*. Posthumous reconstructions of the history of the Institute have almost always striven to make the Horkheimer-Adorno duo the fundamental core of the so-called Frankfurt School. Nevertheless, it was certainly not without reason that they dedicated their masterpiece, *Dialectic of Enlightenment*, to their common friend Friedrich Pollock.

The lifelong friendship of Max Horkheimer and Fritz Pollock began in their teenage years in the Jewish circles of Stuttgart. It developed with the foundation of the Institute for Social Research in Frankfurt and continued with their exile in the USA, their return to Germany during the difficult period of de-Nazification, and lastly, their final, shared exodus, planned down to the last detail, to go to live side by side in a small village, Montagnola, in the Italian-speaking part of Switzerland. Here Max and Fritz, then in their sixties and internationally famous, had two 'twin' houses built. Sharing the same garden, they spent a great deal of time together; they reorganised some of their works and also jointly wrote an aphoristic text (unpublished in English), a sort of diary of their later years, in which they almost seem to revive the Frankfurt Institute's original interdisciplinary programme, despite their altered theoretical and political positions, and real, increasingly radical aporias. They also wanted to somehow bring the legendary *Zeitschrift* back to life and above all to achieve 'freedom from the coercion of the reality principle', to go back 'to dreaming, to the forbidden, to [their] own original truth'. The ongoing desire to be able to live together, the *Beisammensein* which they continued to seek despite the reality of the *principium individuationis*, speaks of a friendship of extraordinary intensity, engaging emotion and intellect, reason and 'instinctual structure'. It was a friendship that led them to place the *decision as to one's own form of life* among the fundamental tasks of philosophy, so that it could acknowledge the due centrality of the relations between critique and existence, philosophy and autobiography, psyche and history, truth and art.

The aim of this book, in which the relationship with eroticism also holds a certain significance, just as it did in the story of Max and Fritz, starting from their youthful and transgressive *île heureuse*, is not to cast the utopia of their form of life – that unobjectifiable and undefinable dimension of existence that they taught in opposition to the era of biopolitics – in stone.

While mainly providing a referential perspective, and often intertwining philosophical theory with biographical aspects, this book reconstructs central moments in the bond between the philosopher and the economist. Not infrequently, the basis is provided by texts and letters never translated into English, and in some cases by documents unpublished or very rarely read even in Germany, such as the jointly written text *Späne*, their *Memorandums*, and not least Horkheimer's letters to the Swiss architect behind their houses, to whom Horkheimer gave planning suggestions which were then meticulously put into practice. Dealing with the 'totally administered society' of 'state capitalism', whose every aspect was supported by the triumph of 'automation' – topics on which at the time Pollock made far-sighted contributions – their *critical theory* then sought, despite it all, to confirm itself and to resist. While throwing themselves back into the practical truth of *nonconformism* and *proximity*, they prefigured the creation of 'collectives that are out-of-season, which can preserve the individual in genuine solidarity' ... even though at times their heterotopia felt obliged to 'descend into the catacombs' and to make their critical theory into a philosophy of survival. In any case, in light of this research, some interpretations aimed at disparaging the later years of Horkheimer's life, reproaching him for sitting back and failing to criticise the existent, as well as his 'inhibited productivity', seem to manifest some limits. Another aspect that can be seen to assume a different significance is their relationship with Judaism, seen as *longing for the wholly Other*, in contrast to the criticism of *statolatric* betrayal which they level against Israel. Indeed, this can be observed in their diagnosis, converging into a stateless ontology, which proclaims the primacy of ethics beyond the self-affirmative identity of being, on one hand reminiscent of the lesson of Schopenhauer, and on the other anticipating Levinas's ethics of proximity. Referential and reconstructive, at the same time the perspective developed in this book does not wish to disavow the partly novelesque nature of the truth.

Acknowledgements

I would like to thank Peppo Brivio, Carla Molteni, Anna Besso, Mathias Jehn and not least Anna Pianezzola Emery for the documents and information that they gave to me and the Canton Ticino Divisione della Cultura e degli Studi Universitari and Fondazione Max Horkheimer for supporting my research. I very much thank Martin Jay for recommending an English translation of the book, Sebastian Budgen for finding the right publishing slot and Karen Whittle for her great work and doggedness in checking the sources. The translation of the book has been made possible by the fundamental support of the Fondazione Max Horkheimer alongside a contribution from the municipality of Montagnola-Collina d'Oro.

Figures

1 Max Horkheimer and Friedrich Pollock on a path in Italian Switzerland (private archive). 227
2 The houses of Horkheimer and Pollock in Montagnola (Switzerland): colour painting, signed by architects Peppo Brivio and Rino Tami. The semi-detached layout shown here was not followed in the end (private collection). 228
3 The final site plan of the twin houses of Horkheimer and Pollock in Montagnola (Switzerland), architect Peppo Brivio (private archive). 229
4 Friedrich Pollock and Max Horkheimer, seated (private archive). 230
5 Carlota Pollock (private archive). 231
6 Horkheimer's house, photographed from the garden, still preserved in its original state (photo M. Peuckert, private archive). 232
7 Horkheimer's house and Pollock's adjacent house which, alas, has been completely transformed in a neoclassical style. Property speculation has nevertheless not aged to completely devastate the traces of the small utopia, still visible today in extremely proximity of the two hoses, as was originally planned (photo M. Peuckert, private archive) 232
8 Cover of the first English edition of F. Pollock's book, *The Economic and Social Consequences of Automation*, Basil Blackwell, Oxford, 1957. 233
9 Cover of the second German edition of F. Pollock's book, *Automation. Materialien zur Beurteilung ihrer ökonomischen und sozialen Folgen*, Europäische Verlaganstalt, Frankfurt am Main, 1964. 234
10 Horkheimer's home, Montagnola (Switzerland), interior: Max Horkheimer's study (photo M. Peuckert, private archive). 235
11 Friedrich Pollock and Max Horkheimer (private archive). 236
12 Pollock's house, Montagnola (Switzerland), architect Peppo Brivio, first-storey floor plan (private archive). 237
13 Horkheimer's house, Montagnola (Switzerland), architect Peppo Brivio, first-storey floor plan; second and final version, changed according to the indications given by Horkheimer. Note the garage moved to the left, the larger study and the doorway from this room to the small bedroom (private archive). 238
14 Above: Horkheimer's house, Montagnola (Switzerland), eastern aspect. Below: Horkheimer's house, Montagnola (Switzerland), southern aspect (private archive). 239
15 Max Horkheimer with Carlota Pollock at a folk festival (private archive). 240
16 Friedrich Pollock and Max Horkheimer at the carnival lunch in Montagnola (Switzerland) (private archive). 241

Translator's Note

A word on the works of Max Horkheimer and Friedrich Pollock translated into English. As mentioned in the introductory note, many of the sources used in this book have not been translated into English before. In particular, there is no translation of Horkheimer and Pollock's *Späne* or *Memorandums*, nor of the youthful *L'île heureuse*. A partial translation exists in English of the *Notizen*, hence those aphorisms that are not included in the volume *Dawn and Decline* are my own translation from volume 6 of the *Gesammelte Schriften*. Of the correspondence referred to in this book, a selection of Horkheimer's letters have been translated in the volume *Max Horkheimer. A Life in Letters*, whereas others appear in English here for the first time, in particular those to the architect Peppo Brivio. With regard to Pollock's text *Automation*, there only exists an English translation of the first edition and not of the overhauled second edition. The first-edition English translation has nevertheless been used as a basis for the translations of the quoted passages where possible.

CHAPTER 1

For Nonconformism

> Philosophical propositions
> cannot simply be regurgitated.
> Here unity of theory and praxis dominates.
> In other words: a theory cannot just be
> classified, it has to be lived.
> M. HORKHEIMER – F. POLLOCK, *Späne*, 1953, own translation

∴

> We could consecrate all our most human parts to our union,
> and no part of the soul, spirit or body
> belonged to the outside world anymore,
> everything – even the common and immediate impulses –
> found satisfaction among ourselves, since Suze
> rejoiced in her sensual beauty and could gift it to us.
> When there were three of us, we were at home,
> that is, we were where you have all you need
> and where you give all you possess.
> M. HORKHEIMER, *L'île heureuse*, 1914, own translation

∵

1.1 Transgression, Autobiography, Philosophy

For Non-Conformism. That society is moving from liberalism which was characterized by the competition of individual entrepreneurs toward the competition among collectives, corporations, commercial and political alliances and blocs is an insight that need not lead to conformism. The importance of the individual is waning but in theory and practice, he may critically intervene in this development. Using up-to-date methods, he can contribute to the creation of collectives that are out-of-season, which can preserve the individual in genuine solidarity. The critical analysis of demagogues would be a theoretical, the union of men who psychologically, sociologically and technologically see through them, a practical element of nonconformism in the present.[1]

This aphorism belongs to the late reflection of Max Horkheimer, at the end of the 1950s, the period when he left Frankfurt, where he had returned after his exile in the USA and covered important academic roles, to move to Montagnola with his friend Friedrich Pollock. Here, on the outskirts of the little village on the Collina d'Oro [Golden Hill], in the Italian-speaking part of Switzerland, almost to round off a friendship which had begun during their adolescence – a friendship closely tied to the theoretical ideas and the vicissitudes of the Institute for Social Research (ISF) of which Pollock was lifelong administrator, and Horkheimer, appointed by Pollock, director – the elderly philosopher and the elderly economist had two houses built alongside each other where they lived until their deaths (see the images in the appendix). Placed right at the end of the *Notizen*, this proposal by the philosopher to form 'out-of-season' collectives, critical for the correspondence between the actual and the rational as an unfulfilled, both theoretical and *practical* legacy of critical thought, seemed to be a bid farewell. Moreover, the aphorism also had an autobiographical meaning, as a reflection on Horkheimer's lasting shared life experience with Pollock, remembering that there is no *singularity* without duality, no self without proximity, no existence without being-together (no *Dasein* without *Beisammensein*).

Only this relational existential structure, however unactual and difficult to actuate, could still defend the single person and reason, prevent their drowning if not their 'enlightened' suicide in the anonymous and solipsistic prospect of instrumental reason, and allow them to survive and differentiate themselves. These were their expectations at least, their need for another place and another life, symptomatic of no small dose of historical and personal suffering. Utopia and suffering, euphoria and depression invoke each other.

Other notes, written jointly by Horkheimer and Pollock, placed right at the beginning of a sort of diary from those years, affirm:

> Inherent in psychoanalysis is the protest against reality. Equilibrium on the basis of inner freedom. *Not conformism.*
>
> Free association. Expectation of the new. Each time a new experience.[2]

---

1 Horkheimer 1978a, 'For Non-Conformism', p. 240. The term used by Horkheimer is 'Nonkonformismus'. The translation adopted in this book is 'nonconformism', written as a single word without a hyphen, to mirror the German.
2 'Miscellaneous Notes', in Horkheimer 1988, p. 306. This is the only note in *Späne* that is entirely in English, left in English by the editors of the complete works of Horkheimer (which consists of 19 volumes). On the composition of *Späne* see later p. 31 and note 79.

And further:

> The task is to do the opposite of what this miserable world prescribes (anti-conformism).³

The following declaration of 'planning' is from 1951 too. Also written jointly, it seemed to augur well for their preparation to retire to Montagnola:

> Our life must be a *testimony*; to create utopia in even the smallest details. We want the other, the new, the unconditional. Our life is serious. Where we live, social laws must not apply. Now, so late in the day, we can no longer waste any time. We must create the conditions in which all our energies can be effective in our very own sense. Especially Max's talent and experience.⁴

In the following years, it would nevertheless become clear that the historical and symbolic costs of this plan were very high. The little nonconformist utopia almost required them to descend 'into the catacombs' and at the same time there was no possible alternative. Otherwise, had they continued to participate in life at the horizontal and exoteric level, according to the prognosis in *Dialectic of Enlightenment*, they would have risked finding themselves capsized, turned into generic beings, and almost swallowed up by the contemporary trend of depersonalisation. More than to a true utopia, the out-of-season collectives in the last aphorism of the *Notizen*, in the same way as the *free association* in the opening note of *Späne*, seem to refer to that melancholy 'Association of the Pitiful Clearsighted' which they had planned in 1959, the parody association heir to their Institute, which seemed to have no other homeland in post-war Europe than in hidden and almost invisible places and shelters. The absent homeland, but now also absence as a homeland, provided shelter for a thought which, while still and forever conceiving of itself as anti-conformist as well as critical, moreover saw itself as *essentially* stateless:

> *For an Association of the Clearsighted.* One should found an association in all countries, particularly in Germany, which would express the horror of those without affirmative belief in either metaphysics or politics.

---

3 'Bon sens' in Horkheimer 1988, p. 308, own translation. The term used here is *Anti-Konformismus*, which Horkheimer uses more rarely than *Nonkonformismus*.
4 'Memorandum Friedrich Pollock-Max Horkheimer', 8 September 1951 in Horkheimer 1985–96, vol. 18, pp. 218–21.

As a humane practice in insane post-war Europe, the latter would seem impossible to them, and the former galimatias. For those who are appalled by the economic miracle, the mendacious democracy, the bribery charges with Hitler judges, the luxury and the misery, the rancor and the rejection of every form of decency, the admiration of eastern and western magnates, the disintegration of spirit, the slide into parochialism of this old civilization, such an association would be a kind of home. They would plot no revolution because it would end in naked terror. But they would nonetheless be the – admittedly impotent – heirs of the revolution that did not occur, these pitiful clearsighted ones who are going into the catacombs.[5]

Writings of a critical-diagnostic nature such as 'State Capitalism' by Pollock, 'The Authoritarian State', *Dialectic of Enlightenment* and *Eclipse of Reason* by Horkheimer and *Automation* again by Pollock, seemed to have registered-announced the *almost* definitive realisation of the conformist-totalitarian threat under the changing but never-ending yoke of 'domination'; the advent, in a sardonic and reversed form, of the end of history; the closure of the real political universe still capable of real history and not just perpetual mediatic administration [*Verwaltung*] and instruction.

As Horkheimer had laid down in his own take on Pollock's concept of 'State Capitalism': 'In the current circumstances, the only clearly logical prognosis that can be made is this: domination [*Herrschaft*] and forever only domination and not its overcoming [*die Herrschaft und immer nur die Herrschaft und nicht ihre Überwindung*]'.[6]

For this very reason, the only thing left open was to try to seek shelter, by almost going underground, in a sort of *katabasis* necessary to stay alive. Otherwise, a praxis could be sought, something like a negative humanism, essentially not open to an idolatrising absolutisation, either of the present or all analogous and foreseeable reproductions of it in the shape of the so-called future.

However off-centre and opaque, their plan for *alternative resubjectivisation* and *nonconformist intervention* nevertheless formed a legacy. It could be called *the other legacy*, somewhere between a continuation and discontinuation of the original vocation of their Critical Theory, which had come about 30 years

---

5 Horkheimer 1978a, 'For an Association of the Clear-Sighted', p. 166.
6 Letter from Max Horkheimer to Franz Neumann, 2 August 1941, in Horkheimer 1985–96, vol. 17, p. 118, own translation.

earlier also in order to deal with 'the yearning for a new interpretation of a life trapped in its individual striving for happiness'.[7]

What still seemed to be able to subsist, despite it all, was the idea-value of a free association or small community of those who could no longer bear any affirmative belief and at the same time expressed their scepticism alongside a critical vocation that had grown up by mixing Marxist social critique with Schopenhauer's critique of the world of representation. And so the idea of a free association or critical collective was reasserted, while at the same time nevertheless highlighting its impossibility, non-actuality, and in short utopian paradoxicality. The idea to plan an out-of-season collective effectively boiled down to their own form of life. Despite this, they continually relaunched it in the idea of a life beyond one's own, a being-there beyond the form of the individual and fractioned subject, a being-there as being-together, a *Beisammensein* capable of transgressing and going beyond trivialised existence following the selfish, bourgeois-proprietary canon of being, interpreted as 'always mine'.

The roots of the friendship between Horkheimer and Pollock went back to their youth, and their story takes us back as far as the start of the 1910s. Pollock, then 16 years old, had moved with his parents from Freiburg to Stuttgart. Owners of a travel and leather goods factory, the Pollocks had made a clean break from the traditional Jewish model, while the Horkheimers, also upper-class entrepreneurs, belonged to the milieu of conservative Jewish families. The meeting between Max and Fritz, as Horkheimer came to affectionately call him, who was 'from somewhere else' and a year older than him, must have opened up 'a new world, beyond religious and conservative traditions' for Max.[8] Pollock was taken aback and irritated when Max invited him to take part in a dancing lesson for the young people of the Jewish community. There was no way he would go back to that conservative environment. He did not hide that he could not see himself in that world, that he was different.

There was thus a certain air of dislike between them in that first meeting, as Pollock noted many years later. It was above all Horkheimer who recognised that the words the two youths exchanged after that invitation made a strong impression and were of great importance for him. For the first time, the young Max felt considered *not* as the son of his father, an established businessman and member of the Order of Merit for Labour, but as a young individual in search of his way in life, his own identity, despite the strong conformist pressure coming from his bourgeois family, in particular the strong father fig-

---

7   Horkheimer, 1993a, p. 7.
8   Wiggershaus 2013, p. 12, own translation.

ure.⁹ And so began the relationship between Max and Fritz. And we must not just underline its 'conspiratorial' purpose, towards Max's father in the teenage and immediate sense. It also prompted a process to break away from the model of the bourgeois individual marked by the 'suppression of instinctual desires', the 'damping of the sensibilities' and the persecution of 'every instinct that did not move in predesignated channels'.¹⁰ In a few years, this model of 'discipline' with the 'asceticism' imposed upon existence that it determines, and the 'human instincts and passions repressed and distorted by civilization' hidden 'beneath the known history of Europe', would be harshly criticised by Horkheimer, philosopher and director of the ISF, much ahead of the times to come. In this connection, his essay 'Egoism and Freedom Movements: On the Anthropology of the Bourgeois', published in 1936, is paradigmatic.¹¹ This critique by Horkheimer of 'tamed' existence was also already explicitly directed at the emancipation of *another form of life* which was 'the task of the historical persons in whom theory and historical practice became a unity'.¹² Not only that, it also presupposed a reference to the level of lived experience, a reference to 'their' decision for a form of life that intentionally could not be likened to the dominant anthropological-social model. If, as we read in the essay from 1936, the 'predominant character' of the bourgeois era embodies the 'principle of coldness and enmity',¹³ or in other words is determined by absorbing the principle of egoism and one's own self-preservation as the psychological, behavioural and ontological norm, and if *solipsistic extraneousness* ends up being the dominant anthropological category,¹⁴ we have to ask ourselves whether, back in the 1910s, with that *friendship* which would last their whole lives long, Max and Fritz were not indeed already creating, anticipating and preparing the theorisation of a sort of practical-existential emancipation from the horizon of interiorised domination.

Conceived of from the start, as we can read in an early 'pact of friendship', as the 'expression of a critical-human impulse' in view of 'creating universal solidarity',¹⁵ their relationship then traversed a good part of the century. Dating back

---

9   For the episode of their first meeting, defined as their 'Urszene', see ibid.
10 Horkheimer 1993d, p. 56.
11 The important and anticipatory 1936 essay by Horkheimer also constitutes the presupposition for the equally important fragment 'Interest in the Body', included in Horkheimer and Adorno 2007, p. 177 and p. 192.
12 Horkheimer 1993d, p. 110.
13 Horkheimer 1993d, p. 59.
14 Horkheimer 1993d, p. 96.
15 This is what we read in a first 'Memorandum' which Gumnior and Ringguth refer to in their *Max Horkheimer* (1997), subsequently in Wiggershaus 2013, p. 14, own translation.

biographically to their adolescence, it was a friendship that started not only from the dance episode, but also from their fantasies, just as the First World War was about to break out, concerning an *island of happiness – île heureuse –* where as a *ménage à trois* they would erotically go beyond the *principium individuationis*. From there, their acquaintance went through the years of the Munich revolution and the subsequent disappointment, then their university studies in economics and philosophy. And henceforth it kept on going through all of the Institute's ups and downs, as far as the creation of their little utopia during their later years in Montagnola.

To deal with this – their longing for *Beisammensein* – is not to make a vain or indiscreet incursion into their lives. Instead, for one thing, it is to try to cast a more complete light on Horkheimer's critique of the *monadic-solipsistic reduction of the subject*, under whose domination *hostility* and the *'performance principle'*[16] had historically been able to impose themselves as a sort of transcendental, a sort of destiny, by decreeing-imposing that 'the extraneous [*fremde*] individual is also experienced as a nullity'[17] and that each person 'is the center of the world, and everyone else is "outside"'.[18]

The result was a rapprochement between *philosophy and autobiography, philosophy and youth, philosophy and the diary*, without reductionism, but also without mystification, without idealising disembodied and nonsensical separations between philosophical reflection and historical existence. In short, at play was what Walter Benjamin indicated as 'overcoming fate', the effort of souls to listen to the 'melody of their youth' as they awaken to despair in the 'emptiness of the present', that is, on the 'first day of the diary', when they manifest their desire-longing, *Sehnsucht*, for another reality, another time.[19]

The critique of the egoistic bourgeois subject, which would also develop in parallel as a practical self-criticism of his own 'autocratic instinctual structure', together with the critique of bourgeois 'ascetic morality' and its nihilistic impoverishment of the life experience, constantly returns in Horkheimer, from

---

16 Horkheimer 1993d, p. 85. It seems almost superfluous to highlight the centrality of these motifs in the subsequent thought of Herbert Marcuse, in particular in his claim to strengthen-free the pleasure principle in the face of the 'performance principle'. See Marcuse 1998.
17 Horkheimer 1993d, p. 98.
18 Horkheimer 1993d, p. 96.
19 'We wish to pay heed to the sources of the unnameable despair that flows in every soul. The souls listen expectantly to the melody of their youth – a youth that is guaranteed them a thousandfold. But the more they immerse themselves in the uncertain decades and broach that part of their youth which is most laden with future, the more orphaned they are in the emptiness of the present. One day they awake to despair: the first day of the diary' (Benjamin 1996a, p. 10).

the already recalled 'Egoism and Freedom Movements', through *Dialectic of Enlightenment*, to the late texts of the *Notizen*. Moreover, on no rare occasion can it also be seen intertwined and *prepared* in the diaries – very soberly called 'Memorandums' – written together with Pollock to define and redefine their friendship, and their existential attempt at *Beisammen-sein*.

Their notion of *Beisammensein* seems to invite the thought that *being together is the precondition for being-there*, its very ethical-affective foundation. On this basis, existence does not appear to be defined by the fundamental concern with possession and self-preservation of our being, but by taking care of relations with others, with the other. The *proximity* theorised at the end of their lives as the key to existence, accompanied by their affirmation of solidarity as the fundamental meta-ontological task, together with the underlying critique of the bourgeois instrumental form of life, also implies a critique of Heidegger's definition of existence. It was a conception well known to Horkheimer, who had attended and appreciated the lessons of Martin Heidegger in Freiburg in 1921–2. Nevertheless, in the inaugural lecture that he held for his appointment as head of the Institute for Social Research in 1931, he already denounced *Dasein*, meant as 'being-for-death and finiteness', as a 'melancholy philosophy'.

If observed and retraced in light of this continual *mixage* between form of life and theory, their *friendship* needs to be thought of almost as a paradigmatic (not necessarily wholly successful) attempt at relational, critical, non-conformist ontogenesis, *autonomous* from the historically dominant phylogenesis. If this is translated into anthropological models and paths of egoistic-solipsistic individuation which also lead 'fatally' to the 'practical destruction of everything joyful and happy' – models also underlying Heidegger's *Dasein* taken in its dark aspect of *Sorge* [concern]— their search for *another existence* had the courage and the coherence to remember and to reclaim the fundamental existential meaning of otherwise devalued and forgotten, or even censured or prohibited experiences too.

While the anti-moralist and anti-repressive essay 'Egoism and Freedom Movements' was under preparation, the anti-conformist motto coined jointly by Max and Fritz to define their attitude towards the world was 'Gaieté, Courage, Fierté' ['Happiness, Courage, Pride']. Besides, almost 20 years earlier, the two men, together with their friend Suze, had played the lead roles in a totally transgressive experience, as they stated that the high and free grandeur present within them, the seed of their redemption, had tired of the offence once and for all. And so they set off for the *île heureuse* where they could not wait to place their imaginaries in the seat of power.[20]

---

20 Nothing seems more appropriate to describe the 'decision' of Max and Fritz than these images from 'Metaphysics of Youth' by Walter Benjamin.

They were able to anticipate and realise that 'higher level of existence' they so longed for, in utopian-hedonistic terms, as the *'universal reality'*. And so on their own small scale, they experienced a 'freer psychic constitution',[21] where the reality principle could unite with the imaginary.

Their life stories speak, with rare intensity and continuity, of an almost 'indissoluble' friendship: when Max was 16 and Fritz just one year older, after that episode of the dance I hinted at earlier, they entered each others' lives, never to leave them again.

We are in Stuttgart, that is, in the same city that provided the setting for that literary gem, *Reunion*. Indeed, for certain aspects, it is also by reading the story by Fred Uhlman that we can best approach the radical sense of friendship that Fritz and Max shared for over half a century.

Max and Fritz, not unlike Hans and as such also Konradin, were *inseparable* in their respective teenage meetings. In each other they found the possibility of *reawakening to life*. They each found in the other the condition for their own life and even potential death, *for their friend*.

After the pact of friendship in 1911, a letter written by Max to Fritz, in Brussels on 14 May 1913, first recorded the story of their radical friendship in extraordinary words.

> Fritz!
>
> My father left this morning. ----
> You're right not to ask me questions about my health; we'll be lacking strength so long as you stay in Stuttgart. ...
> We two would like to wake up at the same time, that is on the evening of 26 May at the 'gare du Nord' in Brussels; n'est ce pas?[22]

The departure of Horkheimer's father, his return to Stuttgart and his business world and the factory that he ran, was hailed as the beginning of a finally free and independent sphere of experience. Now they could live their *friendship* to the full, in an undisturbed if not absolute *being-together, being-one-with-the-other, being-one-for-the-other*, an essential 'uninterrupted' and 'undisturbed' *Beisammensein*, as Horkheimer starts to define it in the letters from those years.

The two young people would moreover openly assert, a few months later, during their stay in Brussels, that their parents intended the trip to boost their

---

21 Horkheimer 1993d, p. 110.
22 Letter from Max Horkheimer to Friedrich Pollock, 14 May 1913, in Horkheimer 1985–96, vol. 15, p. 9, own translation.

knowledge of the world of business, and that they felt as if they had '*escaped*' the rest of the world dominated by the practical interests and bourgeois customs of their families. In this period, they also read their first writings on philosophy, and it was Pollock, after dabbling in some Kant and Spinoza and finding both 'incomprehensible', who pointed towards Schopenhauer, 'a man who instead spoke in German, about real things, concerning what one is, and what one represents, etc.'. So Pollock advised Horkheimer to read Schopenhauer 'and one of the following evenings we went to the German bookshop on the Boulevard du Nord and asked for the *Complete Works*'.[23] Evidently, these readings of Schopenhauer, prompted by the question concerning 'what one is, and what one represents', were destined to combine with their practical search for a different form of life, a different identity. How could they escape the world of will and its patriarchal and commercial manifestations? In the end, even the critique of instrumental reason and its solipsism would have to be traced back to a critique of the world of will and its representations. Meanwhile, in the immediate term, their embryonic philosophy of friendship had to deal with the very possibility of their being together, in very much material and spatial terms too. It was already in the early 1910s that this *being-one-with-the-other* of theirs combined with and reflected the form of their *living*, first of all in the shape of a *Zimmergeschichte*.

And so, again Horkheimer wrote in one of his first letters: 'I'll sort out the story of the room [*Zimmergeschichte*]. You stay in the house opposite or two houses down from mine and thanks to particularly favourable circumstances, we'll probably be able to sleep room to room most of the time because the only lodger in the house travels for six months of the year'.[24] Despite the difficulties, in just a few months the then 18-year-old Max and Fritz managed to settle down as they desired.

In the only surviving letter of those sent by Max to Suzane Neumeier, a distant relative and Max's first flame, he clearly expresses his joy at the possibility of living with Pollock, the only condition that seemed to be able to abate the pressure otherwise exercised by the thousand base claims of the customary world, dominated by interests and antagonisms. Hence, it became Max's desire to also enable Suze, who lived with her bourgeois parents in Paris, to enjoy their different and freer life. And so he formulated his intent to 'get her out' of that place so that she could join them.

---

23 Pollock, 'Biographische Interview, 1965/66' in Wiggershaus 2013, p. 15, own translation.
24 Letter from Max Horkheimer to Friedrich Pollock, 14 May 1913, Horkheimer 1985–96, vol. 15, p. 9, own translation.

Suze,

...

When I read what you write to me and I put myself in your shoes, I suffer like you do – and at times I want to get you out and get you away from these unpleasant trifles and let you breathe in peace and understanding here with us. –

Now we live in the same house – I'm at Fritz's – our dream and boldest longing has come true – *to be together* all the time, with no one to disturb us [*ungestörtes Beisammensein*]. – We've fled the world where you are suffering and our memory of it is just a constant joy that we're rid of it.[25]

It was with these directly expressed words that their first plan for liberation from the world of will and its subjectivistic-instrumental representations was set in motion. But in place of the asceticism of Schopenhauer's *noluntas*, Max and Fritz, soon to be joined by Suze, longed to form a small, integral and uninhibited community, a sort of *three-way existence*, their souls and bodies fully projected beyond the *principium individuationis*. For them, the small community of friends as the condition for freeing themselves and breaking away from the moral and existential prejudices soon became both the field for an engaging experience and food for thought. Indeed, perhaps it provided Horkheimer's first spontaneously philosophical topic of reflection and self-reflection.

The desire to extend their being together, their dual *Beisammensein*, by fostering Suze's escape from Paris to embrace her in their union, by no means remained on paper. Max, Fritz and Suze accomplished it in the warm spring of 1914. First in a room of the Hotel Terminus Saint-Lazare in Paris, then in the dunes by the sea at Fort-Mahon, in Brittany, and lastly, in the interior of a small London flat: despite Pollock's initial reluctance, these were the happy stations of the story of their trinity, which quickly turned into an audacious, no matter how brief, *ménage à trois*:

> we could consecrate all our most human parts to our union, and no part of the soul, spirit or body belonged to the outside world anymore, everything – even the common and immediate impulses – found satisfaction among ourselves, since Suze rejoiced in her sensual beauty and

---

25   Letter from Max Horkheimer to Suzanne Neumeier, 7 September 1913, in Horkheimer 1985–96, vol. 15, pp. 11–12, own translation.

could gift it to us. When there were three of us, we were at home [*daheim*], that is, we were where you have all you need and where you give all you possess.²⁶

More radically than the 'friends' in Plato's *Republic*, who are such because they 'share everything', Max, Fritz and Suze combined spirit and body, sharing both the intellectual and the erotic dimensions. It was thus that they went beyond the *principium individuationis* to the place that they immediately called their *île heureuse*. As to the superior quality of this experience and trinity, they had no doubt. It was Max and Fritz who wrote to Suze that 'the briefest *île heureuse* … was to be preferred to the painful drag of everyday life, as it would be better to die after a few weeks of bliss than prolonging an existence which went against our desires'.²⁷ They had no desire to project the liberating energy of that experience simply into a more or less utopian and in its way mystifying imaginary; rather, while it was underway, they wanted to use this experience to outline their life plan, in view of building a small but also very real heterotopia:

> Let us escape your reality and set ourselves up in some place on this earth, away from your cities; we want to live out our desires [*Sehnsucht*], but don't believe that we think our arms will have to stay still and only our heads produce, no – there has to be work; we believe that human beings have to earn the bread they eat, but not in the way you see it! … Let us do what is good, send us out to another country, where we want to get from the earth what it will give us – we want to remain Free People in free nature!²⁸

This is what the three young rebels, Max, Fritz and Suze, wrote in one of their letters which they also tried to read to their respective bourgeois and conformist parents, but they immediately showed their perplexity and affliction. It was then Pollock, in a rare declaration looking back on this adventure, who hinted at some, nonetheless vague plans that they had discussed to go 'as far away from Europe as possible and become farmers in South Africa and devote ourselves to knowledge during the times of leisure'.²⁹

---

26   Horkheimer 1987, p. 311, own translation.
27   Horkheimer 1987, p. 324, own translation.
28   Horkheimer 1987, p. 317, own translation.
29   'Biographische Interview, 1965/66' which I take from Wiggershaus 2013, p. 19, own translation.

However, the real experience of the *island of happiness* had a brusque and violent epilogue: quickly suffocated by the intervention of the parents of Suze and Max, it resulted in the relative brief arrest of Fritz, the hospitalisation of Max in a *Kurhaus* and the repentance-denial of Suze. It was during that period in hospital that Max felt the need to put down in writing the adventure of their trinity. Thus, in 1914 he drafted his short story *L'île heureuse*, a text that Horkheimer never allowed to be published, and only circulated among a very small group of reader friends.[30]

Despite his reserve in allowing the publication of the text, Horkheimer had the opportunity to refer to it many years later, establishing that

> *L'île heureuse* describes the ideas, achievements and failure of a sworn community [*eine verschworen Gemeinschaft*] of two men and a woman who give themselves to each other without reserve, sharing and binding their spiritual and erotic dimensions, to make their 'free conviction' the measure of all their actions. To hold all material things in contempt was simply our principle of life. While looking at all the changes that fate caused from a cool distance, our goal consisted of reaching the *île heureuse* and living to know the beauty of the world and of our love.[31]

The plot of the short, but not linear narrative, which Max drew from his real experience, without concealing any signs, dates or references, speaks of Max and Fritz's departure from the gloomy, industrial Manchester where they were to have stayed, to go to London. Here they were met by their friend Suze, whom they had already met in the hotel in Paris and among the dunes on the coast of Brittany. Indeed, after abandoning her parents' house in Paris one night, and helped by Max in the journey from the French coast, Suze joined the two friends in a small flat in London, the backdrop for the briefest *ménage à trois*, brusquely interrupted by the repressive intervention of their families.

The parents of Suze, having intercepted a 'secret' letter of hers addressed to her friends, put Scotland Yard on the case and managed to have Fritz held up by two detectives. In the meantime, Max's father, together with a doctor from Munich, Dr Weissbarth, and his firm's accountant, Herr Weiss,[32] in turn arrived in London, alarmed by an incorrect telegram from Suze's parents, which read that Max's life was at risk. The night of the abrupt return to order after that

---

30 See the 'Editorische Vorbermerkung' in Horkheimer 1985–96, vol. 11, pp. 279–91.
31 Horkheimer, 'Aus der Pubertät. Novelen und Tagebuchblätter' in Horkheimer 1987, p. 290, own translation.
32 Horkheimer 1987, p. 325.

episode, Max Horkheimer thought he 'must have been going mad', writing in the short story that for him the following period had been his 'most difficult time'.[33] His effective hospitalisation in the clinic in Villingen, I may add, was one of the consequences of the episode.

The form adopted by the young Max was that of an autobiographical story. However short, it was a *Bildungsroman* in the first person, in which the condition of being-together, *Beisammensein*, came about from the breakdown-overcoming of the *principium individuationis*. It illustrated the complete evasion from the reality principle and bourgeois utilitarian morals, centred around the sublimation of pleasure and the sense of duty oriented towards individualistic self-affirmation. Albeit not principally, this ideal of *Beisammensein* expresses a spontaneous revolt of the pleasure principle and the world *of sensuality*, felt and claimed to be virtuous, against the conformism dominated by the calculating intellect and/or religious morals (represented in the short story by the *illness* of Marcelle Clement).[34]

As said, the small and evanescent space of the *island of happiness* not only coincided with the *dual Beisammensein* of Max and Fritz, but with the more transgressive form of their *trinity*, in certain aspects distantly similar, albeit unconsciously so, to the more tormented and famous experience *à trois* of *fin-de-siècle* philosophy, in the persons of Nietzsche, Paul Rée and Lou von Salomé.[35] Moreover, the tone and tension of the autobiographical narrative of *L'île heureuse* does not fail to be that of a *free spirit*, perhaps one that is already also consciously Nietzschean, and in any case programmatically and radically anti-conformist:

> The most natural necessity, the need that clearly appeared, was honoured. Our path was clear and simple. We loved each other, we wanted to escape society, we wanted to seek the truth – we came together, we took each other's hand and we acted as our religion required. We were free from any prejudice, we fearlessly did what the spirit and the heart deemed right – regardless of habits and reality – virtuously according to *our* senses.[36]

But in order to be understood, this spontaneous and already criticised movement of his/theirs, this going from an all-too-obvious autobiography (Max

---

33 'in der Nacht, die diesem Tage folgte ..., habe ich geglaubt, ich müsste wahnsinning werden, ... es war meine schwerste Zeit', Horkheimer 1987, p. 326, own translation.
34 See Horkheimer 1987, p. 297.
35 See Pfeiffer 1971.
36 Horkheimer 1987, p. 317, own translation.

meticulously added the dates of the events and meetings in the margins of the story) to claiming a full and strong *ethical* aspect 'regardless of habits and reality' and hence also a 'virtuous' dimension, evidently must be isolated neither from the historical-cultural context, nor from the critical-philosophical journey to come. In 1914, year of the composition of the short story I am talking about, with the same destructive flames, the 'atrocious' devastation of the Great War was showing how far the culture of competition and interest, by precipitating into all-out war, could lean to realise its intrinsic barbarity. Individualism had found its pendant and unfurled into aggressive statolatry, nationalistic religion. This, in turn, had to be questioned and criticised by investigating whether there was not rather *another seed* in the essence of humankind: a way of being beyond the asphyxiating reality principle and bourgeois performance, another, more original and liberating way of individuation than this one. What was at play in this also sensual and erotic search for *Beisammensein* was at the same time criticism of the character and the historically dominant anthropological model then also being demonstrated in the brutality of the war. Indeed, this became particularly clear on the last page of the short story, where *proprietary individualism* and *imperialist nationalism* were significantly made to reflect each other:

> Are you not a human being and then a German and as a human being do you not feel that a civilisation that produces similar effects is still barbaric, still immature? Does your heart not tell you how low this whole game of mine and yours is, how crude the life of baseness is? ... Oh you Germans, you had to spill your blood because there are Serbs on the earth but look, I do not want to know anything about states, all states are guilty of a war, and only human beings carry the seed of the salvation [*Keim zur Erlösung*] from this game.[37]

L'île heureuse is a narrative of the 'scandalous' youthful search for an *island of happiness* which questions this '*Keim zur Erlösung*', this possibility and energy of *liberation-redemption*. It is the story of the almost impossible intervention of 'pure Truth', meant as going beyond the Will, in everyday life.[38] Hence, it is also the story of *longing* [*Sehnsucht*] for the alterity of pure truth, its absent values, such as beauty, condemned to disappear no sooner than they arise.[39] Thus, against the background of the atrocious war, the *île heureuse* is a meta-

---

37 Horkheimer 1987, p. 328, own translation.
38 Horkheimer 1987, p. 323.
39 Horkheimer 1987, p. 302.

phor in the form of spatial and temporal secession for this ideal of *going beyond and de-reifying the bourgeois subject*. With the consistency of a mirage, a radical existential utopia, it is spontaneously projected in search of that *Ganzmensch*, that whole person who, as in Schiller's letters on aesthetic education, would come back to anti-bourgeois revolutionary dreams time and again, from Marx to the Marcuse of *Eros and Civilization*.

The 19-year-old Horkheimer and Pollock's overcoming of the bourgeois fractioned subject also doubtlessly took place at an erotic level too. As Max wrote, '[b]ecause Suze was a woman, our relationship had something self-contained, something independent about it; something whole [*etwas Ganzes*]'.[40]

> We were so happy! Nothing could destroy this happiness as we were free and we were strong, nothing could stop our flight ... we saw the world very clearly and everything around us was light, blue and gold. And Suze was a woman: 'What I am, belongs to you, take what I have to give, there is nothing more between us, no prejudice, no false modesty – I want to soothe what is burning and restless in you, I want to soothe your longing and one day, when you will no longer abandon me, when the great, eternal joy will have begun, my body will be yours too!' And we kissed her with passionate kisses and we felt at one with nature, with all this beautiful, clear, flaming fullness.[41]

However much of a one-off, the experience of the *île heureuse* needs to be seen as an experience capable of giving off *other light*, the light of joy and pleasure, and a reference to the immediate, to their lives. From here on, their existence would no longer follow a 'tamed' and 'disciplined' course, but would be characterised by an underlying dissatisfaction with a world placed under the autocratic-solipsistic yoke of the will. This is also why their existence would be conceived of as a friendship, a friendship always involving the critical energy of the *island of happiness*. In short, in the relationship with Suze,[42] the *Bei-*

---

40 Horkheimer 1987, p. 311, own translation.
41 Horkheimer 1987, p. 296, own translation.
42 In the storyline of *L'île heureuse* Suze is in effect accused of betraying their trinity and working a sort of repression-return to order. Suze's answer is expressed in a 'secret' letter dated 31 January 1922, in which she says she is 'disgusted' with her present life (in the meantime Suze had got married to a captain who then went into industry). In it she declares: 'No, Max, Suze has not betrayed her ideal, she acted as she had to do, you'll understand one day and, believe me, it's more difficult to live sacrificing the real me, than following your tastes and ideas. ... If I could fly back to the *île heureuse* at some point, would I stay there forever this time? ...', in Horkheimer 1985–96, vol. 15, pp. 85 ff., own translation from the French.

sammensein of Max and Fritz, their existing according to a configuration that constitutionally went beyond the subject's self-closure, had found its extreme expression and hence in a certain sense its very truth. While Suze seemed to give in to her parents when they called her back into step and to betray the plans for their trinity, Max and Fritz only seemed willing to postpone it. In this connection, the incipit of the story, written by Horkheimer during his stay in the Kurhaus in Villingen, is very eloquent:

> This is the dream that I want to tell and no one from your community will ever understand. Your low thoughts and words are not able to grasp its truth and its meaning escapes you if you compare it with your small desires and intentions. Three human beings woke up, broke out of your chains, became free and rose up towards the blue sky. You aimed your arrows at the three birds, you hit one of them, who dragged down the other two as she fell. But the other two still have wings, they are still alive and are now flying around the sun again.[43]

Horkheimer would implicitly make the palingenetic and in this sense founding experience of the island a motif for reflection, when many years later, in particular again in the essay 'Egoism and Freedom Movements' from 1936, he accused the tamed and internally 'enslaved' bourgeois class of no longer being able to recognise the transforming action of pleasure on life. Pleasure, for the person 'enslaved' internally by morals, the 41-year-old Horkheimer would write, would be reduced, like 'in marriage' to a *function of duty*. Instead of also welcoming the light 'radiating from pleasurable moments' into those parts of life that are by no means delightful, as should be done in a sort of profane enlightenment, the bourgeois subject was formed through the imposition of 'excessive self-denial', where it was understood that 'in order to domesticate the masses, society needed education dominated by religion and metaphysics in addition to physical force. ... [Thus] individuals were subdued'.[44] For the mature Horkheimer, the cultural and moral devaluation of pleasure would be an extreme example of this historical domination over subjectivities. Indeed, 'in the life of the exemplary man, there is little place for pleasure in its most direct form as sexual or, more extensively, material pleasure',[45] and, what is more, it 'has been banished ... to the sad refuge of small-minded obscenity and prosti-

---

43 Horkheimer 1987, p. 293, own translation.
44 Horkheimer 1993d, pp. 56–8.
45 Horkheimer 1993d, p. 57.

tution'.⁴⁶ But this devaluation and repression of pleasure, its reduction to a sin and a 'vice', which implies the mutilation of all comprehensive and happy relationships with the body, generates 'a deep erotic resentment' in society which does not hesitate to express itself as violence towards and the cancellation of those who are different, as well as anti-conformists in general:

> If pleasure, or even just the capacity for pleasure, which they have had to fight in themselves since their youth, is so ruinous, then those who embody this vice and remind one of it in their whole being, appearance, clothing, and attitude should also be extinguished so that the source of scandal disappears and one's own renunciation is confirmed. ... The concept of the alien becomes synonymous with that of the forbidden and dangerous, and the enmity is all the more fatal since its carriers feel that this forbidden thing is irretrievably lost for themselves by virtue of their own rigid character. Petit bourgeois resentment against the nobility and anti-Semitism have similar psychic functions. Behind the hatred of the courtesan, the contempt for aristocratic existence, the rage over Jewish immorality, over Epicureanism and materialism is hidden a deep erotic resentment which demands the death of their representatives. They must be wiped out, if possible with torments, for the sense of one's own existence is called into question every moment by the existence of the others.⁴⁷

The moralistic condemnation of the pleasure principle is unveiled and its effects of sadistically 'disfiguring' the instincts denounced. In this connection, Horkheimer finds quite convincing Freud's original doctrine, according to which 'under the given familiar and general social conditions, [social prohibitions] are suited for arresting people's instinctual development at a sadistic level'.⁴⁸ The act of *internalising* instincts, under the yoke of cultural repression, implies the transformation of mental energies in a radically and unilaterally *destructive* sense. But the sadistic subject, and his or her destructive culture, has in turn to be interpreted and criticised as the upshot of that attitude of 'contempt for ... concrete existence and ... happiness' to which we must give the name of 'nihilism'. It is in these terms that Horkheimer furthers his diagnosis of the *pathology of bourgeois morality*, that is, by taking the Nietzschean critique

---

46   Horkheimer 1993d, p. 58.
47   Horkheimer 1993d, pp. 100–1.
48   Horkheimer 1993d, p. 104.

of 'European nihilism' in a 'specific form' and referring it more directly to analysis of the repression of desirous existence.[49] The traits of a *free spirit* already expressed in the youthful experience of the *île heureuse* are not simply lost along the way or removed, but elaborated theoretically. They lie behind the interesting *anti-nihilistic* terms of the early Frankfurtian project of emancipation and existential liberation, reinforced in the 1930s by their reading of Freud's *Civilization and Its Discontents*. In short, it does not seem at all arbitrary to observe that in his (and their) critical journey, which would see the converging denunciation of the pathology of bourgeois morality and the pathology of instrumental reason, the ideal of the *island of happiness* would remain as a countermelody, as would its excess of aesthetic-erotic energy and the dream of coming together with the beauty and substantial or 'objective' truth of nature, followed as a therapy by nihilism and dominant sadism, and transformed/raised to a *radical critical criterion*, in the wake of Schiller's *whole person* [*Ganz-Mensch*].

Despite its reference to the metaphor common to all utopianism – Utopia has always notoriously been an *island*, ever since Plato, if not Hesiod, a long time before Thomas More[50] – the title of that youthful short story, in French in Horkheimer's original, would seem at this point to also raise a further hypothesis. *L'île heureuse* seems to refer to the poem of the same name by the French symbolist Éphraïm Mikhaël, evoking 'couples of happy lovers' journeying towards the land of delight, where a song of reawakening and joy, that of the mermaids, can be heard. It is the invitation to go to them formulated by the 'sovereigns of the bright marine deserts who cradle the dreams on their enchanted and serene waves':[51] the *île heureuse* seems to be the place where delight and myth combine to promise conciliation and love between people and between people and nature. And the tale by the young Max overflows with figures that can be traced back to the world of myth (like the three masters, an old man, a woman and a naked boy who make a sudden appearance at the end). Here too, it does not seem reckless at all to hypothesise a certain antecedent bond between the youthful and transgressive narrative of *L'île heureuse* and the famous pages on the *Sirens' island* and the repression of their 'promise of happiness' that are fundamentally important in the first chapter of *Dialectic of Enlightenment*. Indeed, these pages denounce the enlightened repression of

---

49 Horkheimer 1993d, p. 100.
50 On the *Island of the Blessed*, happy alternative to Tartarus, see Hesiod 1932, vs. 170–1; Plato 2012, 540 b; and Plato 2004, 523 ff., where we come across the motif of nudity, taking off clothes, as a condition of truth.
51 See Mikhaël 1994, own translation.

the possibility of listening to the Sirens' call by noting that 'humanity had to inflict terrible injuries on itself before the self – the identical, purpose-directed, masculine character of human beings – was created, *and something of this process is repeated in every childhood*'.[52] In the famous work of his mature years, written with Adorno, the episode on shunning pleasure narrated in the *Odyssey* is in short given paradigmatic value in the genealogy of the self-referential subject enclosed within the project of his or her self-preservation. It highlights how this prohibition before the sensual call of happiness is repeated again and again, at the ontogenetic and personal level too.

The adventure narrated in *L'île heureuse*, despite its literary modesty, would therefore seem to hide a layer of directly lived and experienced sense among the multiple layers built up and then condensed in *Dialectic of Enlightenment*: the invincible temptation of the Sirens' song, the ears of the sailors blocked with wax and Odysseus, bourgeois gentleman tied to the mast of the ship, slave at once to a sublimation and sacrifice of pleasure with a frightening existential price.

In an excursus famously written by Adorno, *Dialectic of Enlightenment* would also not fail to add:

> But happiness contains truth within itself. It is in essence a result. It unfolds from suffering removed. The enduring Odysseus is therefore right not to endure life among the Lotus-eaters. Against them he asserts their own cause, the realization of utopia through historical work, whereas simply abiding within an image of bliss deprives them of their strength.[53]

Neither Max Horkheimer nor Fritz Pollock were ever happy with the mere image of bliss, but they sought to make it come true, first of all through the 'historical work' of *criticism*. All the same, the forces encountered in the historical reality then took them back to seek the other space of their decision in the *intérieur*, or even by descending underground.

1.2 Forms of Life

The friends' lives continued in parallel in the years when, as university students in Munich, they possessed 'a substantial house'[54] in Kronberg at the foot of the

---

52   Horkheimer and Adorno 2007, p. 26, italics mine.
53   'Excursus I, Odysseus or Myth and Enlightenment' in Horkheimer and Adorno 2007, p. 49.
54   Wiggershaus 1994, p. 44.

Taunus hills, where they (as Adorno remembered) 'led a sheltered life, but with a tangible aversion towards furnished bedrooms'.[55] The young Horkheimer's appointment in 1930 at the helm of the Institute for Social Research in Frankfurt was then to a large extent decided by Pollock, who had graduated in Politics and Economics at Frankfurt in 1923.

Pollock, who was also among the participants in the Marxist weeks promoted by Felix Weil where the idea for the Institute had matured,[56] had already drawn attention to himself with some essays, and in 1927 had made an important study trip to the Soviet Union in order to analyse (and criticise) the economic conditions ten years after the revolution.[57] When the first director of the Institute, the Marxist Carl Grünberg, had a heart attack, Pollock, who was then his assistant and already held the role of administrator, came up with a formula to entrust the directorship to Horkheimer. In addition, according to what Fritz had laid down, had Grünberg returned, he would nevertheless have had to leave part of the direction to Max. Horkheimer's appointment as the head of the Institute, in many ways surprising seeing as all he had produced up to that point was his habilitation thesis, was therefore to a large extent due to the initiative taken by Friedrich Pollock for his friend. Their friendship, substantiated by transgressive experiences such as those of their youth and important events such as these, was also organised on the basis of texts which they called 'Memorandums', similar in form to 'articles of association' or contracts, akin to the style of their epistolary correspondence, and conceived of to establish

---

55 Adorno mentions this too in the open letter to Horkheimer that he published in 'Die Zeit' (Theodor W. Adorno, Offener Brief an Max Horkheimer, 'Die Zeit', 12 February 1965) on the occasion of his friend Max's 70th birthday. What results is a portrait of a philosopher capable from a young age of dealing with and reconciling the paradoxes of human beings: 'Your face was nevertheless passionately and ascetically thin. You had the appearance of a gentleman, and a refugee, since birth. Your form of existence corresponded to this too. You had rapidly bought a house in Kronberg with Fred Pollock, where you led a sheltered life, but with a tangible aversion towards furnished bedrooms. You knew not only the graveness of life, but also its intricacy. He who was able to look into its intimate mechanism and wanted it to be different was determined and capable of asserting himself, regardless and without giving in. To look critically at the principle of self-preservation as well as wrest one's own self-preservation from understanding – you embodied this paradox. Decades later, on emigrating you said something that I could never forget: we, the saved ones, should have been in the concentration camps. This word is profoundly connected with your strength of survival', own translation.

Nor was the event that led to Horkheimer's taking the lead role at the Institut für Sozialforschung outside this capacity to deal with paradoxes.

56 Jay 1996, pp. 30–1.
57 In this connection, see Chapter 2 in this book.

'the principles of the shared form of life and the conduct to which to aspire'.[58] It was not rare for these 'Memorandums', the first example of which can be found in their 'pact of friendship' from 1911, to include introspective reflections concerning the 'inner disposition of one towards the other and their relationship' together with other considerations as a rule concerning the initiatives to take to somehow deal with the historical and political necessities. The fundamental and almost continuous topic of these texts, which as a whole can never be considered apart from the violent historical background of the *short twentieth century* speaking constantly and at every level in violent affirmation of the will and instrumentality, is without doubt that of *friendship*.

It is a topic that they definitely lived and experienced, but whose psychological layers, link with the libido and sublimation, and long philosophical history are also known. Forty years after their first pact and after *L'île heureuse*, Max and Fritz started one of their 'Memorandums' with these very words: 'We consider our friendship the greatest good [*unsere Freundschaft als höchstes Gut*]. The concept of friendship includes its lasting until death [*bis zum Tode*]. Our action must be the expression of the relationship of friendship and our every principle must adapt to this before all else'.[59]

The primacy of the relationship of friendship over the individualistic organisation of existence, its opening to stronger meanings than those deriving from the individual's finiteness: these topics, which substantiate the definition of friendship in terms of the *most precious good*, as widely propounded in the classics – think of Cicero[60] – often return in these 'Memorandums'. The impression one gets is that their friendship constitutes the authentic presupposition for fully understanding why 'their self-actualization [was] tied to the presupposition of cooperative rational activity' as well as why 'they [could not] avoid suffering psychologically under its deformation'.[61] If the 'normative leitmotif of Critical Theory' is epitomised, as Axel Honneth upholds, by the 'idea of cooperative self-actualization',[62] in short we can ask ourselves if this idea, which also seems to constitute the 'legacy of Critical Theory for today', did not only receive its original impulse from the criticism of the 'social-ontological premises of lib-

---

58 See the editors' note in Horkheimer 1985–96, vol. 15, p. 388.
59 'Memorandum Friedrich Pollock-Max Horkheimer', 8 September 1951, quoted in ibid., own translation.
60 See Cicero 1777.
61 See Honneth 2009, p. 39. I will pose a similar critical question hereinafter concerning the opinion, however bitterly critical, put forward by Jürgen Habermas, in turn centred around the (formal) idea of the cooperation between disciplines as the legacy of the Frankfurt School.
62 Honneth 2009, pp. 27–9.

eralism', but also, and preliminarily, from Max and Fritz's philosophy of friendship, from their *ongoing* criticism of the ontological premises of bourgeois existentialism.

When in 1933 the premises of the Frankfurt Institute were raided by the police to seize the 'subversive material' and an SA squad also occupied the house that Pollock and Horkheimer owned together at Kronberg im Taunus, making it into a guard post, the two friends already found themselves on the way to exile, first to Geneva, then to the United States. Here, right at the beginning of the decade that they would have to spend there, they drew up the long and detailed 'Memorandum', dated New York, August 1935 and entitled 'Materialien für die Neuformulierung von Grundsätzen' ['Materials for the Reformulation of Principles']. Evidently, it came about against the background of the birth of Nazism and the necessity to abandon Germany.

The new context where they found themselves having to live and work now required a sort of re-establishment of the charter of their union, which was also presenting 'small symptoms of crisis'.[63] Moreover, this requirement would repeat itself, in a significant parallel, when at the end of the 1950s they decided to leave Frankfurt for the second time. On reading the 'Memorandum' of 1935, we learn that their most immediate concern was to manage to prevent overly lengthy 'separations' between them in those difficult times, which might somehow jeopardise their mutual knowledge of 'the other's thoughts and activities': 'Longer separations,' they wrote, 'are to be avoided if possible, even at the cost of sacrifices'. In short, their relationship was to pan out according to an 'unbroken figuration [*eine ununterbrochene Gestaltung*]', in which 'the interior always goes before the exterior [*das Intérieur geht immer dem Extérieur vor*]'. The resulting idea was to go beyond 'necessarily partial' opinions, judgements and individual behaviours, in favour of a '*Gesamtsystem*', a strongly shared practical-existential *system*, the expression of a vision of the world based on and substantiated by a radical *gemeinsames Leben*, a *living together* conceived of also and above all as self-criticism of their own, at times still contrasting, individual 'instinctual structures'. The youthful desire for *Beisammensein* – metaphysically youthful, in the sense of Benjamin – was therefore anything but exhausted in this period too, a time when they were also organising the Institute's new course in the USA. At this time in particular, the 'security of not being alone and isolated', as well as the security that 'one can absolutely count on the other, not only

---

63 'Our letters show small symptoms of crisis, that mutual understanding which is the vital element of our relationship does not dominate between us', letter from Friedrich Pollock to Max Horkheimer, 14 July 1934 (which I quote from Campani 1992, p. 204 note 37, own translation).

in the great questions, but also in the things of everyday life', required the establishment of the 'necessary detailed measures concerning our contrasting instinctual structures [*unserer konträrer Triebstrukturen*]'. The 'supreme truth' expressed by '*unser Gesamtsystem*', the attitude towards the world following the motto 'Gaieté, Courage, Fierté', had to be achieved by defining and first of all working on *das Intérieur*. In this work 'of self-knowledge' [*Zur Selbsterkenntnis*], unreserved criticism of one's own '*autocratic instinctual structure*' was to lead to *Identifikation mit dem Anderen*, 'identification with the other', wherein 'each one of the other's failures, is also one's own'. Furthermore, to the same extent, it seemed equally possible to access and fully share *the other's joy* as 'joy felt for the other [*die Freude am andern*]'.

Divided into 13 articles-principles, in turn divided into numerous paragraphs, this text, *trans-authored* in its method and *trans-subjective* in its underlying merit, was defined as and strongly felt by Pollock and Horkheimer, then 40 year olds, to be '*our decision* [*unser Entschluss*]': 'Living on the basis of our convictions and doing everything in our power to achieve the values we recognize. This *decision* [*Entschluss*] goes before everything else'.[64] They established this not only in relation to *das Intérieur*, but also to that *intermediate space* in which they situated the Institute, then, moreover, waiting to be reopened. Without doubt, the attempt to overcome the separation between fields of competence in the Institute also derived from the radical *trans-individual* thrust of their existential project. In short, in part at least, their notion of *Beisammensein* also provided the springboard for that 'cooperative' project of theirs to abolish the positivistic-bourgeois fractioning of knowledge and to 'merge the social sciences in the burning glass of critical theory' which Jürgen Habermas then interpreted as their 'original answer, opposed to that of Heidegger, to the "end of metaphysics"'.[65] That same 1935 'Memorandum' already put it clearly:

> The rigid division of the spheres of life according to 'competences', where only the expert can have a say in the matter, is a limit for all moral spheres, as well as for many [other] spheres. It is the consequence of a bourgeois error, that is, the overestimation of the possibilities of the division of labour. Instead, to a certain extent, in a community, the whole must be expressed in every sector, every person is equally responsible for this whole ....[66]

---

64 Horkheimer 1985–96, vol. 15, p. 388, own translation.
65 'Max Horkheimer: Zur Entwicklungsgeschichte seines Werkes' in Habermas 1991, p. 93.
66 'Memorandum Friedrich Pollock-Max Horkheimer', August 1935 in Horkheimer 1985–96, vol. 15, p. 382, own translation.

As proof of the fact that the friendship between Max and Fritz, starting from these premises, was effectively also of no secondary significance in the innovative 'interdisciplinary' set-up of the Institute, it must be highlighted how once again in the 1935 'Memorandum', the project for their *gemeinsames Leben* is directly transposed into a consideration on the definition of the nature of the Institute. As the twelfth principle sets out

> living together must also be expressed in the sharing of everyday joys and concerns, not only in affliction over the great problems. For example, the disposition towards the Institute, its works and collaborators. The Institute is not a company [*kein Geschäft*], nor an institution [*keine Institution*], but a group [*eine Gruppe*] with *shared* outlooks and aims [*mit gemeinsamen Anschauungen und Zielen*]. A shared watch must be kept so that the core of the Institute is as homogeneous as possible [*möglichst homogen*], as well as utmost care over the choice of the closest collaborators.[67]

This extension of the shared life project, *gemeinsames Leben* and *Gemeinschaft*, to the Institute, referred to by the term 'group' – perhaps less sociologically exacting than the Tönnesian, organicistic *Gemeinschaft* – hence also implied the establishment of limits and closed doors to preserve its homogeneity. Opening up beyond the *intérieur* and the intermediate space of the Group-Institute, which could ultimately easily be traced back to the same, was the expanse of a historical-political *extérieur*, populated by dangers and enemies. And now more than ever all excessive or naïve confidence in this *extérieur* had to be avoided.

In this sense, it was indeed a matter of *de-ciding* [*ent-scheiden*], of *separating* oneself from that society which still or already in the 'Memorandum' of 1935 was described as the *Gesellschaft* of falsification and egoistic, universally instrumental individualism. It was only by making that 'de-cision', that 'separation', which was anything but simple to do, also owing to the problems of the instincts and character of the *intérieur*, that a 'suitable disposition towards society' could be created, oriented by the awareness that

> in today's society all human relations are false, all kindness, all agreement, all benevolence, in the end is not to be taken seriously, only the struggle

---

67 'Memorandum Friedrich Pollock-Max Horkheimer', August 1935 in Horkheimer 1985–96, vol. 15, pp. 387–8, own translation.

for competition within a class and the struggle between classes are serious things. All recognition, all success, all apparently kind interest comes from gaolers who indifferently allow those with no success or power to die, or torture them till they bleed ... Consequence: never on the same level as the gaolers, solidarity with the victims (N.B. in this society, in addition to the officials, there are also human beings, above all among women).[68]

Although there are reasons for wondering if what is meticulously prescribed in the long 1935 'Memorandum' was not then disregarded in the behaviours both of the *extérieur* and the *intérieur*,[69] it is above all worth underlining that the topics of going beyond the self and decision-separation [*Entscheidung*], and in short *gemeinsames Leben*, all of which were essential and already encountered in the midst of their youth, would then return in their 'Memorandums' in the 1950s, connected to their shared exile in Switzerland.[70] And yet, as I have already hinted, in these *existential* prior to organisational motifs, can we not perhaps hear a potential *countermelody* to, and hence also an echo of, *Sein und Zeit*? In Heidegger's 1927 work, is it not maybe a 'decision' [*Entscheidung*] that *Dasein* should make to avoid dejection in the anonymous horizon of human beings and to assume its *being-for-death* and ontic-ontological project? Between 1921 and 1922, Horkheimer spent a semester in Freiburg where the young Heidegger made a strong impression on him with his philosophy that was not abstractly intellectualist – unlike what his master, the neo-Kantian Hans Cornelius had accustomed him to – but faithful to experience, even everyday *Erlebnis*. In a letter from November 1921 Horkheimer writes:

> The more philosophy captivates me, the more I distance myself from what is understood as philosophy at this university [that is, in Frankfurt, trans-

---

68 'Memorandum Friedrich Pollock-Max Horkheimer', August 1935 in Horkheimer 1985–96, vol. 15, pp. 386–7, own translation.
69 This can be gleaned from their next 'Memorandum' of 1936, which also includes some bitter criticism above all against Pollock's character, lacking in warmth, sympathy and identification. It also expresses disappointment in their failure to create their *Gemeinschaft*, which at the same time is underlined as 'the most important thing we have in the world', see 'Memorandum Friedrich Pollock-Max Horkheimer', 'Notizen auf Beach Bluff', August 1936, in Horkheimer 1985–96, vol. 15, pp. 606–10.
70 It is a topic that not only returns in the 1955 passage in *Späne* 'Unsere Beziehungen' ['Our Relationships'], but also in the *Notizen* – see the last aphorism, cited in Part 1.1. It is also expressed in the 1935 'Memorandum', which invites to *always keep your eyes open* – an exhortation that will be found again in the *Notizen* – in order to denounce the *falsification* that looms over all social relations in the context of the dominant *Gesellschaft* and to be capable of other visions and actions.

lator's note]. We must search for substantive expressions about our life and its significance rather than formal epistemological laws, which are basically terribly unimportant. I know now that Heidegger was one of the most significant personalities whose philosophy spoke to me. Do I agree with him? – How could I, since I actually only know one thing about him for sure: that for him the impulse to philosophy does not stem from intellectual ambition and a preconceived theory but springs anew each day from his own experience.[71]

In Horkheimer's inaugural lecture for his 1931 appointment as director of the Institute, this impression was then elaborated in critical terms, namely, as the requirement to distance himself from '*melancholy philosophy*', in other words, from the philosophy of finiteness of *Dasein* and being-for-death.

Also in light of his acquaintance with Heidegger during the 1921–2 semester, the hypothesis of a critical echo of Heidegger's motif of *Entscheidung*, *decision*, in the 1935 'Memorandum' appears anything but unfounded. However, the most important aspect must immediately be specified, namely, that where Heidegger speaks of *decision* for *Sein zum Tode* and *Dasein* understood as '*in any case mine*' [*Jemeinigkeit*],[72] the 'Memorandum' instead speaks very differently. Indeed, in line with everything that went before it, the 'Memorandum' talks of *decision* to enable the subject to take him or herself *beyond the individual*, of decision to go beyond the primacy of *instrumental self-preservation*, of decision to go past one's '*autocratic instinctual structure*'. And the outcome that is aspired towards speaks of 'joy', 'happiness', shared pleasure, of overcoming the 'nihilistic consequences' of morality[73] and then of a structure of original 'solidarity', namely going beyond the ontological subject to attain *being-for-the-other*, the *proximity principle*. The lesson of Heidegger, in other words, seems to be taken up on one hand as a possibility of faith in *Erlebnis*, and rejected on the other as succumbing to the melancholy solitude of the 'tamed' subject incapable of *feeling* the other.

It can be added that this *dual movement* towards the perspective opened by *Sein und Zeit* also comes to light where Horkheimer on one hand demon-

---

71   Letter from Max Horkheimer to his wife Maidon (on Horkheimer's wife, see pp. 139–40) from 30 November 1921, in Horkheimer 2007, p. 22.
72   'We are ourselves the entities to be analysed. The Being of any such entity is *in each case mine*. These entities, in their Being, comport themselves towards their Being. As entities with such Being, they are delivered over to their own Being'. Heidegger 1962, p. 42.
73   These are the terms used in the 1936 essay 'Egoism and Freedom Movements' (Horkheimer 1993d).

strates his desire to reopen human knowledge *beyond the reduction effected in the sphere of natural sciences*. Indeed, as he has it, they all too hastily assert that the 'supreme good is self-preservation' and the 'supreme evil is death' for human beings in the same way as for natural *presences*.

> Knowledge of human beings becomes a specialized problem of natural science. ... it is based on the view that for everything in nature, and thus for the body and its indwelling soul, to perish [*der Untergang*] represents the greatest evil, while self-preservation and all actions toward that end constitute the highest good. ... This seemingly unprejudiced concept of nature was in reality individualistic in that it maintained each being's self-preservation to be its law and standard, corresponding to the social existence of the bourgeois individual. What starts as a conception of non-human nature ... is eventually projected back onto human beings.[74]

With the same gesture used here to seemingly, in his own way, draw from *Sein und Zeit* to criticise the reductive effects of scientific objectivism and Cartesian ontology which puts human beings down to a mere presence among presences, at the same time Horkheimer also critically distances himself from Heidegger's perspective. If we are to radically reopen the question of the definition of existence, we have to go past the *existence-self-preservation* or *existence-care for one's own being* pairings and denounce their limited historical-bourgeois origins. This also has to allow us to recognise that other *experiential possibilities* open up and have always opened up beyond the economy of individualistic *Selbsterhaltung* [self-preservation], possibilities marked by a radical happiness, *beyond concern for one's own survival* or *for one's own whole return to the self*. Finiteness speaks of the decline [*Untergang*] of the self. Nevertheless, this becoming passive, and going past the self, can correspond to the very concept of happiness, with its essential *excess* with respect to the calculating existential-bourgeois economy of the ego:

> Human beings and probably animals as well are hardly so psychologically individualistic that all their instinctual impulses are necessarily founded in immediate desire for material gratifications. Human beings may, for instance, experience a sort of happiness in the solidarity with like-minded souls that makes it possible for them to assume the risk of suffering and death ... nonegoistic instinctual impulses have existed during all periods.[75]

---

74   Horkheimer 1993d, p. 50.
75   Horkheimer 1993b, p. 123.

The right approach to society – *'die richtige Einstellung zur Gesellschaft'* – in short has to translate not only into a project of collaboration-blending between the disciplines to give an original response to the 'end of metaphysics', but also, and as a priority, into a radical *existential difference*. This difference, in turn, has the task of making a separation, a *'change in level'*, an anti-conformist transcendence/resistance with respect to the individualistic and always calculating dominant reality. From the *falsification* of existence, conceived of as hostility and instrumentality aimed at treating other people as means and disavowing them as ends unto themselves, it is necessary to focus the energy of friendship in order to achieve *proximity* to the victims and solidarity with others. This is the truth of an existence (as the 'Memorandum' from 1955 would set out) *'beyond one's own death'*.

In other words, under the omnipresent threat of 'falsification' and the horizon of the historical world – harbinger of hostility – what is needed is *critical decision*. This *ethical-existential* decision alone can allow us to escape reclusion in anonymous integration in the imposed social mechanisms, and to live in the truth of shared *Dasein*, beyond being calculated-planned-kept as *'in any case mine'*.

As the text from 1955 would say, to follow this route, and assume one's perishing would be to strive to go beyond the 'coercion of the reality principle'. In short, a philosophical expression needs to be made of that seeking to go beyond the *principium individuationis* already begun with the anti-moralistic and hedonistic figures of *L'île heureuse* and 'Egoism and Freedom Movements'; figures which in their way speak of an *Untergang* – connected to the pleasure principle[76] – and which ultimately develop into the interrogation of the topic of *proximity*, fostered at the same time by Jewish and Schopenhauerian, as well as experiential elements.

Without doubt, if the dominant society is the society of 'gaolers', those who risk making this 'decision' and make *'identification with the other'* their ethical imperative will experience a situation of exodus and disorientation, a condition of *Unheimlichkeit* and uprooting. For this reason too, before the unjust and imprisoning *Gesellschaft* – here in the 'Memorandums' use is made of Tönniesian terminology – the communitarian dimension of the Group, or *'unsere Gemeinschaft'*, and of the *'menschliche Gemeinschaft'* in general, can only take the shape of the *'intérieur'*, that is, an *inner place* that has to be guarded like a shelter-retreat from an im-possible *ethical community*. Indeed, outside this *intérieur* – a place of a trans-psychic, but also physical decline-going bey-

---

76 See Freud 2003.

ond, a place of meeting beyond one's own, a place of unity beyond the *principium individuationis* – Exteriority imposes itself and grows as an economic, authoritarian, depersonalising *Gesellschaft*. Despite the falsification of individualistic *society* and in the face of its sinister *Unheimlichkeit*, the relationship-identification with the other, with that particular neighbour – respectively called Max and Fritz – and, starting from here, *identification with others* in general, should enable the experience of another *existence*, another *theory*, another *living*. Hence one can achieve an existence beyond individualism, a theory beyond theory, an ethic along with the 'coercion of the reality principle' capable of also challenging the economic concern with one's *Dasein* as the principle of all action.

'The concept of friendship', Max and Fritz wrote in 1935, 'includes its lasting until death'. Truly bound during all the vicissitudes that followed on from Horkheimer's appointment, from the exile in the USA, through Geneva and Paris, to their return to Germany in 1946, in the 1950s together the two friends again started to feel – not just as the 'clearsighted' ones of the abyss – the need to abandon that disappointing and disturbing Germany. Hence, on one hand, anticipating the late project of forming 'out-of-season collectives' which brings the *Notizen* to a close, and, on the other, picking up their original endeavour towards union, they meticulously prepared the possibility of again sharing their existences in the 1950s in the closest way possible.

Together, in September 1951, Fritz and Max established:

> Our life must be a *testimony*; to create utopia in even the smallest details. We want the other, the new, the unconditional. Our life is serious. Where we live, social laws must not apply. Now, so late in the day, we can no longer waste any time. We must create the conditions in which all our energies can be effective in our very own sense. Especially Max's talent and experience.[77]

At this point, their work itself seems to consist of the elaboration of their *form of life*: the end of their engagement, the construction of a *shared form of life* capable of giving itself its own conditions and its own character, freed from the coercion of the reality principle, that is, from the ontological destiny of the subject in his or her isolation.[78]

---

77 'Memorandum Friedrich Pollock-Max Horkheimer', 8 September 1951 in Horkheimer 1985–96, vol. 18, p. 218, own translation, italics mine.
78 See Benjamin 1986, 'Fate and Character', written in Lugano, but in 1919. The reflection on 'forms of life', present not only in Horkheimer (see for example 2004, p. 24), but in many

As a *testimony*, the work had to remain a *practice and form of life*, the realisation of *utopia in the smallest details*, whose protocols and documents would consist of texts, memorandums and diary entries but also physical spaces, houses, rooms and refuges. These documents are all necessary and inevitable, and at the same time inadequate and always on the point of betraying the supra-individual sense of this practical-existential design in dead letters and works. As part of this search for the form of life and testimony as a task, alongside the *Notizen* and their numerous 'Memorandums', we must therefore also thoroughly take stock of the aphorisms and diary entries of *Späne*: a collection of fragments which document the chats between Pollock and his friend Horkheimer during their years in Montagnola.[79] 'Freely annotated' by Pollock, with respect to the traditional authorship logic these *fragments* or *crumbs* resulting from those night-time chats appear an 'impure' text and form a work which fundamentally *does not distinguish* what comes from the philosopher and what comes from the economist. And so it is that this work – hitherto the most neglected, ignored even – holds particular interest. Its very form in the end is *testimony* to their continuous *being-with*, their fundamental *Beisammensein*. We might also ask ourselves if, not so much because of its contents, but its dual authorship, that is, because of its genesis and its very form, this spurious or 'nonconformist' text in the end does not constitute an extreme expression of that *programme for interdisciplinarity* around which, along with Pollock in the early 1930s, Horkheimer already sought to build his directorship of the Frankfurt Institute for Social Research.[80] Nevertheless, over 20 years after

---

authors, amongst whom Simmel, Wittgenstein, Foucault, Tugendhat and Habermas, has recently been enriched by two further contributions: the first of these, Jaeggi 2018, is directly linked to the Frankfurt circles and also significantly refers to the early critical theory while other stimulating theories can be found in Agamben 2016, which develops the nexus between 'form-of-life' as *dynamis* [potential] and 'inoperativity', see pp. 245 ff.

79   *Späne. Notizien über Gespräche mit Max Horkheimer, in unverbindlicher Formulierung aufgeschrieben von Friedrich Pollock*. The *Späne* are notes of shared conversations, mainly held at night, put down in writing by Friedrich Pollock, lifelong close friend and colleague of Horkheimer. Since they are notes made at the time which were annotated or summed up later on, they can only relay Horkheimer's thinking to a certain degree. Nevertheless, they transmit a rich and lively image of the later Horkheimer's thought. Especially as of 1959 when the two lived in neighbouring houses in Montagnola, Pollock visited his friend almost every evening. Except in a few cases, the notes cannot be considered records of the discussions in the strict sense, but summaries of Horkheimer's reflections, with which Pollock was almost always in agreement. Just one entry contains the explicit note: 'Some of Horkheimer's considerations which Pollock does not deem reasonable', 'Editorische Vorbemerkung', in Horkheimer 1985–96, vol. 14, p. 171, own translation.

80   On this basis too, I cannot wholly agree with the interpretation put forward by Jürgen

the formulation of that project, no complete accomplishment, no work could in itself sum up their original endeavour towards a *form of life*, a utopian thrust that seemed to lead from the field of works to one of experience-existence. And here, in a potential, fragmented, 'bitty' way, they were able to recollect a historically lost ideal – the ideal of philosophy as *practical philosophy*.

1.3   Psyche and History

That 'practical philosophy is continually losing its importance and interest', and that indeed 'it is becoming increasingly difficult to establish any connection between theoretical, philosophical ideas, and practice', is denounced in the *Notizen* and in *Späne* as a 'characteristic of our time'.[81] If, after Kant, the presupposition for the very possibility of practical philosophy depended upon the idea of an autonomous subject *ultimately responsible for deciding* upon his or her moral action, as things stood, this same presupposition had been eliminated by the contemporary state of affairs. The form of autonomous subjectivity had been replaced by a subjectivity that was merely functional, also because at that point 'the ultimate decision' had become 'so narrowly prescribed that speculative thought [was] no longer required'.[82]

The endeavour towards a form of life would have to combine once again with the motif of *de-cision*, because it was only by separating oneself from the depersonalising homogenisation that was taking place, driven by the generalised introduction of 'automation', that it was possible to reformulate a philosophical idea of subjectivity and practical truth as testimony. The proposal to form out-of-season collectives capable of criticising the present day and 'preserv[ing] the individual in genuine solidarity' is what could still result from practising 'decision'. Moreover, Horkheimer and Pollock had already attempted and planned to practise this decision on several occasions, while also involving it at the origin of the first steps of the critical theory.

Besides, the genesis of *critical theory* was not 'just philosophical', nor, from the outset, was its intention to provide a purely theoretical answer. In the figures of critical theory, they had sought to convert, or at least react to their elaboration of the various historical and political disappointments they had

---

Habermas, which maintains that the end of interdisciplinary cooperation was what generated what he indicates as the 'inhibition' in Horkheimer's writings in the almost three decades following the war. See Habermas 1991, p. 93.

81   Horkheimer 1978a, 'The End of Practical Philosophy', p. 226.
82   Horkheimer 1978a, p. 227.

lived through and experienced directly – the failed 1919 revolution in Munich, supported by both Pollock and Horkheimer – or witnessed in various ways – the Weimar Republic and the increasingly dramatic subsequent events, and Pollock's first-hand assessment of the betrayed ideal in the USSR in 1927. The figures and forms of critical theory were certainly not 'melancholy' and quietist like those in *Sein und Zeit*, but *ab origine* were in turn marked by a historical-epochal sense of great unease, also resulting from their direct experience. They marked the laceration between the *intérieur* and the *extérieur*, the struggle between *decision* and the imposition of the reality principle, and between 'critical imagination' and the particular 'addition' of bourgeois repression. History and its aporias, contradictions and lacerations extend into psychologies, into the so-called 'pathologies'.

This is another reason why critical philosophy and autobiography always continue to implicate each other. So much so that one might also wonder if, when Horkheimer placed 'the question of the connection between the economic life of society, the *psychic development* of individuals, and the changes in the realm of culture in the narrower sense' at the centre of his first project of social philosophy,[83] he was not *also* taking some elements of his/their lives, marked by a primary split between the personal and the historical-political dimensions and somehow aimed at overcoming it, to the level of critical and conceptual understanding. The young Horkheimer was afflicted by what his biographer describes as an illness: 'he was ill due to the conflict between what was and what – he thought – should have been'.[84] It was then that he approached Schopenhauer's *Aphorisms on the Wisdom of Life*. In those years, it was the experience of the *île heureuse* which enabled him to temporarily combine ideal and real, which Schopenhauer saw as being split, overcoming the *principium individuationis* in a radically anti-conformist proximity that went somewhat against Schopenhauer's asceticism. But, beyond the fleeting *île heureuse*, would it be historically possible to actually overcome this principle? The critical and self-critical seizure of the 'autocratic instinctual structure' testifies that despite the critical commitment and 'historical work' dear to Adorno, even many years after that first experience, *overcoming the self* remained a task destined to evolve and evaporate into 'utopia'.

Despite his opposition, in 1914 Horkheimer had to sign up for the army. Even though he never went to the front, this also helps us understand that his unease and unhappiness did not 'simply' have an endogenous or private origin, nor

---

83 Horkheimer 1993a, p. 11, italics mine.
84 Gumnior and Ringguth 1997, p. 16, own translation.

express an absolute ontic-ontological *Befindlichkeit*. By then taking the connection between the economic life of society and individual psychic development as a theme, Horkheimer also intended to explicitly respond, again, to Heidegger's phenomenology of existence. Horkheimer's involvement in the revolutionary movements of 1919 that led, like a passing elation, to the *Soviets* of the Bavarian Republic, had in fact been 'mediated' – distanced – by a sort of suffering or convalescent 'standing by the window', moreover, in effect, a standing by the window in the home for 'mental illnesses', where in that very period he found himself interned following his escape to the *île heureuse* ...

The person who allows us to get to the bottom of what the official biography barely hints at,[85] benefitting from a veil of romantic fiction but not without some underlying truth, is Germaine Krull. Later to become one of the most interesting figures in international photography, Krull was a friend of Horkheimer and Pollock from the Munich period right up to the years in Montagnola, and hence a witness to that youthful period. We are in Schwabing, the most bohemian of neighbourhoods, where Chien fou [Mad Dog] – as Krull was called by her friends owing to her highly irregular moods and passionate nature – was going from a meeting with Rilke to one with Kurt Eisner, the leader of the Bavarian revolutionaries killed in 1918. It was immediately after the proclamation of the general strike and a large demonstration that Chien fou met the young Horkheimer in Munich. Introduced to her by a friend, Horkheimer gave her the impression of a 'good-looking, tall and slim young man' who 'looked like he came from a good family'. In the span of a few sentences, the young Horkheimer confided to Krull:

> My father has had me shut up in a care home because he didn't want me to end up in prison for my ideas. There are thousands of little birds on the branches of the trees outside my window. I spend all day with them because I'm not allowed to go out, you can't go out when you've got serious mental illnesses like mine. My family pays a sackload of money to keep me in there. It's true, don't laugh, I'm 'mental' and prone to breakdowns. The doctors really love me, almost as much as they love my family's money ...[86]

Despite his father's fears concerning his strange, anti-conformist and subversive ideas – then alternating between a transgressive hedonistic dream and the

---

85 Gumnior and Ringguth 1997, p. 20.
86 Krull 1992, p. 50, own translation.

telos of *'rational social organisation'* which he started to read of in Marx – *even at such an early stage*, in practice he could not find in either the real proletariat or the idea of class the subject or historical figure that would guarantee to fight for the realisation of this organisation.

The *extérieur*, contemplated from the window of the care home with that spectacle of thousands of birds, was not dialectically reflected at all in the climate among the masses. Indeed, with respect to the masses, in the end Max and Fritz would always remain similar to those two birds freed into the air that they described themselves as in *L'île heureuse*.

In other words, despite reaching a higher level than the window in the care home, the window of the nascent 'critical theory' never wholly overcame that feeling of distance and separation. Instead, and necessarily, it became an almost constant object of theoretical reflection; that *distance* and that separation between inside and out, existence and history, morality and reason, them and the others, instinctual structure and the tyranny of self-preservation, metamorphically returned again and again in the midst of almost constant *Sehnsucht*.

Also because of this real suffering, to him Heidegger's existential analytics seemed to elude and disguise the problem of the historicity of *Dasein*, by speaking abstractly and almost again metaphysically of 'inner historicity' and interpreting *Dasein* as a mode of being in the ground of Being.[87] Laid down in such a way, the connection of *Dasein* with the *real historical process* was distanced, sublimated by imagining a relationship with a 'purely apparent' dimension from an ontological-fundamental perspective. And yet, Horkheimer objected, '[j]ust as engagement with external history illuminates the individual beings [*das jeweilige Dasein*], the analysis of individual existence [*das jeweilige Existenzen*] conditions the understanding of history'.[88] Rather than evoking a mysterious ontic-ontological relationship, it was a matter of recognising that existence in its 'particularity' is indissolubly implicated in exterior history and its contradictions. In other words, subjectivities and psychologies are produced by real and material history, and in their turn psychologies and subjectivities work back on the real historical relations, reproducing them or seeking to criticise them and change them, by separating and de-ciding themselves from them.

The object of psychology – the soul, the instinctual structure – in short is not solely biological or natural, nor abstractly existential, but rather a quite radic-

---

87   Horkheimer 1993b, p. 112.
88   Horkheimer 1993b, p. 113.

ally *historical* fact. The city of history and economy finds its way into the subjects and expands there, to then condition and direct the multiform dimension of action and the '*gaieté*' of forms of life, imprisoning them in a repressive autocratic universe marked by a disposition towards masochism as well as sadism.

Horkheimer would again come back after the war to critically thematise this classic isomorphism, upon which Erich Fromm[89] would also concentrate his attention, between the psyche and history. At this later stage, Horkheimer no longer dealt with Heidegger's ontological 'abstractions' alone, but also with the 'psychologistic' interpretations of culture. In 'The Lessons of Fascism', one of his most complete and perhaps most successful essays from the 1950s, a comparison is drawn between psychology, meant as the 'positive science of mental process', and the 'present situation of the world'.[90] Despite attesting to a remarkable sensitivity on his part for psychological analyses and the non-authoritarian educational practices that these should lead to on the practical institutional level, this comparison between psychology and history brings Horkheimer to methodologically clarify that 'the exclusive concentration on psychological phenomena and psychological explanations is one-sided and relativistic, as not a few psychologists have realized. ... Social analysis offers a necessary corrective to psychologism'.[91] Otherwise '... we run the danger of replacing in our minds the real human beings in their world of conflicts by a fictitious type, a kind of universal man, or even the "neurotic personality" of our time'.[92]

The motifs already encountered in the critique of Heidegger's 'ahistorical' existentialism, then also present, as we shall see, in Horkheimer's criticism of Kant's moral theory, return in this critique of psychologistic abstraction and reduction. And once again, the criticism is also levelled from a very real *practical* concern. Since we are conscious of the limits of the 'science of mental process', evidently 'we can then ... expect to find the answer to social and political tensions by mere psychological analysis'.[93] In other words, the psychological therapy route, whose Stoic origin Horkheimer highlights, cannot be understood and proposed as a suitable solution to problems that are also and foremost historical and social.[94] But at the same time, according to a line of

---

89 For a factual reconstruction of Fromm's brief relationship with the Institute, see Wiggershaus 1994, pp. 52 ff.; 'Break with Erich Fromm', pp. 265 ff.
90 Horkheimer 1950, p. 209. To compare with the following text by Adorno, similar in many aspects, entitled 'The Meaning of Working Through the Past', Adorno 2005b.
91 Horkheimer 1950, p. 215.
92 Ibid.
93 Horkheimer 1950, p. 218.
94 See Horkheimer 1950, p. 240.

thought already present in the texts of his youth, which would remain constant in his work, it also needs to be recognised that the here seemingly obligatory political route appeared heavily compromised. Not just that, it seemed to contain a historically insuperable aporia, since the irrational powers seemed to have started defining people more and more coercively, deeply influencing the *intérieur*, the 'instinctual structure' and this all the more so since '[c]*ircenses* of all kinds have in many historical situations taken the place of *panis*'.[95] The Frankfurt School, which would be epoch-making in its critique of the *cultural industry*, was formulating its first criticisms of ideology, for the moment explicitly distancing itself from a rigid reading of Marx and Engels to lay down that 'even the situation of the proletariat is, in this society, no guarantee of correct knowledge'.[96]

This means that the question of the subject historically capable of fighting for emancipation is posed and complicated in the interlacing of history and psychology. This mix of social and psychological problems also had to be tackled in the form of a *radical criticism of demagogy*, in the awareness that neither the social roots of the phenomenon, nor the psychological structure of the masses had simply been 'swept away' with the military defeat of Nazism and Fascism.

> The specific task of the leader is to carry the already existing tendency to intellectual and spiritual passivity one step further, to convert the masses into 'followers', to lure them into blind, masochistic obedience. He transforms his audience into a submissive, uncritical, and highly critical mass, held together by identification with the speaker or leader.[97]

With these observations, once again in the 1950s Horkheimer seems to take up that programme on the psychological *humus* of Fascism already developed under his directorship in the early 1930s in 'Studien über Autorität und Familie' ['Studies on Authority and the Family'].

It is significant that he himself felt the need to resume that programme and relaunch it in terms of a critique of demagogy as the historical legacy of that Fascist past. Indeed, it was still deemed very topical: it did not seem to want to pass, but instead appeared to manage to survive and bring itself back up to date:

---

95   Horkheimer 1993b, p. 124.
96   Horkheimer 2002d, p. 213.
97   Horkheimer 1950, p. 232.

> In the thirties, much valuable research had been started on the techniques of demagogy. Then came the war, and the investigations dropped off, as if the whole problem was going to be ended for all time by the military defeat of the fascist aggressors. The agitator and his audience have been relegated to the archives of history. Yet it is easily demonstrable that neither the underlying social roots nor the psychological structures have been swept away .... I would argue vigorously for a serious re-examination of the techniques and psychological aspects of demagogy.[98]

Evidently, for the appropriate resumption and renewal of this critical programme, already launched in the 1930s, the condition was that, in spite of everything, there had been no clean break between the two historical periods and, above all, between the two political forms succeeding each other in Germany. No difference had come about in kind, rather than in degree, as many instead would have liked to believe. This is why, on externalising what would then be the reasons leading to his fresh abandonment of Germany in the late 1950s, in 'The Lessons of Fascism' Horkheimer feels the need to

> point to the generally recognized failure of the de-Nazification program. Even though the top criminals have been tried, condemned, and in some cases executed, the majority of Germans who sympathized with National Socialism are better off today than those who remained aloof from fascism. So true is this that it is correct to say that the institutionalization of de-Nazification achieved the opposite of what it was intended to accomplish. The man with Nazi contacts was able to speed up his de-Nazification trial, pay a fine of a few thousand worthless marks, and promptly regain his old position. Only a few of those who were morally strong enough to risk their lives by resisting the Party now have governmental or professional positions.[99]

While criticised for having been 'established overnight' upon his return to Germany,[100] with observations such as these, Horkheimer is capable of a critical gaze filled with an essential solitude, a gaze in certain ways not unlike the one given by Heinrich Böll to the characters in his novels.

---

98 Horkheimer 1950, p. 232.
99 Horkheimer 1950, pp. 236–7. Horkheimer expresses himself in similar and even more radical terms in the 'Brief an den S. Fischer Verlag' from 3 July 1965 preceding Volume II of his *Kritische Theorie* writings (1968b, pp. VII–XI).
100 Wiggershaus 1994, pp. 442 ff.

The critical questioning of the German transition seems to extend the discussion on 'state capitalism', in particular the effective possibility of its democratic variant, developed as of the 1940s under the stimulus of Pollock's fundamental concept of the same name. Between totalitarian and democratic state capitalism does there not seem to be a sort of *grey area*, which makes democracy apparent and 'false'? With the advent of 'state capitalism', was another form to that of domination [*Herrschaft*] possible? Maybe a domination disguised-sublimated as welfare and total administration? And was this question not to be raised in Germany in particular, that is, where the economic miracle *co-existed* with corruption trials presided over by judges who had backed Hitler? As Horkheimer writes, on planning his association of the clearsighted and preparing his second expatriation together with Pollock:

> For those who are appalled by the economic miracle, the mendacious democracy, the bribery trials with Hitler judges, the luxury and the misery, the rancor and rejection of every form of decency, the admiration of eastern and western magnates, the disintegration of spirit, the slide into parochialism of this old civilization, such an association would be a kind of home.[101]

The task of critical theory, in a sort of *permanent exodus*, would be to keep this fundamental critical question open at least. At the same time, of course, it would also have to seek to maintain a separation between the two *variants*, of authoritarian state capitalism and democratic state capitalism, while claiming the importance of those values of personal freedom which were reaching their twilight. Nonetheless, no emphasis was to be placed on any particular reality, instead fostering a strong 'longing for perfect and consummate justice' with respect to each of them.[102] *The theoretical and practical possibilities* that this question on state capitalism and its variants implies and stirs up, *from a theoretical perspective*, correspond precisely to the relationship between Pollock and Horkheimer, attesting to their distinction but also their hence not only existential but also – as we will see in detail later on – intellectual and theoretical *inseparability*.

Many years before, Horkheimer had moreover already defended and practised the autonomy of critical thinking, doing so at the price of placing his critical theory in historical solitude, against all ruinous conciliation and myth-

---

101   Horkheimer 1978a, 'For an Association of the Clearsighted', p. 166.
102   Horkheimer 1975, pp. 70–1.

icisation of the present. Then, he had dared to advise that an attitude which was not in the condition to act in what were the true interests of the proletariat, but instead drew its orientation from the ideas and moods of the masses, would find itself in a state of servile dependence on the existent.

> The intellectual is satisfied to proclaim with reverent admiration the creative strength of the proletariat and finds satisfaction in adapting himself to it and in canonizing it. He fails to see that such an evasion of theoretical effort (which the passivity of his own thinking spares him) and of temporary opposition to the masses (which active theoretical effort on his part might force upon him) only makes the masses blinder and weaker than they need be.[103]

Horkheimer had already dramatically suspected that the bearers not only of *thought* but also of a *critical attitude*[104] therefore increasingly risked finding themselves 'isolated' and 'thrown back upon themselves'.[105] He also suspected that it was less and less possible for the truth to be safeguarded and realised in the masses, and that rather it could only find *refuge* in the form of 'small groups',[106] and 'numerically small groups of men'.[107] They were thoughts that had arisen at the same moment that the elaboration of (his own) history had also led to the elaboration of the original separation-opposition between *traditional theory* and *critical theory*. Even then, methodologically speaking, Horkheimer's criticism of the *alienated* character of traditional theory and its *quietist* and *conformist*[108] implications made reference to the *activity of soci-*

---

103 Horkheimer 2002d, p. 214.
104 It is necessary to underline 'critical attitude', the expression that Horkheimer uses to further differentiate Critical Theory and its position beyond the reification of objectivity and subjectivity typical of traditional theory. On the 'critical attitude' see in particular Horkheimer 2002d, pp. 206–9.
105 '... the kind of thinking which is most topical, which has the deepest grasp of the historical situation, and is most pregnant with the future, must at certain times isolate its subject and throw him back upon himself', Horkheimer 2002d, p. 214.
106 '... under the conditions of later capitalism and the impotence of the workers before the authoritarian state's apparatus of oppression, truth has sought refuge among small groups of admirable men. But these have been decimated by terrorism and have little time for refining the theory. Charlatans profit by this situation and the general intellectual level of the masses is rapidly declining.' Horkheimer 2002d, pp. 237–8.
107 'In the general historical upheaval the truth may reside with numerically small groups of men'. Horkheimer 2002d, p. 241.
108 Horkheimer 2002d, p. 229.

ety as a transcendental power,[109] hence not only latching onto the legacy of Kantian idealism, but also the Marxian *critique of the political economy*.[110] Nevertheless, the theorist from Frankfurt was totally aware that he may or would *have to* 'find himself in opposition to views prevailing even among the proletariat'.[111] It was a contrast and conflict – Horkheimer writes in an anticipatory answer to a criticism which would later often be aimed at him, from Brecht first of all – that had nothing at all to do with 'the theoretician's social position' nor his 'income'.[112] 'Engels', Horkheimer ironically underlines, was, like him, 'a businessman' by birth too.[113] That contrast and conflict – and the connected radically *minority* or even *aristocratic* position of critical theory – were instead the result of loyalty to the '*very essence of thought*'. He was not willing to functionally reduce it into a *useable* theory, nor to ensnare his *longing for the future* in the framework of an absolutised reality principle repressing all *fantasy*.[114] In this refusal he was the steadfast guardian of the transformative autonomy of critical thought, on both the existential and the historical-political level:

> The hostility to theory as such which prevails in contemporary public life is really directed against the transformative activity associated with critical thinking. Opposition starts as soon as theorists fail to limit themselves to verification and classification by means of categories which are as neutral as possible, that is, categories which are indispensable to inherited ways of life. Among the vast majority of the ruled there is the unconscious fear that theoretical thinking might show their painfully won adaptation to reality to be perverse and unnecessary. Those who profit from the status quo entertain a general suspicion of any intellectual independence. …[115] The demand therefore for a positive outlook and for acceptance of a subordinate position threatens, even in progressive sectors of society, to overwhelm any openness to theory. The issue, however, is not simply the theory of emancipation; it is the practice of it as well. …[116] But conformism in thought and the insistence that thinking is a fixed vocation, a

---

109   Horkheimer 2002d, p. 203.
110   Horkheimer 2002d, p. 219, p. 246.
111   Horkheimer 2002d, p. 221.
112   Ibid.
113   Ibid.
114   Horkheimer 2002d, p. 220.
115   Horkheimer 2002d, p. 232.
116   Horkheimer 2002d, p. 233.

self-enclosed realm within society as a whole, betrays the very essence of thought.[117]

It was with these words that he concluded the text-manifesto of 1937, 'Traditional Theory and Critical Theory', and we should underline the almost staggering continuity – thanks to the continuism of history, despite the 'Lessons of Fascism' – between these assumptions and the ones that would finally be collected in *Späne* and the *Notizen*. The awareness that psychologies are *produced by history* already achieved in 'History and Psychology' nevertheless enabled a close criticism of the psycho-biologistic naturalisation of utilitarianism made by those rationalistic psychological theses which sustained that, by nature, 'human beings supposedly act exclusively on the basis of their material advantage'.[118] This 'psychological abstraction' he traces back to 'economic egoism ... historically conditioned and subject to radical change',[119] while also asserting, on the basis of the Freudian distinction between the immutable and the *plastic impulses*, that

> [m]odern psychology has long since identified the error of asserting that the human instinct of self-preservation is 'natural' .... Human beings and probably animals as well are hardly so psychologically individualistic that all their instinctual impulses are necessarily founded in immediate desire for material gratifications. Human beings may, for instance, experience a sort of happiness in the solidarity with like-minded souls that makes it possible for them to assume the risk of suffering and death.[120]

Becoming aware of the interlacing between *history* and *psychology* did not only produce a difficult or even aporetic consequence at the level of identifying the historical subject of change. Instead, reflection and self-reflection on the historical character of psychologies and behaviours was also able to lead to the critical seizure, relativisation and deconstruction of the naturalisation of the impulse towards self-preservation. In other words, it could lead to questioning, also self-critically, 'the autocracy of one's own instinctual structure' and thus cast a new light on the question of the meaning and possibility of crit-

---

117   Horkheimer 2002d, p. 243.
118   Horkheimer 1993b, p. 123.
119   Ibid.
120   Ibid. On the importance of these reflections and on the relationship with Fromm, see Dubiel 2001, pp. 41–6. Also remember the relationship of the young Horkheimer, as a student, with Gestalt psychology: see Gumnior and Ringguth 1997, p. 22.

ical behaviour, that is, of authentic, anti-nihilistic and nonconformist *moral action*. It is precisely in Horkheimer's recurrent critical comparison with *Kantian morality* that the also directly experienced nexus between history and *psyche* develops and deepens. Life is elaborated and interrogated philosophically, and in turn philosophy is traced back to history and life. From this point of view too, there are profound links between Horkheimer's 'diaries' and his best-known philosophical essays. With his imperative, Kant enters the stage like the seismographer of separation and the inner struggle of consciousness, and, in order for them not to remain ideological abstractions, his recordings need to be understood by repositioning them materialistically in connection with the external historical world. If, as Kant has it, the distinctive sign of moral action oriented by the categorical imperative is the 'renunciation of all interest', so that the moral subject may '[a]ct only according to that maxim by which you can at the same time will that it should become a universal law',[121] well, historically, this same distinctive sign of disinterest can only translate into a mental situation characterised by *continual uneasiness* and endless reflection, and inner conflict that is 'fundamentally impossible to overcome', and hence also aporetically paralysing. Indeed, the moral imperative 'leaves the individual with a certain uneasiness and unclarity. Within the soul, a struggle is played out between personal interest and a vague conception of the general interest, between individual and universal objectives'.[122] And 'since this problematic tension playing itself out in the inner lives of human beings necessarily derives from their role in the social life process, Kant's philosophy, being a faithful reflection of this tension, is a consummate expression of its age'.[123]

Seeing as the action and the Dasein requested by the *social life process* are historically oriented towards *unleashing the possessive instincts and continually satisfying the instincts for self-preservation*, the upshot is that '[t]he basis of the spiritual situation in question is easily recognized upon consideration of the structure of the bourgeois order'.[124] But if the foundation and root of the *moral aporia* paralysing the subject is thus recognised within the instrumental bourgeois attitude, coherent consequences will have to be drawn. It will be necessary to go back *from inside to outside*, from the *psyche to history*, and elaborate that previously introjected pain in the social space as critical decision and *praxis*: 'In this society of isolated individuals, the categorical imperative,

---

121   Horkheimer 1993c, p. 18, which quotes Kant's *Groundwork of the Metaphysic of Morals*.
122   Horkheimer 1993c, p. 19.
123   Ibid.
124   Ibid.

as was suggested above, runs up against the impossibility of its own meaningful realization. Consequently, it necessarily implies the transformation of this society'.[125] The moral root of critical theory appears evident here, and, together with this, the fragility of its relationship with real historical-political projectuality. The transformation of society seemed to be deduced almost as a 'consequence' aimed at saving the sense of the categorical imperative. However much of a compensation, this conclusion seemed to naively evade the nevertheless already highlighted historical antinomy, concerning the integration and *psychopolitical* production of that historical subject who in theory should have enacted the transformation of instrumental society. As a consequence, instead of being able to observe and aid the evolution of practical reason into a transformative critique and externalised political struggle, Horkheimer was to increasingly observe and denounce that the essential feature of the historical times in which he and Pollock found themselves leading a tendentially more and more withdrawn life was the most radical elimination of all moral orientation. Under the yoke of an 'automated' principle of self-preservation – and Pollock would dedicate his later works to the *era of automation* – the real increasingly split from the ideal and comparison with the question of sense until, with the reduction of the ego to a function, it prompted the most total *eclipse of moral possibility*.

History by no means allows the Kantian mental conflict to be resolved in a neat conclusion, it does not mitigate it, but rather submerges it and no longer even lets it appear in the automated *extérieur*. No laceration appears, only homogeneous and depersonalising function. The production of life consists of producing the surface. Instrumental reason builds the world of total administration by submerging the radical anti-conformism of practical reason and radically driving it away from appearance, and in so doing, it takes the same 'irreconcilable contradictions' of the Kantian system to their extreme consequences.

> Kant's concepts are ambiguous. Reason as the transcendental, supraindividual self contains the idea of a free coexistence in which human beings organize themselves to form the universal subject and resolve the conflict between pure and empirical reason in the conscious solidarity of the whole. The whole represents the idea of true universality, utopia. At the same time, however, reason is the agency of calculating thought, which arranges the world for the purposes of self-preservation and recognizes

---

125 Horkheimer 1993c, p. 25.

no function other than that of working on the object as mere sense material in order to make it the material of subjugation. The true nature of the schematism which externally coordinates the universal and the particular, the concept and the individual case, finally turns out, in current science, to be the interest of industrial society. Being is apprehended in terms of manipulation and administration. Everything – including the individual human being, not to mention the animal – becomes a repeatable, replaceable process, a mere example of the conceptual models of the system.[126]

Hence, Kant's morality remains a victim of its own contradictions.[127] This is why *Dialectic of Enlightenment* highlights how the attacks soon made against him in the same sphere of enlightened thinkers were not lacking in coherence.

Once harnessed to the dominant mode of production, enlightenment, which strives to undermine any order which has become repressive, nullifies itself. This is expressed in the early attacks of the current form of enlightenment on the 'all-crushing' Kant. Just as Kant's moral philosophy sets limits to his enlightened critique in order to rescue the possibility of reason, unreflecting enlightened thinking has always sought, for its own survival, to cancel itself with skepticism, in order to make room for the existing order. In contrast to such precautions, the work of Sade, like that of Nietzsche, is an intransigent critique of practical reason, beside which even that of Kant himself appears like a revocation of his own thought. It pushes the scientific principle to annihilating extremes.[128]

If the pathology of enlightened reason as such generates monsters, all that remains to morality, to the *intérieur*, to contact without instrumentality is the part of the *other*, that is, that *other reason* which is exiled in suffering and madness as the extreme and solitary manifestation of morality. The memory of the *Kurhaus* and psychiatric clinics also seems to have to return in the years in Montagnola as the expression of uninterrupted suffering, a personal malaise that expresses and reflects the suffering of an era:

Now that liberalism is declining and social reasons for moral behavior become less compelling in an increasingly administered world, and con-

---

126   Horkheimer and Adorno 2007, p. 65.
127   Horkheimer and Adorno 2007, p. 64.
128   Horkheimer and Adorno 2007, p. 74.

formist reactions, what is still necessary today, function *automatically* so that criminality begins where they end, morality has become historical and faithfulness a romantic category. Given the encompassing transitoriness of all things, the wholehearted devotion to another, happiness that conflicts with personal material interests, is a *delusion* that derives from the residue of earlier social forms. The psychoanalyst has the last word. Morality stands in need of therapy. And despair and bliss need it even more.[129]

Now distance and diversity are reclaimed, in some way reconciling affliction and happiness, identity and alterity, morality and antiutilitarian madness.

Albeit transformed, in the end what is still being expressed is the metaphysics of youth, his *Sehnsucht* for another reality:

> *Comical old people.* Old people often develop preferences and aversions that seem absurd to other people, attachments to things and relationships that are pointless, sensibilities without any apparent reason; as one might say, they become comical, singular, and in the best of cases pitied. In truth, the same could be said of culture *per se*, insofar as it has to be something more than a simple means for co-existence or a tool of social relations, of traffic. The difference between sex and love, veneration and obedience, heroism and collective interest, the objective meaning of this difference, its own and so-called absolute sense is imaginary; and those who seriously devote themselves to others, obliviously and without high-sounding discourses on eternal values, distinguish themselves from those comical old people, from the *'characters'*, as the Americans say, only because their particular qualities are shared by a greater number of people; and that is it. But happiness and sorrow are serious for both; madness is serious, it is reckless not to live in madness.[130]

It is a sort of extreme self-portrait, which reuses that biographical method we owe to the great Edgar Allan Poe, according to which in order to find the traces

---

129   Horkheimer 1978a, 'Historicity of Morality', p. 226, italics mine.
130   Horkheimer 1991, 'Komische Alte', p. 393, own translation. Adorno is much more often given credit for the historical significance of this result than Horkheimer (as Honneth 2009 does, p. 26), in particular with regard to the aphorisms on offended life in *Minima Moralia*. Indeed, Horkheimer is often greatly undervalued for these results too (see Habermas 1991; Wiggershaus 1994; but also Ponsetto 1981, pp. 368 ff.).

of superior individuals in past history one has to 'search carefully the slight records of wretches who died in prison, in Bedlam, or upon the gallows'.[131]

In one of his last texts, Pollock also concentrated on growing old as a sociological problem, highlighting the increasing loss of social utility and social position of 'old people'.[132] These texts are also mirrors, in which one can perceive the memory of friends and unknown people who died in the concentration camps,[133] in the same way as one can also make out the image of Carlota Weil, Pollock's wife and cousin of the patron who enabled the adventure of the Institute (see Figures 5 and 14). During the years in Montagnola, Carlota was admitted to a clinic for mental disorders on several occasions, and she would pass away there in 1983.[134] At the start of the 1970s, just after Fritz's death, Max had the chance to recall, not without some nostalgia, his lifelong friend. He would use these words: 'If you'd asked Pollock the place he felt he belonged to most, he'd have replied: at Max and Maidon's, we had a unique feeling, as a three [*ein Gefühl von Dreien*]. And so, despite it all, we achieved the *île heureuse*'.[135]

1.4   Biopower and the Hidden Faculties of Existence (Eroticism, Friendship, Art)

'Vernunft und Selbsterhaltung', in English 'The End of Reason', an important essay by Horkheimer from 1942, begins with this powerful incipit: 'The fundamental concepts of civilization are in a process of rapid decay'.[136] Starting from here, this essay, which makes up the original core of the subsequent work *The Eclipse of Reason*, shows how the same central concept of *'reason'* undergoes a drastic *change*, to be interpreted as *an emptying, a loss of sense*. The word 'reason' has not been cancelled from the vocabulary, but the concept of 'objective reason', central for the whole epistemic-metaphysical tradition, in effect collapses and 'reason itself appears as a ghost that has emerged from linguistic

---

131   Horkheimer 2004, p. 108.
132   Pollock 1958.
133   Horkheimer 2004, p. 109.
134   After the First World War, Carlota Pollock, née Weil, Argentinian citizen, was also behind interesting initiatives in favour of the poorest children in New York, preparing an art education programme for the Manhattanville Day Care Center which also involved representatives of the Museum of Modern Art: see C. Pollock 1946.
135   'Biographische Interviews Max Horkheimer-Mathias Becker, 1971–72', Max Horkheimer Archiv X 183 a, quoted by Wiggershaus 2013, p. 227, own translation.
136   Horkheimer 1978c, p. 26.

usage'.¹³⁷ From the organ of eternal ideas and unchanging truths that it was in itself and for itself, reason is reduced to being a *mere adding machine*, called upon solely to adapt the means to the ends, within the growing domination of an economic rationality that presupposes profit to be the ultimate end of all ends. 'Objective reason', aimed at dialectically overcoming the whole sphere of *doxai* and at apprehending universal ends and values, is thus reduced and betrayed, becoming *calculating reason*, and the discussion-definition of *ends* is overturned into the mere calculation of *means*. This crisis, or, in Horkheimer's words, *eclipse* of reason, is the pathology of rationality that flares up when its relationship with the truth and with the realisation of an existence possessing sense is denied, while the term is preserved in a purely rhetorical and formalistic manner in false idolatry of the economic *doxa*.

With this eclipse, reason has 'been reduced to its pragmatic significance much more radically than ever before',¹³⁸ and, to use classical terms, it hence seems to celebrate the victory of Thrasymachus and sophistry. It asserts *the usefulness of the strongest* as right or rational, to the detriment of the dialectical, Socratic-Platonic search for justice in itself. Besides, in modern terms, this change of reason, its ridding of sense, seems to reflect that usurpation of the ends by the *means*, which become *ends unto themselves*, and *end up overturning rationalisation, changing it into irrationality*, as already written by Max Weber (whom Horkheimer does not fail to quote). Indeed, already for Weber, '[t]his reversal marks the whole of modern civilisation, whose arrangements, institutions, and activities are so "rationalised" that whereas humanity once established itself within them, now it is they which enclose and determine humanity like an "iron cage"'.¹³⁹

And again, as Horkheimer writes, in contemporary terms, but not without classical overtones, with reason 'all ideas that transcend the given reality are forced to share its disgrace. ... It is [now] a pragmatic instrument oriented to expediency, cold and sober. The belief in cleverness rests on motives much more cogent than metaphysical propositions. ...'¹⁴⁰ With the eclipse of the dialectical-epistemic dimension, reason hence becomes 'a kind of adding machine',¹⁴¹ whose exclusive activity is to calculate in function of the dogmatically presupposed and hypostatised historical end, an end without end: to

---

137   Horkheimer 1978c, p. 27.
138   Horkheimer 1978c, p. 28.
139   Löwith 2003, p. 68.
140   Horkheimer 1978c, p. 28.
141   Horkheimer 1978c, p. 31.

increase profit and power. This end goes without question. Presupposed as a dogma or sacred taboo, it overrules all reasoning around sense:

> When even the dictators of today appeal to reason, they mean that they possess the most tanks. They were rational enough to build them; others should be rational enough to yield to them. Within the range of Fascism, to defy such reason is the cardinal crime.[142]

Instrumental reason hence proves to be closely linked to praxis. There can be no preventing criticism of its absurd self-purposiveness, and as such it *is* realised and reflected in an 'iron cage', to take up Weber's image, but in the case of our authors, the cage is by no means metaphorical, it is that of the *authoritarian state* and *totally administered society*. By upsetting the original, essentially disinterested and non-violent traits of the *theorein*, the *adding machine of reason* is entirely transformed into an instrument to seek *interest* and boost power. In this historical situation, in the same way those *qualities* that were seen as a person's *virtues* become mere instruments of interest too. In short, in light of these analyses it appears that the overall historical passage towards the 'totally administered' form of society, prepared by the advent of monopolistic capitalism and the 'authoritarian state', was also ordaining an *anthropological change* so radical as to lead to the individual's transformation, decline and, lastly, elimination.

> The crisis of reason is manifested in the crisis of the individual, as whose agency it has developed. The illusion that traditional philosophy has cherished about the individual and about reason – the illusion of their eternity – is being dispelled. The individual once conceived of reason exclusively as an instrument of the self. Now he experiences the reverse of this self-deification. The machine has dropped the driver; it is racing blindly into space. At the moment of consummation, reason has become irrational and stultified.[143]

What is 'dropped' and brusquely exonerated from a productive totality racing towards the conjunction of automation and self-purposiveness is the person-subject as such, and in particular his or her essential attribute which is 'spontaneous action'.[144]

---

142 Horkheimer 1978c, p. 28.
143 Horkheimer 2004, p. 87.
144 Horkheimer 2004, p. 97.

As Joseph Schumpeter had already suggested in the socio-economic field, this process of marginalisation of subjectivities ends up concerning not only the workers but the entrepreneurs too, since as Horkheimer observes, '[i]n this age of big business the independent entrepreneur is no longer typical', and in substance, '[t]he ordinary man finds it harder and harder to plan for his heirs or even for his own remote future'. The only person who can prevail is the 'submissive type'.[145] Hence, the upshot at the sociological level is that '[b]ecause modern society is a totality, the decline of individuality affects the lower as well as the higher social groups, the worker no less than the businessman', with evident effects of 'integration in the general system' of those labour forces who should have transformed or demolished it. Hence 'individuality loses its economic basis' and is absorbed and assimilated into *purely pragmatistic totalities*'. In turn, this translates into a radically conformist homogenisation of the members of the working class too, whose 'minds are closed to dreams of a basically different world and to concepts that, instead of being mere classification of facts, are oriented towards real fulfilment of those dreams'.

The overall consequence, going from the sociological to the anthropological level, is that 'the individual subject of reason tends to become a *shrunken ego*, captive of an evanescent present, forgetting the use of the intellectual functions',[146] to the point that 'specificity (uniqueness), the element of particularity from the standpoint of reason, is completely repressed or absorbed'.[147] The human being lacking in 'uniqueness' necessarily comes to lack *qualities* too; the individual has been brought down to a functional, totally conformist generic being, absorbed in the horizon of the 'purely pragmatistic totalities' of the late industrial era. The domination – from the viewpoint of reason – of 'the general' is realised by incorporating subjectivities into the generic being, leading to a regressive change which greatly harms not only social concepts and relations, but also the dimension of affections, instincts and characters. *Distinction, courtesy, composure* and *loyalty* lose their purposiveness and indeed become impossible, since, like reason, they are implicated in a parallel process of ruinous emptying. All those tendencies towards disinterest remain as mere ornaments, like those utilitarian objects which were still preserved at the beginning of the machine age, even though at this point they were only a reference to obsolete production techniques and no longer counted for anything.

Now, so long as they do actually remain, *human qualities* are only *an empty ornament*, marked by an essential impotence. Forcibly eclipsed, they risk ex-

---

145   Horkheimer 2004, p. 95.
146   Ibid., italics mine.
147   Horkheimer 2004, p. 100.

tinction, being wiped out completely, as, moreover, also happens to 'theoretical thought',[148] 'the esthetic delight of ... contemplation'[149] and all those activities deemed 'unproductive' which are hence, owing to their dysfunctionality, devalued, controlled and repressed, like 'a kind of vice'.[150] In short, do not be deceived, not only the calculations of reason, but also *self-preservation* is 'at the root of the variety of attributes characterizing individuality'.[151]

As a consequence, *totally* administered society means that all the spheres of society are subsumed within the process of its irrational 'rationalisation'. In other words, all rapports, relationships, feelings and social expressions become functions and moments of the realisation of this *totality* of means that proceed in a technocratic, or rather, autocratic manner. This global subsumption-assimilation also happens because, more and more often, *'that which is outside is inside'*. The laws and requests of totality – 'that which is outside' – are increasingly *introjected* into the deepest and most *unconscious* dimensions of the masses and people. End of the *intérieur*. It is a long-term historical process. However, in this process, more and more

> [t]he individual has to do violence to himself and learn that the life of the whole is the necessary precondition to his own. Reason has to master rebellious feelings and instincts, the inhibition of which is supposed to make human cooperation possible. Inhibitions originally imposed from without have to become part and parcel of the individual's own consciousness – this principle already prevailed in the ancient world. What is called progress lay in the social expansion of it. In the Christian era, everyone was to bear the cross voluntarily. The slaves were forced to work by outside violence. Instead, in the Christian era, all persons have to take it upon themselves. In the end, the reform transferred the requirements of the church into the consciousness.[152]

Both on the global and the microsocial scale, the affirmation of 'rationalisation', ultimately in the form of the totally administered state, no longer seems to allow any room for singularity or relationships between *uniquenesses*: 'all of this is surpassed, the units are too small, history has no room for them, we are

---

148 Horkheimer 2004, p. 106.
149 Horkheimer 2004, p. 103.
150 Horkheimer 2004, p. 102.
151 Horkheimer 1978c, p. 32.
152 Horkheimer 1978c, p. 30. Translator's note: The last three sentences are not found in the English version of the text, hence they are my own translation.

heading towards broader actions. What is individual must perish'.[153] And the way in which that which is single is incorporated and its singularity suppressed pans out as a *process of assimilation*, a process that is realised and fulfilled in the *psychotechnical reduction of the intérieur*.[154]

The work attesting to how far '*for the rulers ... human beings become mere material, as the whole of nature has become material for society*' was that of Marquis De Sade, which must be seen as erecting 'an early monument to [the totalitarian trust-makers'] planning skills'.[155] After the window of liberalism, with the totalitarian monopolists and the establishment of mass society, planning aimed to create 'organization ... which was to encompass the whole of life', rationalised 'even in its breathing spaces'. Thus, according to Sade's vision, the result was that 'the government itself must control the population. It must possess the means to exterminate the people, should it fear them, or to increase their numbers, should it consider that necessary.'[156] The organisation of life becomes an end unto itself: neutral with regard to objective ends, which are rid of all their sense, it establishes its domination as total calculation and coordination, in a sort of total functionalistic organisation, unmasked-parodied in the image of a *continual and coerced sexual performance*:

> Reason is the organ of calculation, of planning; it is neutral with regard to ends; its element is coordination. More than a century before the emergence of sport, Sade demonstrated empirically what Kant grounded transcendentally: the affinity between knowledge and planning which has set its stamp of inescapable functionality on a bourgeois existence rationalized even in its breathing spaces. The precisely coordinated modern sporting squad, in which no member is in doubt over his role and a replacement is held ready for each, has its exact counterpart in the sexual teams of Juliette, in which no moment is unused, no body orifice neglected, no function left inactive.[157]

Within this transformative process, pleasure becomes mechanical and depersonalised, and passion is devalued to illusion and deceit. 'Here, the inevitable consequence implicit in the Cartesian division of the human being into think-

---

153   Horkheimer 1991, 'Hindernis Europa', p. 287, own translation; but see also Horkheimer 1978c, 'History and Future of the Individual', pp. 168–9 and *infra*.
154   Horkheimer 1972, *passim*.
155   Horkheimer and Adorno 2007, p. 68, italics mine.
156   Horkheimer and Adorno 2007, pp. 69–70.
157   Horkheimer and Adorno 2007, p. 69.

ing and extensive substance is expressed with total clarity as the destruction of Romantic love. The latter is taken to be a mask, a rationalization of the physical drive',[158] in turn stripped down so far as to become an 'object of manipulation', of a quantitative nature, increasingly subject to hormonal therapy, in a historical dynamic aimed at seamlessly transforming the debauched, unillusioned Sade, cynical roué, into 'the open-minded practical man who extends his affirmation of sport and hygiene to include the sex life'.[159]

By drawing up a 'story of the individual' – one he keenly felt to be lacking – in these terms, from triumph to fall,[160] Horkheimer did not fail to very sharply cast light on 'a crucial difference between the social units of the modern industrial era and those of earlier epochs'.[161]

In previous epochs, the 'patterns of organization' of the ideologies in power had met a wall when they came to face 'forms of material life'. In short, the patterns and devices of organisation did not manage to dominate the totality of individual experience 'point for point': *'life itself'* managed to preserve some margin of difference. Instead the *modern* form of the social unit and its specific 'domination' appears as a totality without walls or exteriority. 'Life itself', 'wretched life',[162] is completely integrated into the totality and the individual has no room to sidestep it. Life itself, and individuals' former various 'walks of life' now fell under the technical horizon of *productive superorganisation*, after of course passing through the preliminary 'control' and 'discipline' of every desire that was not integrated or could not be framed in the existing patterns. The *productive assimilation of the living being*, Horkheimer specifies, is accomplished by filling the gap between *culture and production*, and between *life and production*:

> The objective and universal validity claimed for the ideologies of the older collective units constituted an essential condition of their existence in the body of society. But the patterns of organization, such as that of the medieval Church, did not point for point coincide with the *forms of material*

---

158   Horkheimer and Adorno 2007, pp. 84–5.
159   Horkheimer and Adorno 2007, pp. 85–6.
160   Horkheimer 2004, p. 88.
161   Horkheimer 2004, p. 97.
162   There is a remnant in 'wretched life' which, despite everything, one 'can never quite control', but now it only appears in 'the convulsive gestures of the tortured' and in the flight reactions and swarming of the lower animals. 'In the death throes of the creature, at the furthest extreme from freedom, freedom itself irresistibly shines forth as the thwarted destiny of matter. It is against this freedom that the idiosyncratic aversion, the purported motive of anti-Semitism, is ultimately directed', Horkheimer and Adorno 2007, p. 151.

life. Only the hierarchical structure and the ritual functions of both clergy and laity were strictly regulated. Apart from that, neither *life itself* nor its intellectual framework was completely integrated. The basic spiritual concepts were not entirely amalgamated with practical considerations; thus they maintained a certain autonomous character. There was still a cleavage between culture and production. This cleavage left more loopholes than modern superorganization, which virtually reduces the individual to a mere cell of functional response.[163]

By focussing on this 'basic difference' between the field of exercise and attack of *premodern* and *modern* power, and locating the threshold of the technical-productive investment of life itself in the latter, Horkheimer seems to very precisely anticipate what, starting with his courses and writings from 1976–7, Michel Foucault would indicate as the modern transformation of politics into *biopolitics*. The French thinker would thematise this transformation by clarifying that '[f]or millennia, man remained what he was for Aristotle: a living animal with the additional capacity for a political existence; modern man is an animal whose politics places his existence as a living being in question'.[164]

This comparison with the concept of *biopolitics* obviously cannot be sufficiently developed here. However, it seems legitimate to observe that it is in this attitude of attention to enrolling the very lives of populations into the production practices of modern power that we must see the proximity to the Frankfurt School expressed by the French thinker: 'If I had known the Frankfurt School at the right time, I would have been spared a lot of work. Some nonsense, I wouldn't have expressed and taken many detours as I sought not to let myself be led astray when the Frankfurt School had already opened the ways.'[165]

This is another motive for underlining that, after already identifying and focussing on certain aspects of this route in the essays from the 1930s (for example in 'Egoism and Freedom Movements'), as well as in the considerations on the 'story of the individual' present in *Eclipse of Reason*, and those on Sade and enlightenment developed in *Dialectic of Enlightenment*, Horkheimer continued along this same path in the critical reasoning of his later texts too. In recording and criticising these anthropological transformations, in the *Notizen* his attention not infrequently also returned to the topic of *love, sexuality, passions* and the loss of *friendship*. Wholly similar considerations are often found

---

163   Horkheimer 2004, p. 98, italics mine.
164   Foucault 1978, p. 143.
165   Lotringer 1989, pp. 241–2.

in *Späne* too. His reflections, like those in Adorno's *Minima Moralia*, are considerations on *offended life*, offended insomuch as it is substantially *produced*. In them, he proposes a sort of critical analysis of the *transformations of existence* linked to the advent of a 'one-dimensional society'.[166]

In the very first aphorism of his *Notizen*, the emancipation of women that was taking place in western countries is seen and criticised as *assimilation*, as a moment of expansion of the tendency of that time towards homogenisation.

> On my journey to France I realised two things. Both concerning women. – The reason why I do not like the fashion of trousers. Now women walk just like men, cigarette in mouth, corners of the mouth turned down, wrinkled forehead: just like the owner of this civilisation that is treading nature underfoot. It stresses their equality with men, but the civilising role that men have played does not suit women at all. Women have assimilated and reveal all the evils of the oppressor.
>
> In this licensed freedom, the erotic is simply denied – contrary to the old role of trousers ...[167]

If this aphorism is from 1950, in an aphorism from 1966 the assimilation of women is insinuated and asserted not only in the form of their clothes and habits, but also through the *automation* of housework:

> Women's work – infinitely vague, usually subtler and at the same time more exhausting than that of their husbands – is now becoming automated too, while the rest appears a useless torment. Women are equalised, or rather levelled: to that which for some time has only been a step backwards. ... The wife of old belongs irreversibly to the past, like love! *Ratio* is alive and kicking! With the disappearance of 'the housewife's care', men are becoming even colder, and women are imitating them.[168]

---

166 The picture of correspondences drawn thus far between the internalisation of instrumental rationality and the 'repression of the instincts' stimulated criticism of the reality principle in Herbert Marcuse too. 'Conservative' in their contents, and at times effectively so (as has all too often been highlighted), methodologically speaking the late Horkheimer/Pollock nevertheless continued to be highly critical (as shown, despite everything, by Marcuse's debt towards them).
167 Horkheimer 1991, 'Falsche Hosenrolle', p. 189, own translation.
168 Horkheimer 1991, 'Zerfall der bürgerlichen Ehe', p. 407, own translation.

In Horkheimer's diagnosis, the historical levelling of the *gender difference* not only combines with the extinction of eroticism but also with the banning of 'all positive ties among human beings', with the advent of a totality that no longer respects *any limit between the public and the private spheres*. It is even on the verge of totally *planning* sexual bonds. In other words, it is about to make the whole of life into its *product*:

> *The End of Individual Love.* Today individual love is socially surpassed or even nullified. And so the subject has been dropped, much more than in the cheap novels already existing a century ago, which were still taken seriously. The readers of illustrated weeklies already suspect that it is over. ... In order to have a meaning for someone, that something has to concern the person directly, and today these things are just career, success, power; everything else takes second place. The sexual bond can play its part, but alone it is no longer a goal with a greater meaning; hence even reserve has gone, love is insipid and de-eroticised; it would be high time to have it planned.[169]

The whole aesthetic-existential dimension linked to *fantasy* and *pleasure* is hence condemned to being paradoxically rationalised – and absurdly even 'planned' – and thus forced to vanish. Even though it has not gone out, the other light of erotism and the imagination turned on with *L'île heureuse* seems a long way off.

Not only the manifestation of the pleasure principle in forms of *art* too, but the very possibility of its original experience in *childhood*, are seriously under threat.

> *Without Love.* Erotic love is paling, and with it all positive ties among human beings and everything that is not means to an end. Erotic love was the basis of art, of the ideas of something other than empirical reality, of the imagination. In the family anchored in love, the child experienced that happiness and that grief, that longing which – though always rare – is now fading into nothingness. Material needs and pragmatic collaboration can be no substitute for it. Without love which ultimately owes its

---

169 Horkheimer 1991, p. 389 'Das Ende der individuellen Liebe', own translation. On gender difference and 'man as ruler refuses to do woman the honor of individualizing her', see also the observations already put together by Horkheimer and Adorno 2007, pp. 87 ff.

existence to the erotic, community engenders the collective creed which tends toward fanaticism.[170]

Among the positive relationships that people have with each other, which are, however, threatened with *extinction* under the triumph of instrumental logic, Horkheimer could not fail to also mention *friendship*. Since 1940 Horkheimer had been observing that character traits come from nothing other than *self-preservation*. And so it comes as no surprise whatsoever to then read in the *Notizen* that

> What is decisive today is the alignment of interests, i.e., the constantly changing constellation of prospects for power and advancement. ... Relationships between individuals, *friendliness, indifference and hatred* are precisely tuned to the constellation, and impulses to resist, let alone convictions, no longer arise. What is not intended instrumentally seems necessarily the outgrowth of *superstition, weakness, a parochial frame of mind*. The necessary result is the marked attenuation of every other quality in social intercourse. Dialectic of Enlightenment. The eternal values are idle delusion, yet life without loyalty that is not *purposive* becomes as vapid as that delusion.[171]

This diagnosis in no way goes against what had already been established in his numerous previous writings. All non-instrumental relationships between individuals, feelings and *human qualities* take a definite step backwards, in an upset that identifies the ruinous dialectic of enlightenment and manifests it at the existential level. The *self-referentiality* of reason, its solitude, is expressed in *self-preservation* as the supreme principle, the principle without principles that instrumentalises everything and hence excludes, *a priori*, the possibility of an orientating-originating, constitutional and moral relationship with the other, with others. A reaction of this kind is discarded *a priori* and repressed as a sign of the subject's '*minority*' and inadequacy.

Indeed, in Kant's words, enlightenment 'is the human being's emergence from self-incurred minority. Minority is inability to make use of one's understanding without *direction from another*'.[172] In contrast to the relational condition that binds the subject to the other, a condition that, when the prin-

---

170 Horkheimer 1978a, 'Without Love', p. 236.
171 Horkheimer 1978a, 'Power of Interest', p. 221, italics mine.
172 Horkheimer and Adorno 2007, p. 63, italics mine.

ciple of identity is absolutised, is conceived of (and devalued) *a priori* as a condition of dependence and 'minority', is the *system of reason*. This, on the other hand, is guaranteed instrumentally by the schematism of the intellect, and aimed at that 'form of knowledge which most ably deals with the facts, most effectively assists the subject in preserving nature. The system's principles are those of self-preservation. Immaturity amounts to the inability to survive. The bourgeois in the successive forms of the slave-owner, the free entrepreneur, and the administrator is the logical subject of enlightenment'. The solipsistic self-referentiality in which this subject encloses him or herself achieves its paradoxical fulfilment in 'totalitarian order' that 'has granted unlimited rights to calculating thought and puts its trust in science as such. Its canon is its own *brutal efficiency*'. Now, this result has also found its disenchanted truth, beyond Kant and beyond Nietzsche too, as we have seen, in 'moral enlightenment', as Horkheimer provocatively writes about the author of *Justine* and *Philosophy in the Bedroom*. Indeed, complementarily to what had already been observed on the banning of all feelings,[173] we need to recognise that, better than any other, 'the work of the Marquis de Sade exhibits "understanding without direction from another" – that is to say, the bourgeois subject freed from all tutelage'. He asserts a subject in whom 'rather than with tenderness, pleasure makes its pact with cruelty'. In this movement, civilisation seems to lead back to the 'terrors of nature', in whose sphere 'with both the male and the female, ... "love", or sexual attraction is originally and preeminently "sadic"; it is positively gratified with the infliction of pain'.[174]

If, with this outcome, the dialectic of enlightenment 'only succumbs more deeply to that compulsion',[175] it can be understood that all drives and desires in the opposite direction will be devalued and repressed as if lacking any sense. In the triumph of the world of will, quality and feelings such as *compassion*, *empathy* and *closeness* would be viewed with 'suspicion' at the least, if not accused of being 'womanish and childish' with respect to that '*manly competence*' which 'from Roman virtus through the Medici to efficiency under the Fords, has always been the true bourgeois virtue'. So, in the end, all disciples of Schopenhauer are suspected, as already admonished by Kant in his own way, of 'a certain soft-heartedness' and of lacking 'the dignity of virtue', that is, the suspicion of transforming the human being, according to Clairwil, into

---

173 Horkheimer and Adorno 2007, pp. 65–8, italics mine.
174 Horkheimer and Adorno 2007, pp. 88–9.
175 Horkheimer and Adorno 2007, p. 9.

'a tender-hearted idler'.[176] But if this is the bill of health of the absurd will, in reality it leads to the more drastic emptying of existence. In other words, we need to underline that 'yet' which appears in the last aphorism quoted from *Notizen* which opposes his own diagnosis from the inside: '... yet life without loyalty that is not *purposive* becomes as vapid ...'. The capable existence of that 'yet' is not a simply resigned existence, unable to break the conformist-manly-solipsistic circle of reason and self-preservation. If interest drains reason and sensitivity, to remember a *lack of purposiveness* and to extend the criticism to behaviour will be to want to retrieve the moral sense of existence in the face of biopower and its totally pervasive codes. In the forms of love, family, friendship, as well as in those of art and religion, by analysing their transformations and criticising them *dialectically*, Horkheimer increasingly tries to *save* this moral sense. This is another reason why these topics always recur in his late reflection. Lastly, by making a hybrid and anti-conformist combination of Judaism and Schopenhauerian ethics, it is in the idea of *proximity and solidarity* that the elderly Horkheimer would seek a way to break the bond between reason, interest and self-referentiality and to preserve the moral sense of existence, by freeing it *for the other*.

One could continue to go through the *Notizen* starting from these existential and moral themes – love, friendship and proximity. But in the meantime, how can these late aphorisms be read as a whole? Are they just the spasms of an old man who has become seriously conservative and hence suddenly mourns the traditional institution of the family? To respond and to realise further that, in reality, something much deeper is at stake, first of all we need to remember that reflection on the world of social bonds, from the couple to the family, from erotic love to love for children, played an important role right from the start in the writings and research of the Frankfurt School.

Under Horkheimer's guidance, in the early 1930s the members of the Frankfurt Institute for Social Research had taken part in work dedicated to reflecting on the meaning and the historical condition of affective bonds, specifically family ties, in the face of the authoritarianism that was enforcing itself in the political dimension, in particular from the crisis of the Weimar Republic up to the advent of national socialism.

In 1936, when the authors had already emigrated, the result was an important volume entitled *Studien über Autorität und Familie*. Horkheimer authored its 'general part', publishing a long essay in it. It is worth recalling the underlying theses, traces of which can also last be found in the *Notizen*.

---

176   Horkheimer and Adorno 2007, pp. 79–80.

The presupposition for and outcome developed in the essay is a certain model of shared community. First of all, however, it must be stated that it involves a sort of historical diagnosis around *authority*, seen as the *dominant category in the conceptual apparatus of history*, and yet, Horkheimer sustains, quite rarely thematised as such.[177]

Authority 'has, in fact, as Hegel says, "much greater weight in determining men's opinions than people are inclined to believe". The great attention presently being given to authority may be conditioned by the special historical circumstances of our time and especially by the rise of the so-called *authoritarian forms of the State*. But in this historical situation we are nonetheless confronted with a reality that has been decisive in the whole of past history as well'.[178]

In other words, an *authoritarian form of state* was becoming established. At the same time, private liberal capitalism was in crisis and monopolistic structures corresponding to the phase of 'state capitalism' were taking central stage.[179] This came after the invocation and acceptance – following bourgeois thought, the Enlightenment, the lessons of Descartes, Kant and Fichte – of a *principle of authority* and relationships of *domination*, already beratable as a mark of a wholly reactionary and regressive position. And now they had been brought to their extreme and radical expression.[180] This *regression* underway was actually also made possible by the modern thinkers. It was down to the *abstractness* of the category of 'individual' to which they had referred, and their undue hypostatisation of a category genetically linked to the market economy, marked, but only in an early, now surpassed phase, by free competition. By proceeding as such, an ideological image of liberal society had developed which *disguised* that, in reality, authoritarianism and domination had always continued throughout the bourgeois period. They had specifically taken root in the necessity to which the poor classes were bound, as they were obliged to

---

177 As such, see also Kojève 2014, p. 30. It must be added that since the original publication of this book, some contributions published in France have added to the literature on critical theory. Although it has not been possible to adequately take them into account herein, it is necessary to point them out if only to attest to the current lively interest, in particular in French-speaking areas, towards the history and legacy of the Frankfurt School's thought. They are the monograph by Katia Genel (2013), in which the concept of authority is attentively followed as the 'central object of the Frankfurt School's programme', and the two generous collective issues of the journal *Illusio* under the direction of Patrick Vassort (2013 and 2014). In the first, please see in particular the essay by Voirol (2013).
178 Horkheimer 2002c, p. 68, italics mine.
179 On the centrality of this concept, borrowed from Pollock, see Chapter 2 in this book.
180 Horkheimer 2002c, pp. 69–74.

bow down to imposed economic relations and sell their labour force: 'For the reigning authorities were not cast down from their place, but had simply hidden themselves behind the anonymous power of economic necessity or, as the phrase was, behind the voice of the facts'.[181]

But, in addition to the constant threat for salaried workers of losing their jobs, these facts of the bourgeois era also implied 'mass executions of tramps' and the connected industries, with orphanages, mental asylums and hospitals, places of constriction and horror.[182]

In other words, the process of the original accumulation of capital (as Marx had already said) oozed with violence, it was the fruit of throwing farmers off their land and was accompanied by widespread practices of discipline, repression and surveillance, using devices that tended to bind the factory to devices of repression and even prison.[183] As can be seen, the topics that Foucault would develop in *Discipline and Punish*, thematising the nexus between panopticon and production, were already present in embryonic form in these pages by Horkheimer. In short, the modern autonomy of the individual was essentially revealing itself as abstract and formal and not at all *substantial*. Horkheimer, here using Marxist language, concludes: '... The freedom claimed in philosophy is an *ideology*, that is, a condition that seems necessary because of a specific form of the social life-process'.[184]

In the resolute terms of this essay, the critique of ideology is hence developed as a criticism of the authoritarianism of the bourgeois era. It points out the contradictions of the era, confirmed again and again and actively reproduced in institutional situations and cultural activities such as the church, school, literature and so on. Wherever it was reproduced, the relationship of authority and subordination was reaffirmed and consolidated based on the social pattern of differences in ownership.

But precisely because so much progress had been made in the 'comprehensibility of the apparatus of production' and because of the contemporaneous growth in human capacities and social wealth, in a historical-materialist analysis it appears that in reality domination 'is bereft of every meaningful necessity'.[185] Authority responded with force to this crisis of historical legitimacy linked to the evolution of the *modes of production*, which in reality, according to Horkheimer, should already have enabled *participative production relation-*

---

181 Horkheimer 2002c, p. 87.
182 Horkheimer 2002c, p. 83.
183 See Foucault 2019.
184 Horkheimer 2002c, p. 89, italics mine.
185 Horkheimer 2002c, p. 93.

ships.¹⁸⁶ This power grew after the liberal phase, intensifying, becoming domination and leading to '*the rise of the so-called authoritarian forms of the State*'. And against this historical background, the *family* seemed to be called upon to block or 'freeze' it in a violently reified form, to ensure its *unchangeability*, by taking the stamp of domination *right into individuals' mental lives*.¹⁸⁷ So domination managed to conceal its historical senselessness, and could be *internalised* and lived as an unchangeable natural fact:

> People have for over a hundred years abandoned the view that character is to be explained in terms of the completely isolated individual, and they now regard man as at every point a socialized being. But this also means that men's drives and passions, their characteristic dispositions and reaction-patterns are stamped by the power-relationships under which the social life-process unfolds at any time. The class system within which the individual's outward life runs its course is reflected not only in his mind, his ideas, his basic concepts and judgments, but also in his inmost life, in his preferences and desires. Authority is therefore a central category for history.¹⁸⁸

The family in its position, so to speak, as a filter between the *social exterior* and the psychological interior, is hence defined as having an '*authority-promoting*

---

186   Horkheimer 2002c, p. 92.
187   One must note that the distance between the Frankfurtian diagnosis and the orthodox Marxism diagnosis of collapse and revolution began in the texts of Pollock from the late 1920s (which we will look at in the next chapter). The works on the history of the family, and on the imaginary and authority in general, which developed in the Institute in the 1930s, grew up from that diagnosis which speaks of freezing dialectics, despite the existence of historical presuppositions that were also structurally to the contrary.

   In a consideration on the method, Giacomo Marramao lastly described the Frankfurtian position as 'a Marxist orthodox that we could define as "frozen", kept as if in hibernation' (Marramao 2013, pp. 134–5). If the orthodoxy looked towards collapse and revolution, to assign the Frankfurtian position to orthodoxy is evidently to some extent intentionally forced, but in a certain sense it does not lack a paradoxical truth. We are indebted to Marramao for the very first interpretation, together with that of Helmut Dubiel, concerning the role of Pollock's theory of *State Capitalism* in the development of the Frankfurt School's positions. His, in particular, is the observation with regard to the tragically ironic ['*beffardo*'] outcome of the blocking of the collapse hypothesis in Adorno, whom the Italian scholar admonishes for 'forgetting the barycentre of reification: the modern factory'. See the introduction to Marramao 1973; see also the 'Einleitung' by Helmut Dubiel, 'Kritische Theorie und politische Okonomie', to the anthology Pollock 1975.
188   Horkheimer 2002c, p. 69.

function'. It is the breeding ground for obedience to power linked to the deep inculcation of a *masochistic* nature.

In short, it is in this sphere, under the gaze of an authoritarian father and under the threat of a loss of protection, that the future citizen learns a paradoxical pleasure, namely that of submission.

But *on the other hand*, under the lens of Horkheimerian criticism, in the *Studien* the family is already at the same time seen as the place where the reified subject, reduced to a pure economic function in the totality of the authoritarian order, was somehow able to or could resist and prefigure a human community. This better collective could then interrupt the relations of domination and instrumental relations in general, in which we each see the other as solely the *means* to realise our own interests and never as an end unto him or herself. A device generating an instinct of '*subordination*' and 'the *masochistic* inclination to surrender one's will to any leader whatsoever, provided only he could be described as powerful', *on the other hand*, according to the perspective of the 1936 essay, the family is also a place where the individual's harmed interest can find a '*retreat*', and 'could put up some *resistance*'.[189]

The critical theory in this text therefore does not only develop as a criticism of the profound and structural implication between the reproduction of patterns of authority and of the bourgeois family. It also seeks to indicate a dialectical movement in the direction of *alternative*, post-bourgeois and *post-authoritarian forms* of community and existence. The pages of Marx and Engels on the dissolution of the family and its flipside as a source of the development of human qualities echo on both sides of this movement.[190] However, what is also striking in Horkheimer's analysis is its continuous, almost introspective attention:

> But the fact that in the average bourgeois family the husband possesses the money, which is power in the form of substance, and determines how it is to be spent, makes wife, sons, and daughters even in modern times 'his', puts their lives in large measure into his hands, and forces them to submit to his orders and guidance. ... The despair of women and children, the deprivation of any happiness in life, the material and psychic exploit-

---

189 'Even in the golden age of the bourgeois order, it must be remembered, there was a renewal of social life, but it was achieved at the cost of great sacrifice for most individuals. In that situation, the family was a place where the suffering could be given free expression and the injured individual found a retreat within which he could put up some resistance'. Horkheimer 2002c, pp. 110–14.

190 See Marx 1976, pp. 620–1.

ation consequent upon the economically based hegemony of the father have weighed mankind down no less in recent centuries than in antiquity except for very limited periods, regions, and social strata.

The spiritual world into which the child grows in consequence of such dependence, as well as the fantasies with which he peoples the real world, his dreams and wishes, his ideas and judgments, are all dominated by the thought of man's power over man, of above and below, of command and obedience. This scheme is one of the forms understanding takes in this period, one of its transcendental functions. The necessity of a division and hierarchy of mankind, resting on natural, accidental, and irrational principles, is so familiar and obvious to the child that he can experience the earth and universe, too, and even the other world, only under this aspect; it is the pregiven mold into which every new impression is poured.[191]

His criticism of the *patterns of domination* and their colonisation not only of real experience but also of the intellect and above all the imaginary, also seeks to postulate an *overcoming*. In its dimension of sexual *love* and above all *maternal* care, *the other family*, the other unit of sharing and *Beisammensein*, the future moral community, is already indicated in 1936 as the place where, unlike what happens in the bourgeois world, the life of the single person, in his or her uniqueness, can receive a *positive form*. It is where the immoral reduction of the other as a simple means that prevails in civil society but also in the authoritarian state, can and must be interrupted:

> Within the family, however, unlike public life, relationships were not mediated through the market and the individual members were not competing with each other. Consequently the individual always had the possibility there of living not as a mere function but as a human being. In civic life, ... common concerns ... had an essentially negative character, being mainly concerned with the warding off of dangers. But common concerns took a positive form in sexual love and especially in maternal care. The growth and happiness of the other are willed in such unions.[192]

The difference expressed and claimed here between public life and private-intimate life seems on one hand to announce the difference between instru-

---

191 Horkheimer 2002c, pp. 105–6, italics mine.
192 Horkheimer 2002c, p. 114.

mental reason and objective-moral reason, while on the other it seems to refer to that 'original' separation between the external world and the space of the *intérieur*, expressed first of all with the spatial separation of *L'île heureuse* and then reformulated or sublimated in the internal/external distance of the 'Memorandums'. I do not want to simplistically reduce their thought to a reflection of their lives, but it must nevertheless be noted that motifs and terms recur in the *Studien* – for example that identification with the other, *Identifikation mit dem Anderen*, in which 'each one of the other's failures, is also one's own', and in which, to the same extent, it seemed possible to access and fully share *the other's joy* as 'joy felt for the other' [*die Freude am andern*] – which were already at the centre of the Pollock-Horkheimer 'Memorandum' from 1935 looked at earlier.[193] In that text the attempt was made to 'decide' [*entscheiden*] their community of 'being together', extended to the group, from the society in which 'all human relations are false, all kindness, all agreement, all benevolence, in the end is not to be taken seriously' and hence it was a matter of never being 'on the same level as the gaolers'. In the *Studien*, on the other hand, it was also apparently a matter of converting the nostalgia for the paradise lost of one's childhood into a social prefiguration, or even into historical-cultural projectuality. Here the interior seems to offer the seminal forces to imagine another external world, not seen as the negation and repression of the interior, but as its 'rational' realisation:

> To this extent, the family not only educates for authority in bourgeois society; it also cultivates the dream of a better condition for mankind. In the yearning of adults for the paradise of their childhood, in the way a mother can speak of her son even though he has come into conflict with the world, in the protective love of a wife for her husband, there are ideas and forces at work which admittedly are not dependent on the existence of the family in its present form and, in fact, are even in danger of shrivelling up in such a milieu, but which, nevertheless, in the bourgeois system of life rarely have any place but the family where they can survive at all.[194]

According to the 1936 essay, the contrast between these forms of affection and the external reality, the tension between the private sphere and bourgeois civil society dominated by interest, seemed liable to become greater, to the point of once again becoming a contradiction that could produce the future. Endeav-

---

193   See earlier in the chapter, pp. 22 ff.
194   Horkheimer 2002c, pp. 114–15.

ouring to go beyond the bourgeois family, place of subordination to authority and masochistic mental internalisation of domination, this contradiction could make new forms of future moral communities possible. In short, the historical-social dialectic, here a touch providential or more simply utopian, seemed to be able to somehow still promise relations, *Eros*, the other's happiness and solidarity as the future pattern of existential and indirectly political orientation, evidently in criticism of all totalising and totalitarian outcomes. Clearly, behind this there was also the attempt to save happiness and the subjects' relational freedom, the 'dark natural background' of the family, from their subjugation or dialectical *absorption and elimination* (to take up an expression from the Hegelian Giovanni Gentile),[195] in the now blinding homogeneous light of the authoritarian state, the paradoxical historical truth of Hegel's ethical state.[196] A residual historical hope and the achievement of another form of life still seemed to be able to combine and lead to the realisation of the *intérieur* and the wider realisation of its principle. Nevertheless, if the *intérieur*, as the 1935 'Memorandum' postulated, was to have the better over the *extérieur*, the rational society that this should have prompted, lacking all capabilities of effective synthesis, very much risked only being asserted as a memory and the longing – *Sehnsucht* – for the *island of happiness*.

Remembering the tragedy of Antigone, the advocate of the ethical state deemed the *death ceremony* and *funeral* to be the place where the family, struck by the 'dialectical' effects deriving from the realisational contact with totality, could still carry out its positive – but also just desolate and impotent – ethical action towards the single person. However, Horkheimer objected that if the *contrast* was to become unbearable, the family itself – starting from that proletariat subjected to continual violence by the ruling classes – could develop a sense of community and an *'explosive'* solidaristic logic that would be the harbinger of a *'new community'*. Hence, as he saw it, ethical action towards the single individual could be achieved, not in the funeral, but in this living community.

> The demands of extensive industrialization do away with the pleasant home and force husband, and often wife as well, into a difficult life out-

---

195   In a conference held in Berlin in 1931, Giovanni Gentile, Fascist minister of education, stated that 'the state cannot be achieved unless it absorbs the family into itself and eliminates it', Gentile 1987, pp. 103–20, own translation.
196   'In relation to the spheres of civil law [*Privatrecht*] and private welfare, the spheres of the family and civil society, the state is on the one hand an *external* necessity and the higher power ... on the other hand, it is their *immanent* end ...', Hegel 1991, p. 283.

side the house. There can no longer be any question of a private existence with its own satisfactions and values. ... the family becomes ... a source of multiplied anxieties.

Yet this last state of the family, when the original orientation to the family has largely disappeared, can be the basis for cultivating the same sense of community as binds such men to their fellows outside the family. That is, the conception of a proximately possible society without poverty and justice, and the consequent efforts to improve conditions and to make such a society a reality, replace the individualistic motive as the dominant bond in relationships. Out of the suffering caused by the oppressive conditions that prevail under the sign of bourgeois authority, *there can arise a new community of spouses and children, and it will not, in bourgeois fashion, form a closed community over* [sic] *against other families of the same type or against individuals in the same group. Children will not be raised as future heirs and therefore not be regarded, in the old way, as 'one's own', as binds such men to their fellows outside the family.* ....[197]

It was almost a word-for-word quote of the considerations on the family in the first book of Marx's *Capital*.[198] The oppressed *intérieur*, threatened by the irruption into its space of the conflicts and logics of the city, seemed to be able to react and manage to *work through the suffering, overcome it in the principle of a common feeling with a universal vocation.*

But more than a dialectic of historical powers, all in all, here too, the movement thus evoked by Horkheimer seemed to remind one of, or even copy, from a formal point of view, the overcoming of the world of the will as outlined in Schopenhauer's ethics. For this reason too, it comes as no surprise that this *diagnosis-utopia*, which sought for the relational form of love and the *meta-individual intérieur* a kind of higher stage or level or *island* outside the instrumental totality of state domination and the struggle of the wills in civil society, would immediately clash with the opposite historical reality, that is, with the advent and fulfilment of a totalitarian biopolitical reality in which the *intérieur* and individuals were no longer granted any margin of difference or freedom. The Nazi family policy, aimed at building the *Volksgemeinschaft*, as also documented by recent historical studies, led to unlimited interference in the sphere of those families who were approved and urged to increase their offspring. Indeed, the interference got to such a point that it went the other way. It

---

197 Horkheimer 2002c, p. 124, italics mine.
198 See Marx 1976, ch. 15.

became a ruthless war, a striving towards the elimination, with negative eugenics for example, of the so-called 'racially alien'.[199] It must be highlighted that, despite having already emigrated at that point, Horkheimer managed to be an extremely lucid critic of these implications, and that as a result his contribution on the matter must not only be recognised in relation to the *Studien*.[200] He saw perfectly how, in a certain sense, in the sphere of the *authoritarian state*, it was not only affection and love that were reaching a twilight but, paradoxically, that the authoritarianism of the family meant as a specific and distant phenomenon was coming to an end too. Children, he observed, are placed before a society that *immediately* enters the home and marks and destroys the *intérieur*, remoulding it and producing to its measure, even attacking the intimacy of 'life itself'.

> The contrast between the social and the private is blurred ... In the twentieth century, the population is surrounded by large trusts and bureaucracies; the early division of man's existence between his occupation and family ... is gradually melting away. The family served to transmit social demands to the individual, thus assuming responsibility not only for his natural birth but for his social birth as well. It was a *kind of second womb*, in whose warmth the individual gathered the strength necessary to stand alone outside it.[201]

But 'today' – and we are in 1940 – this function of mediation and protection-shelter, is *wiped out*: 'Totalitarian governments are themselves taking in hand the preparation of the individual for his role as a member of the masses'.[202] The authority of parents is thus totally stripped of its protective and formative role, replaced by the Balilla and Hitlerjugend youth movements, but also invaded by 'routines supervised to the last detail', even in 'the pleasures of the ball park and the movie, the best seller and the radio', which 'has brought about *the dis-*

---

199 See Ginsborg 2014, pp. 353–96.
200 Despite being considered extremely suggestive, the recent book by Paul Ginsborg quoted earlier only considers the work of the Frankfurt School in relation to the *Studien*, see pp. 394–5. In the Conclusions to his mighty volume, the author then complains how '[g]iven their undeniable importance, it is all the more surprising that families are hardly mentioned in the very considerable literature on totalitarianism. It would require an entire historiographical essay to explain why this is so. Here a glance at the most influential and intellectually distinguished treatment of the subject, Hannah Arendt's *The Origins of Totalitarianism* (1951), must suffice'. Ginsborg 2014, p. 436.
201 Horkheimer 2002e, p. 276, italics mine.
202 Horkheimer 2002e, pp. 276–7.

appearance of the inner life'.²⁰³ It is in the essay 'Art and Mass Culture' that, linked on one hand to Pollock's analyses on state capitalism, and on the other somehow preannouncing Foucault's critique of biopolitics, Horkheimer further develops his particularly appropriate diagnosis of the destiny of the family in the sphere of the affirmation of the authoritarian state, which he had already outlined in the *Eclipse of Reason*. He repeats how the sphere of the family and the *intérieur* in general, which 'made the individual aware of other potentialities than his labor or vocation', have been *drained*, and how their seizure has threatened the very possibility of preserving a different *moral sensitivity* to that imposed by the current totality. Instead, before then, the single person '[a]s a child, and later as a lover, ... saw reality not in the hard light of its practical biddings but in a *distant* perspective which lessened the force of its commandments'.²⁰⁴

In short, in this way too in the context of the affirmation of the *authoritarian state*, a sort of 'plastic surgery' is performed *'which carves all men to one pattern'* and seems capable of amputating every 'other potentiality', every dimension of personal and ipso-facto anti-conformist excess that diverges from the plane of adaptation and functionality. *And yet*, Horkheimer observes once again in this essay on 'Art and Mass Culture', the experience of *love* and *art* constitute that *'hidden faculty'* whose autonomy and absolute laws can give rise to 'another world'.²⁰⁵ Life itself, wretched life, pursued into its most intimate recesses by biopolitical and eugenic totalitarianism, seems to be able to find a sort of escape route in those eminently creative and transcendent dimensions of *art* and *Eros*.

An additional biographical element was probably at work in this suggestive association between the secret meaning of *art* – of 'new' or 'other' art – and that of *Eros*. It was an element linked both to childhood and youthful memories (when he was very young, Horkheimer's family gave him an early pastel by Picasso, and, in their home in Kronberg Pollock and Horkheimer owned works by Chagall, Klee and Franz Marc) and to an episode of violent expropriation of some masterpieces owned by the pair which the National Socialist authorities judged to be 'degenerate'.²⁰⁶

---

203   Horkheimer 2002e, p. 277, italics mine.
204   Horkheimer 2002e, p. 274, italics mine.
205   Horkheimer 2002e, p. 273, italics mine.
206   In the period before the First World War, Horkheimer's father had played an important role as a friend and patron of the Stuttgart school of painting. Later figuring among the founders of the Deutschen Museum in Munich, he also possessed a collection of authors from Württemberg – artists such as Landenberger, Haug and Reinige – and, around 1910,

In any case, in the rule of the authoritarian state, not only was *new art* under accusation and prohibited, all nonconformist existential expressions were banned and condemned too. The authoritarian state accused the non-imitative and anti-traditionalist Neue Kunst of being degenerate language, *entartete Kunst*, and hence banned it. In its stead, it promoted 'Great German Art' – for example, the then celebrated 'Farming Family from Kalenberg' by Adolf Wissel – with its emphasis on harmonious family portraits, and rural and organicist atmospheres.[207] But in the same way, people's relationships with *sexuality* were also subjected to an active 'normalisation', and as such intimacy was repressed with intense manipulation and appropriated by the state. 'Social regimentation of the relations between the sexes had gone far before racial *eugenics* consummated this process; it was expressed by the *standardized normalcy* in all spheres of mass culture'.[208] The outside thus took hold of the *inside* and violated its secret, also in a tragically parodistic manner: '[u]nder National Socialism extramarital intercourse is among the activities encouraged by the state as socially useful forms of labor. Love is organized by the state'.[209] The total mobilisation was achieved by violating the inner life, not only in principle, but also in deed: '[u]nder National Socialism, the girl's refusal of herself to men in uniform is deemed to be as unbecoming as ready surrender formerly was'.[210]

But it is evident that this 'prescribed sexual freedom', this instrumental sexuality which prior to Nazism seemed to have found, as we have seen, its paradox-

---

Max remembers falling in love with painting and literature. To further encourage this inclination of his, he remembers in a letter written in Montagnola in 1966, his parents decided to add a more modern section to the family collection and therefore bought a nice pastel drawing by the early Picasso. Hence, very directly educated in the family sphere to love art – that which he would later call 'new art' – the young Horkheimer then became a collector himself for a period. And together with his friend Pollock, as Max again wrote in the letter from 1966, he purchased some modern works, first by Klee and Chagall.

Horkheimer and Pollock then became the owners of the famous watercolour 'Der Blaue Reiter' by Franz Marc, which they had already sold before the 1920s.

With the advent of Nazism, the family's whole art collection was seized and disappeared forever. In 1966 all that remained of Picasso's pastel was a photograph. Other details on the disappearance of the collection and the role of a 'forwarder' [*Spediteur*] from Stuttgart are found in a letter from Horkheimer to Dieter Koepplin, 10 May 1966, in Horkheimer 1985–96, vol. 18, pp. 624–6.

207 On the Great German Art exhibition inaugurated in Munich in 1937 and the preference for family portraits, see the observations in Ginsborg 2014, pp. 377 ff.
208 Horkheimer 1978c, p. 42, italics mine.
209 Horkheimer 1978c, p. 42.
210 Horkheimer 1978c, p. 43. See hereinafter in Chapter 2 the similar and anticipatory observations by Friedrich Pollock (1941) in his essay 'Is National Socialism a New Order?'.

ical truth in De Sade, merely constitutes a 'scorn of love', that is, the suppression and totalitarian expropriation of its destabilising energy.

In reality, the *state coercion* consisted of the pointed attempt to biopolitically suppress *Eros*, that is, to extinguish and invade every 'hidden faculty' of relational subjectivity wishing to transcend the self. Since *Eros* cannot be reduced to this manipulated sexuality, employed for and forced into the 'labour of childbirth', Horkheimer invites us to recognise that it can nevertheless still emerge in its excess and thus fracture the rule of instrumental totality, not recognise its laws and anthropological and moral repercussions, and not lie down to the surgical and eugenic *diktats* of the authoritarian state. Also or above all by hiding, love – transcendent denial of the identity myths triumphing on the outside, '*tryst of those who cannot change their ways*' – achieves a *moral* form of difference, that of *being-for-the-other*. Not fulfilled in *being-for-oneself, it overturns this trend*, and, by freeing itself, attacks the purity of the race and the overall myth of autocratic and racist *self-preservation*.

> Love is the irreconcilable foe of the prevailing rationality, for lovers preserve and protect neither themselves nor the collectivity. They throw themselves away; that is why wrath is heaped upon them. Romeo and Juliet died in conflict with society for that which was heralded by this society. In unreasonably surrendering themselves to one another, they sustained the freedom of the individual as against the dominion of the world of things. Those who 'pollute the race' in National Socialist Germany remain loyal to the life and death of these lovers. In the inhuman world of National Socialism, which reserves the name of hero to clever yet beguiled youths who in conceiving, begetting and dying are but victims of a monstrous population policy, the racial crime resurrects what once was called heroism, namely, loyalty without prospect and reason. The sad tryst of those who cannot change their ways is blinded to the rationality which triumphs outside.[211]

Hence, what comes to light is an irreconcilable conflict between a more and more radically *biopolitical*, manipulating and absolutely (genetically) encoding totality, and the hidden relational faculty of *Eros*, whose unshakable law, the 'tryst of those who cannot change their ways', in effect breaks down the racist order of the city. Here, *Eros* – a relation outside totality, interiority in exteriority – shows the truth of *subjectivity*, namely that it is a *tryst*, that it forms and

---

211 Horkheimer 1978c, p. 43.

occurs outside authority, outside the finiteness and autocratic preservation of static identity. As the 'tryst of those who cannot change their ways', *Eros* puts the critical theory of subjectivity into practice, it forms its dynamic and permanent realisation.

Similar to this condition of transcendent and subversive formativity and subjectivation is the condition of art – *other* or *new* art – in the context of totality. In the same way as desire for the other calls the subject outside totality and attacks the purity of the race, class, gender and identity, with its autonomous language, new art attacks the veneer of rationality that has covered all human relations, and proposes itself as the other language, the language of the other who criticises-meets-transforms the same. 'New art' pursues *the absolute of its formal law*, its free, forming shape. Hence, it recognises no definitive authority in the imitation-reproduction of the present or in any simply presupposed or preconstituted given. And so this 'other' art declares its faith in a freedom that denounces the oppressing and nihilistic falsity of encoded communication. 'To the extent that the last works of art still communicate, they denounce the prevailing forms of communication as instruments of destruction, and harmony as a delusion of decay'.[212] 'In giving downtrodden humans a shocking awareness of their own despair, the work of art professes a freedom which makes them foam at the mouth'.

In the same way as authentic *Eros*, *new art* is the realisation of the subject beyond identity, it expresses the victory of transformation beyond all assimilation-reification functioning in totality, it is the expression-manifestation of non-mimetic potentiality, the formativity that remains *outside* the current totality of codes. And as such, it too bears witness to the *other*, the *unconditional* and *discordant self-formativity* as elements of authentic subjectivity:

> Today it [art] survives only in those works which uncompromisingly express the gulf between the monadic individual and his barbarous surrounding – prose like Joyce's and paintings like Picasso's Guernica. The grief and horror such works convey are not identical with the feelings of those who, for rational reasons, are turning away from reality or rising against it. The consciousness behind them is rather one cut off from society as it is, and forced into queer, discordant forms. These inhospitable works of art, by remaining loyal to the individual as against the infamy of existence, thus retain the true content of previous great works of art and are more closely related to Raphael's madonnas and Mozart's operas than

---

212   Horkheimer 2002e, pp. 279–80.

is anything that harps on the same harmonies today, at a time when the happy countenance has assumed the mask of frenzy and only the melancholy faces of the frenzied remain a sign of hope.[213]

Shakespeare, Goethe, Proust, Joyce and above all Picasso are the artists who 'awaken memories of a *freedom* that makes prevailing standards appear narrow-minded and barbarous' and hence keep the permanently critical and self-critical truth of subjectivity alive. Not only that, they are also, and more deeply, the artists who, owing to the alterity and difference from totality preserved in their language, bring us to observe that '[a]rt, since it became autonomous, has preserved the utopia that evaporated from religion'.[214]

In the same way as *Eros*, art also speaks of another form of life – as also seen, moreover, from its 'very close' bond with the sphere of religion. Indeed, while also reflecting on this bond and this *cultural origin* of art, we need to recognise that, insofar as it announces another reality, its significance by no means stops at the single works. Instead, it is of a *practical-existential* kind. In order to preserve *utopia*, to gather it up from religion, a link with praxis still needs to be preserved. By asserting this, the elderly Horkheimer demonstrates that, no less than Adorno, he is still able to reflect deeply on the role of avant-gardes and neo-avant-gardes:

> Art goes beyond the actual existence of the single work – not towards the dominant reality, but towards *the unconditional* in a certain sense guaranteed by the internal perfection and harmony of the work. Every work testifies to a different principle to that of the world ... But one cannot arrive at art through mass culture and find peace in it, in its harmony or disharmony. Indeed, art identifies with *truth*, and this forces us to tackle the real praxis, the endless and uneven battle for every creature.[215]

On the same basis as this practical-existential understanding, it must be added that, if on one hand Horkheimer greets the autonomy of art as a possibility of freedom and unconditionality, on the other he recognises that it is not immune from potential contradictory outcomes, which could cause that ornamental emptying which Adorno would later indicate as the phenomenon of the *de-artification* of art.[216]

---

213   Horkheimer 2002e, p. 278.
214   Horkheimer 2002e, p. 275, italics mine.
215   Horkheimer 1991, 'Kunst und Kino', pp. 198–9, own translation, italics mine.
216   See Adorno 2013.

While in his 1941 text Horkheimer observes that, with its autonomy, new art preserves the utopian moment and hence also preserves the bond with existence deriving from its historical bond with religion – '[a]rt, since it became autonomous, has preserved the utopia that evaporated from religion'[217] – in his later aphorisms he instead appears more inclined to highlight the many risks in understanding autonomy in terms of abstraction.

The emancipation from naturalism and every denotative task in effect seems to have led not only to *other* art – meant as an experience of freedom and renewal of sense thanks to a continual resignification – but also to a formalistic drift that reduces art to a mere consumer good and ornament. Other art becomes banal and ends up showing its decline by arousing nothing but *boredom*, that is, the denial of an alternative and transcendence onto the existential level. Significantly, his criticism continues in this direction, as he no longer finds a space in art separate from praxis where an existential liberation can be imagined. In short, it is the drift into formalistic and institutional encoding that resolves

> the puzzle of why *other art* is boring. Abstractionism had a language when it defied naturalism, and even impressionistically and expressionistically progressive naturalism. Now that the works of the nineteenth century have become petrified museum pieces, abstract art pales, turns into a consumer product, an ornament. It is becoming insipid and conformist, however rebellious its gesturings. 'There should be a spot of color on this wall', says the up-to-date bank director. 'Look how funny', says the American employee of a Picasso, 'that woman has three eyes, doesn't she'. The artists won, but it was a Pyrrhic victory. In times such as these, art survives through its defeats.[218]

With this diagnosis as to the paradoxical counterpurposiveness that seems to turn the modern autonomy of art into a brand new and destructive heteronomy, ultimately putting art at the mercy of the market and of market ideology,[219] Horkheimer's awareness and far-sightedness take him beyond the more enchanted visions produced on this, also later, by Herbert Marcuse, in particular in *The Aesthetic Dimension*.[220] The implicit presupposition of his diagnosis as to the *Pyrrhic victory of art* should instead be identified as an essentially

---

217 Horkheimer 2002e, p. 275.
218 Horkheimer 1978a, 'Too Abstract', p. 163, italics mine.
219 See Horkheimer 1978a, 'After Voltaire', p. 120.
220 See Marcuse 1979.

theological-cultural and hence also and ever more critical-practical conception of art (akin in certain aspects to that of Walter Benjamin).[221]

As we have seen, in the forms of art, as well as in the forms of *Eros*, an encounter, a tryst takes place with *alterity* that can resist the self-referential and autocratic rule of totality. Horkheimer's later reflection would also give the name of *Judaism* to this relationship with the ab-solute that goes beyond all totality and identity, all sovereignty both political and otherwise. Moreover, as Horkheimer often underlined, Judaism too implies *the end of representation*, and as such it would not seem wrong to think that by destructuring all naive mimeticism, 'new art' could place language in a similar condition of critical and self-critical openness, just as critical theory itself more directly and explicitly wanted to do as the apophantic theory of truth. Nevertheless, this purpose of representation can in no way be likened to the hegemonic sphere of abstraction. If anything, it is the antithesis.

> Why is art reduced to an abstract ornament? Because the emotions that found their full expression in the nineteenth century – think of the poems of Justinus Kerner, but also of all the music, painting and literature – are already surpassed; they are considered romantic and sentimental. Their decline is a symptom of the lesser significance of the individual, the historical necessity of his or her negation. The mentality that corresponds to this process is positivism, which now, in this phase of transition, also includes contempt, hate for love and compassion, and for all non-pragmatic feelings in general. This aversion is historically no less justified than the equally as dubious practice of turning away from theology and religion.[222]

The formalisation of art, its 'escape into so-called abstraction', runs parallel – despite the historical process of autonomisation – to the devaluation both of theology and religion and of the subject's every feeling and passion, as well as to the negation-planning of the transcendency of Eros. The forced decline of these crucial experiences of the tryst and transformation of the identity and the

---

221 From this point of view, he also remembers Walter Benjamin, even though in some aspects his final, negative diagnosis seems the opposite (as would happen in Adorno) to the diagnosis – not positive but at least full of (revolutionary) hope – that his friend (with Brecht) attributed to the overcoming-realisation of the *auratic* condition, by technical-reproductive as well as social means. See Benjamin 2008.

222 Horkheimer 1991, 'Kunst als Ornament', p. 422, own translation, see also 'Intervista di Dudu Gobba: Arte e religione' (Interview by Dudu Gobba: Art and Religion), p. 28, December 1971, TSI (Italian Swiss Television), now in van de Moetter 1990, p. 124.

twilight of critical thought in the face of technicist positivism reflect the end of all messianic endeavour towards a different form of life realised in the sphere of 'state capitalism', dictated by the biopolitical yoke of total automation. But precisely because he sets it out in these terms, Horkheimer's diagnosis takes us directly to that of Pollock, in a further expression of the formative nature of their tryst.

CHAPTER 2

The Era of State Capitalism: Morphology and Genesis Starting from Friedrich Pollock

> The systematic use of all technical resources in the workshop as well as the office, the draw towards an increasingly capital-based mode of production, the clear tendency towards a person-free workspace or at least with a scant human presence, lead to the 'structural' unemployment of numerous 'hands' and heads, and at the same time to a clear differentiation between the employed people themselves.
> Indeed, a relatively regular job is becoming more and more of a privilege ....
> The annihilation of the working class's capacity to resist is therefore completed through this differentiation among the unemployed, between those who can still hope for a job and the 'unreliable elements' who are temporarily or constantly denied this privilege.
>
> FRIEDRICH POLLOCK (1933), 'Bemerkungen zur Wirtschaftskrise', in Pollock 1975, own translation

∴

2.1   Friedrich Pollock's Ideal Type

The affirmation of the Horkheimer-Adorno duo, which in reality formed rather late on and was consecrated by the success of *Dialetik der Aufklärung*, placed important moments and personalities in the story of the so-called Frankfurt School very much in the shade. One of these is the undeniably *vital* role of Pollock.

The intention of the dedication printed in the front of the first edition of *Dialektik* – 'To Friedrich Pollock on occasion of his fiftieth birthday' – may not have been exclusively to express an intellectual debt, which of course is no small thing, but a sort of reparation at the personal level. That dedication, repeated and 'renewed' in the subsequent editions, was the sign of an ongoing dialogue, without which the Institute and the book would have been different. Indeed, without Pollock's diagnoses, including those dating from way before the 1940s, the Frankfurt School's theories might not even have taken shape.

It was Adorno himself who acknowledged this, in a way, in spring 1964 when, together with the full-length recording of Richard Strauss's *Salome* directed by Georg Solti, he sent a letter full of friendship and gratitude to Pollock for his seventieth birthday in Montagnola:

> I think of you with all the warmth and friendship, not only stemming from a frame of mind or from subjective behaviour. Instead, it draws its substance from a long life, which I cannot imagine without you and which – may I be so presumptuous to think – would be hard to imagine without me either; at least in the sense that otherwise each of our lives would not have become what it is. Shy as you are, you will surely not want to hear that this feeling has now been joined by gratefulness, since, were you not around, in all likelihood I would have fallen into ruin; but allow me to say this to you, just this once, *with so many words*.[1]

Proof that their dialogue concerning *Dialectic of Enlightenment* did not remain on this level of deep but generic gratitude, and did not only refer to their general relations with each other, but instead actually involved a more active and direct intervention by Pollock, is duly provided in another letter, this time sent from Montagnola to Horkheimer's address in Frankfurt. Dated 24 January 1961, it shows a Pollock intent on voicing his opinion as a consultant and 'expert' in judging and intervening on the text of *Dialektik*, so much so that he even pointed out to Horkheimer those passages and expressions which in his opinion needed revising with a coloured pencil. In effect the letter was a note rounding off a list he had drawn up concerning the places in *Dialectic of Enlightenment* he thought needed changing in a new edition.[2]

While short, this note is in many aspects very significant. Dated Montagnola 24 January 1961, it expresses the disenchanted and realistic, soberly pessimistic even, vision of the late Pollock. It seems right to reproduce it in full here:

> Reacquaintance with *Dialectic of Enlightenment* leads distressingly to two conclusions: How many significant ideas are contained in it, and in an adequate and convincing form, and how little or, rather, how much less than fifteen years ago, one can say without incurring the fury of the mob.

---

[1] Letter from Theodor W. Adorno to Friedrich Pollock, 20 May 1964, in Horkheimer 1985–96, vol. 18, pp. 568–9, own translation.
[2] As the editor of Horkheimer 1985–96 remarks in note 3 on p. 502 of volume 18.

The reasons for the parts underlined[3] in green are self-evident: to be true, I should have marked a lot more. My question marks and crosses predominantly indicate misgivings about the too-unguarded use of language. Only in a few places did I think it necessary to express doubts, as an 'expert', on the correctness of the content. All in all, I come to the dismal conclusion that the content of *Dialectic* is not suitable for mass circulation. However, individual chapters, somewhat amended here and there, should be republished in the planned collection. Of the two copies attached, one (the one with the parts underlined in green) is an old copy of mine that I have modified.

All right. F.[4]

In the same way as the letter mentioned above from Adorno for the economist's seventieth birthday, this letter and the attached list show – without reserve – that during the Montagnola period Pollock was still deemed a very important interlocutor, a sort of mentor even, and that he was aware of this role, without however ever belying that reserved and modest character noted by those who had dealt with him in the past.[5] Pollock must also have had an important role in the workshop where *Dialectic of Enlightenment* came into being in the first half of the 1940s, directly suggesting to Horkheimer which interventions to censure and/or self-censure,[6] also inspired in part by a certain intellectual Nicodemism. While this tendency has to be contextualised in a period that was always difficult for the Institute, perhaps it should also be seen as the exoteric face of an esoteric and more radical dimension of the critique that it seemed right to reserve for the *intérieur*.

---

3   In a copy of the first print edition, published in Amsterdam by Querido Verlag in 1947, already underlined in pencil. See Horkheimer 1985–96, vol. 18, p. 502.
4   Letter from Friedrich Pollock to Max Horkheimer, 24 January 1961, in ibid. The letter is transcribed, minus the sentences on the parts underlined in green, in the Editor's Afterword to Horkheimer and Adorno 2007, p. 243.
5   'A pleasant man, overflowing with cordiality, Max Horkheimer, and his more reserved friend, with a more austere appearance, Fritz Pollock; but he too let transpire what lay behind his composure ...', as described by the man of letters and theatre critic Ludwig Marcuse (1975, p. 115) in a passage referring to a meeting between them when they were youths; but on Pollock's character see also the passages earlier in the book on what can be read in some 'Memorandums'.
6   The 'scissors method' applied by Horkheimer to the parts of *Dialectic of Enlightenment* written by Adorno, in particular to his first draft of the chapter 'Odysseus or Myth and Enlightenment', has been highlighted on several occasions, most recently by Petrucciani 2000. The discourse should be developed while also taking Pollock's role into consideration.

The first question to obviously spring to mind is this: on what basis did his friends and colleagues from the Institute grant to Pollock this position of great skill and authority? Beyond his merits as administrator of the Institute, Pollock had won this role thanks to his earlier theoretical contributions, amongst which, in particular but not exclusively, those on the concept of distant Engelsian descent, *state capitalism*. Despite being genetically linked to the attempt to critically interpret National Socialism, the concept of 'state capitalism' put into circulation by Pollock resembled and indeed set out to be an *ideal type*, so much so that his use of the expression 'era of state capitalism' already seemed legitimate. In other words, this category of his proved relevant, urging a critical reading of the contemporary world to be drawn up in which, beyond the totalitarian and/or democratic pictures and devices, a *continuist picture* could appear that coldly enclosed the dependent variables of a single *dominion*. Although in truth Pollock distinguished, quite firmly, between a *totalitarian* and a *democratic* possibility of 'state capitalism' – with the second variant intending to indicate (and at a certain point also to defend) the Keynesian forms of welfare – compared to the more phenomenal distinction between totalitarianism and democracy, the stabilisation and uniformity that his basic concept implied almost seemed to offer a path to the noumenal, to the historical thing itself. For this reason too, his *State Capitalism* aroused numerous and contrasting reactions among the members of the Institute. Indeed, at first only Horkheimer defended it, showing his appreciation for that very same broadness and inclusiveness that allowed it to gather up the complexity of socio-political events in their ambivalent entanglement rather than simply see and resolve things in dualistic terms. Among the members of the Institute, not only the economist Henryk Grossmann and the historian Franz Neumann, but also Theodor Adorno, who was much closer to Horkheimer than the latter, quite harshly criticised Pollock's essay.

In summer 1941, at the very time when Pollock was still completing his essay, later to be published in issue number IX of the *Zeitschrift*, there was an interesting exchange of letters between Adorno and Horkheimer and between the two and Pollock. Hoping that he would not misunderstand him and relying on his extreme discretion, Adorno, in New York at that point, set out his concerns regarding Pollock's writing to Horkheimer. Pollock had sent 35 pages of it to Adorno, and in a 'truly touching' way was putting 'every new paragraph' to him in order to obtain his opinion. So Adorno addressed Horkheimer to express his unease at this situation: despite acknowledging the fact that he was not an economist and therefore did not possess the required authority to intervene, he wrote that he did not feel comfortable 'for psychological reasons above all' letting Pollock know what he really thought about his essay. Beyond all formality, it seriously worried him. Adorno's judgement was so negative that he was convinced that its publication 'would damage not only and particularly Pollock's reputation, but that of the whole Institute'. 'The best way to sum up my opinion', Adorno wrote to Horkheimer, 'is to observe that Pollock's essay is an inversion [*Umkehrung*] of Kafka. Kafka represents the hierarchy of offices as hell: here hell is transformed into a hierarchy of offices'. This first comment seems to parody the change, effectively diagnosed by Pollock, in the hierarchy between the political and the economic sphere. Pollock's model of state capitalism almost turned the Marxist picture on its head as the economic sphere effectively reacquired a role *dependent* on the political, technical and administrative fields. In other words, according to Adorno's critical metaphor, it had come to depend on the hierarchy of offices, whose role otherwise would only have been as a superstructure.

However brilliant from a literary and not arbitrary point of view, in itself this observation by Adorno did not possess such critical force as to justify his 'serious concern'; at most, it could convince on the presupposed basis of a structurally determinist, orthodox Marxism alone. In any case, Adorno sought to add to his criticism, continuing his letter as follows:

> Furthermore, everything in the text [of Pollock] has an assertive and peremptory nature. To express myself in the sense of Husserl, it is formulated from above, and hence lacks all efficacy; notwithstanding the fact that it then implies the non-dialectical presumption that a non-antagonistic economy is possible in an antagonistic society. I see a truly aporetical situation.[7]

Hence, in Adorno's view, both the method and the content of Pollock's text shared an aspect that was to be criticised and radically reviewed. Such was his fear that according to him the only way to avoid that disappointing result, and to also face up to the internal adversaries Adolph Lowe and Franz Neumann, would be to have Horkheimer intervene directly in reviewing and rewriting Pollock's essay. What is more, again in Adorno's opinion, Pollock seemed not only to have clearly derived the arguments of his essay from those already developed by Horkheimer in the essay 'The Authoritarian State', but in doing so he had 'simplified them and rid them of their dialecticism', in effect turning these arguments on their heads. The way out from this situation

---

7   Letter from Theodor W. Adorno to Max Horkheimer, 8 June 1941, in Horkheimer 1985–96, vol. 17, pp. 53 ff., own translation.

would therefore have to be found by 'blending the two pieces' and jointly signing the new text, even though Adorno did not fail to add that he could well imagine this proposal may not have really tickled Horkheimer's fancy … Despite the expectations and these discreet but certainly not harmless urgings by Adorno, on reading Pollock's text a month after Adorno's crushing letter, in truth Horkheimer expressed himself in a very different way. Indeed, his reaction could be deemed symmetrically opposite, almost reversing every word of what Adorno had observed and wished for. On sending his observations on the text of 'State Capitalism' to Fritz Pollock, Max took care to immediately point out that the 'overall appearance' [*Übersichtlichkeit*] of the essay seemed 'positive', and able to 'grasp the complexity of what is happening'. And he continued, observing that

> to use an expression of old Husserl, it allows us to go back the things themselves. The thesis is convincing: economic development everywhere is showing a tendency towards state capitalism. The totalitarian form is just one of its possible forms. Let us define its essence, its structural core, and ask ourselves if it is fundamentally able to take capitalism beyond the difficulties of its private phase. With a similar analysis, we recognise *state capitalism* to be the economic form that is most effective and most in line with the present time. By just naming the problem, and determinedly indicating its technical resolvability, the essay fulfils an important disenchanting function [*eine wichtige entzaubernde Funktion*]. I consider it a significant step in the direction of the very much needed new Manifesto.[8]

As can be seen, not just the generalising method, but those same heterodox aspects characterising Pollock's essay attracted Horkheimer's anything but detached endorsement. His primary intent was to promote its '*entzaubernde*' function. In short, he understood that as a diagnosis which also included a 'technical resolvability' of the contradictions – which surely did not mean their dialectical overcoming – Pollockian state capitalism could play a realistic and critical role which could disenchant the revolutionary collapsism of orthodox Marxism. So, in that same *Entdialektisierung* for which Adorno at first sight wanted to reprimand Pollock, Horkheimer instead seemed to find the baseline for setting out a necessary new *Manifesto*.

---

8   Letter from Max Horkheimer to Friedrich Pollock, 1 July 1941, in Horkheimer 1985–96, vol. 17, pp. 90 ff., own translation, italics mine.

In this light, it must then be underlined how, alongside some advice concerning the formulation of Pollock's text – deemed not always incisive and slightly stiff as well as verbose – in his letter Horkheimer also expresses the underlying desire for the text to give more emphasis to the entanglement [*die Verflochtenheit*] and the ambivalence [*die Zweideutigkeit*] of the phenomena that it deals with, as well as the transition or the passage [*der Übergang*] from one formation to another, that is, from the democratic to the totalitarian form of state capitalism.[9] In short, the distinction between the two forms should not outshine their original and fundamental entanglement.

Therefore, these letters show that Pollock's essay, first considered worrying and almost embarrassing by Adorno, found an empathetical ear in Horkheimer. Indeed, such was his endorsement that it became the basis for the plan (formulated in March 1942) to directly involve Pollock too in drawing up what was to become *Dialectic of Enlightenment*.

Moreover, Adorno slowly changed his opinion from his initial rejection and ended up adopting Pollock's original view. In another letter, sent to Horkheimer in July 1941, he expresses what in his opinion is the main strength of Pollock's essay:

> In actual fact I think that the central problem of the essay [by Pollock] is the question whether the tendency that it draws up, towards a crisis-free economy governed from above [*einer krisenlos von oben gelenkten Ökonomie*], effectively expresses the objective tendency of reality, or if the ideal purity of this construction is in principle to be excluded for the future too, owing to the antagonistic condition of the present. I really do not feel able to respond to this question. My instinct on the matter is something like this: the correct aspect of this concept is its pessimism, that is, the perception that there is a greater possibility of domination continuing in its immediately political form than of it being left behind. Optimism is wrong, also for the others: what continues does not seem so much to be a new state of relative and in a certain sense even rational stability, but instead an endless series of catastrophes, chaos and horrors for an endlessly long period, thereby also including the possibility of an explosion, which is [instead] slim in the Egyptian vision.[10]

---

9   Ibid.
10 Letter from Theodor W. Adorno to Max Horkheimer, 2 July 1941, in Horkheimer 1985–96, vol. 17, p. 96, own translation.

In line with this, Horkheimer then spoke of Pollockian state capitalism as a sort of *'negative utopia'*. And, in August 1941, Adorno took from the overall notion of state capitalism the fundamental idea according to which 'one could even say that in state capitalism the old concept of superstructure [*Überbau*] is no longer valid'.[11] So, *à la* Pollock, the hierarchy of offices therefore needed to be fixed as the sphere in which the so-called superstructure assumed a new and paradoxical significance, imposing itself and dominating owing to its capacity to even liquidate culture through the manipulated forms of mass consciousness.[12] In the horizon of state capitalism, Adorno now concluded, 'nothing is harmless anymore and even the smallest of thoughts seems to contain such a potential explosive force [*Sprengkraft*] that as a consequence thought must be directly abolished'.[13]

A few months later, in 1942, Adorno then used Pollock's category as a sort of conceptual analogue to Aldous Huxley's fictional dystopia in *Brave New World*.[14] In the end, there was indeed truth in the consequence of inverting Kafka's hell. The non-antagonistic economy was not yet accompanied by a really antagonistic society. Instead, the society was preliminarily the result of a eugenic selection, like in Huxley's nightmare, or cultural sedation and crystallisation, blocked in a technically non-dialectical reality. And it was effectively so beyond all mere optimistic presumption which now Adorno would also certainly have ascribed 'to the optimism of official Marxism'.[15]

In its very generality, Pollock's ideal type – which Pollock himself nevertheless criticised and questioned – was in short taken as an implicit structural, somehow counterfactual base for that dystopian manifesto entitled *Dialectic of Enlightenment*. And this implicit fact was to occupy an explicit part in the work, through the intense and direct collaboration of Pollock (together with Felix Weil) to give it 'the necessary precision and concreteness', in particular in the 'economic and political sections'.[16] Horkheimer wanted *Dialectic of Enlightenment* 'to be stuffed to the bursting point with historical and economic material',[17] for no other reason than to avoid ending up being a mere theoretical-philosophical *raisonnement* that might be incapable of highlighting the 'eco-

---

11   Letter from Theodor W. Adorno to Max Horkheimer, 30 July 1941, in Horkheimer 1985–96, vol. 17, p. 112, own translation.
12   Horkheimer 1985–96, vol. 17, p. 113.
13   Ibid., own translation.
14   See Adorno 1983, pp. 95–118.
15   Letter from Theodor W. Adorno to Max Horkheimer, 18 August 1941, in Horkheimer 1985–96, vol. 17, p. 132, own translation.
16   Letter from Max Horkheimer to Felix Weil, 10 March 1942, in Horkheimer 2007, pp. 203–4.
17   Horkheimer 2007, p. 204.

nomic significance' of what it was upholding. This important programmatic desire from March 1942 evidently did not come to be, however. So, when a few months later Horkheimer started to put down the *Dialectic* with Adorno, this desire to delve into its economic significance translated into the sober, very much laconic and minimalist dedication to Pollock at the start of the work.

This in some respects reductive, unfaithful perhaps, reception and assumption of Pollock's concept, with all its about-turns, gives more reason to concentrate hereinafter on its long genesis, slow evolution and morphology.

From the second half of the 1920s to the start of the 1940s, Pollock constantly dealt with the crisis of the self-regulated market and the political attempts to respond to it launched in different national contexts. In this connection, he wrote a substantial number of analytical contributions accompanied in 1941 by the essay with a clearer ambition, as shown in its title: 'State Capitalism'. This, thanks to the ideal type that it models, is his most famous and influential essay. His previous contributions instead dealt more analytically with the genesis of the various forms of state regulation of the economy, almost the moment they took place, starting from the attempts at a planned economy implemented in the USSR. These earlier interventions of his must hence be read both as chapters in a sort of *diary of the world crisis of private capitalism and of the Soviet model*, and a *preparation and foundation* for the 'negative' ideal type which he perfected in 1941 (therefore, it can neither chronologically nor genetically be traced back to or said to be simply derived from Horkheimer's essay 'The Authoritarian State', as Adorno instead maintains in the 1941 letter).[18] Methodologically, Pollock himself explicitly means the concept of 'state capitalism' to be 'a model' in the sense of Max Weber's 'ideal type'. It is an ideal-typical construct to interpret and classify the formations called upon in the broad and heterogeneous movement of the early decades of the twentieth century – for some a sort of nebula – to respond to and take over from *private capitalism*, towards its redefinition in the wider term of *social state*. Pollock quickly understood that the state was not only intervening here, there and everywhere to perform functions hitherto carried out by private actors in the market sphere – 'state capitalism is the successor of private capitalism' and in it 'the state assumes important functions of the private capitalist'[19] – but he also understood that it was doing this task by intertwining, albeit in distinct and different or even opposing ways, economic intervention with the *socio-political* (mainly authoritarian) reorganisation of the state.

---

18   See the letter from Theodor W. Adorno to Max Horkheimer, 8 June 1941, commented above.
19   See Pollock 1978, pp. 71–94, in particular p. 72.

According to Pollock, the principle of *planning*, in all the different guises it was taking on, led to the redefinition of the rules and economic ends, which now needed to be corrected or politically manipulated. 'State capitalism replaces the methods of the market with a new *set of rules* ... A *general plan* gives the direction for production, consumption, saving and investment'.[20] From the tendency to control production, determine prices and profits, all the variables in the market system are administered and governed on the basis of a preliminary and presupposed decision. This restriction and absorption of the variables within a pre-decided scheme – the plan – implies some important consequences. It generates some *effects of subordination* which ultimately influence the very identity of the economic subject. In the new context, the interests in personal or group profit which hitherto directed that person's action on the market would find themselves strictly 'subordinated' and to a large extent 'sacrificed' to the realisation of the 'general plan', the expression of the 'interest of the ruling group as a whole'. In other words, what is called radically into question with the affirmation of (totalitarian) state capitalism is the '*role of the individual*' as an economic subject and therefore also as a subject. In this connection, Pollock's view coincides with that of Horkheimer and goes further, combining critical observation of the sacrifice of individual interest and property rights with the denunciation of a further subjugation hitting on the 'physiological and psychological' dimension in which the total state cleverly grants 'forms of satisfaction' and transgression of taboos in exchange for the elimination of the personal dimension. These forms of *compensation* did not weaken but intensified the power. They aimed to prompt 'the release of instincts and impulses operating against the enemies and scapegoats of the regime, such as cruelty against the weak and helpless (Jews, feeble-minded and "unfit" persons), hatred of racial aliens',[21] using racism and identity to offer sadistic as well as 'masochistic' compensation for the economic de-individualisation that was being put into practice.

But Pollock understands this *political economy of the instincts*, in which 'even sexual relationships' and 'extra-marital affairs' become 'tools' to implement the policies of the Third Reich, to be a particular element of the fundamental principle according to which

> where the interest of single groups or individuals conflicts with the general plan, or whatever serves as its substitute, the individual interest must

---

20 Pollock 1978, p. 75, italics mine.
21 Pollock 1941, p. 445.

give way. This is the real meaning of the ideology *Gemeinnutz geht vor Eigennutz*. The interest of the ruling group as a whole is decisive, not the individual interests of those who form the group.[22]

Now, in Pollock's model, the factor defining the ruling group is no longer the 'profit motive', which nevertheless remains an 'incentive', but rather the 'power motive'. The interest in forming and imposing a political hierarchy, a structure of command, first of all implies an interest in building a 'political set-up', a people's community [*Volksgemeinschaft*], in place of a simple *Gesellschaft* supported by relations of mutual separation between subjects bearing economic interests.

Indeed, while in private capitalism 'all social relations are mediated by the market', what happens in (totalitarian) *state capitalism* is that the people no longer encounter each other as separate and formally equivalent economic subjects, but as members of a 'political set-up' whose construction and organisation is imposed as the preliminary *raison d'être* for their action and their hierarchical relations:

> Under state capitalism men meet each other as commander or commanded; the extent to which one can command or has to obey depends in the first place upon one's position in the political set-up and only in a secondary way upon the extent of one's property. Labor is appropriated directly instead of by the 'roundabout' way of the market. ... the profit motive is superseded by the power motive.[23]

On this Pollockian basis, it is easy to understand why historians in more recent years would speak of the '*Aryanisation of the economy*' that happened in Germany, on their part using this category to recognise the superimposition of a preliminary and definite (racist) political restriction over economic relations under National Socialism.[24] But to say this would be to begin to suggest that, despite presenting itself as an ideal type and epoch-making concept, Pollock's model of 'state capitalism' displays features that are directly and principally, perhaps even exclusively, ascribable to the National Socialist picture. As a result, it becomes difficult to use, without stretching it too far, to describe the 'democratic' variant, which Pollock always at least formally distinguished. In other words, when Pollock defines 'state capitalism', he does so by nevertheless

---

22   Pollock 1978, p. 76.
23   Pollock 1978, p. 78.
24   See Aly 2016.

also referring to the preliminary (exclusivist) construction of a 'political set-up'. What is more, in effect he already seems to be implicitly proceeding to outline a concept of 'command society' and 'command economy', which he indeed later would recognise as referring exclusively to the totalitarian, and in particular the National Socialist, version of state capitalism.

While I will come back to this, it is necessary to underline once more that according to Pollock the twilight of the market system not only leads to the eclipse of the centrality of individual interest but also to a metamorphosis in the relations between the economic and political spheres, resulting in a shift in priorities and 'structural' balances. 'The introduction of the principle of planning into the economic process means that a plan is to be constructed for achieving on a national scale certain chosen ends with all available resources. ... The genuine problem of a planned society does not lie in the economic but in the political sphere, in the principles to be applied in deciding what needs shall have preference'.[25]

> Performance of the plan [is] enforced by state power so that nothing essential is left to the functioning of laws of the market or other economic 'laws'. This may be interpreted as a supplementary rule which states the principle of treating all economic problems as in the last analysis political ones ... [which] changes the character of the whole historic period. It signifies the transition from a predominantly economic to an essentially political era.[26]

As already hinted, Pollock is aware that this ambitious frame of interpretation of his – which even aspired to recognise the traits of a 'new era' – had to be assumed *generically*. Then, from here *species and subspecies*, that is, political forms, degrees and types of 'state capitalism', had to be distinguished. Indeed, '[b]etween the two extreme forms of state capitalism, the totalitarian and the democratic, numerous others are thinkable'.[27] His 1941 text nevertheless does not manage to avoid a certain ambiguity in this sense; an ambiguity, a space of inquiry which in the end would prove to be extremely productive. On one hand, Pollock claims to have drawn his model of interpretation from extensive historical points of reference – the left, right or democratic; on the other, he adds that it is quite difficult to specifically describe a suitable model for the *democratic* form of state capitalism, since, as far as this form is concerned,

---

25 Pollock 1978, p. 75.
26 Pollock 1978, pp. 77–8.
27 Pollock 1978, p. 90.

'our experience gives us few clues'. The built model would therefore in actual fact mainly refer to the form on which experience in Europe, but also in the USSR, was providing more clues, that is, the *totalitarian* form of state capitalism.

While it seemed almost necessary to suspend judgement on the *democratic* form, and at most specify that it would have to *distinguish itself* from the totalitarian form because it would have to involve the possibility of citizens *controlling the state power* and its planning, the upshot was that the aspirational 'epoch-making' ideal type in effect almost remained restricted to the totalitarian form of state capitalism alone. It was from this that the concept received its *main form*.

> It refers here to a model that can be constructed from elements long visible in Europe and, to a certain degree, even in America. Social and economic developments in Europe since the end of the first world war are interpreted as transitional processes transforming private capitalism into state capitalism. The closest approach to the totalitarian form of the latter has been made in National Socialist Germany. Theoretically the totalitarian form of state capitalism is not the only possible result of the present process of transformation. It is easier, however, to construct a model for it than for the democratic form of state capitalism to which our experience gives us few clues.[28]

For this reason too, the 1941 text did not prevent the possibility of somehow solely *hypostatising* the totalitarian variant of the concept of state capitalism. Hence, it left open the risk and/or opportunity of absolutising a category lacking a solid methodological base, that is, a sort of synecdoche with little attention to the meaning of the morphological distinctions. This result was without doubt also linked to the historical and genetic circumstances behind Pollock's text, being part of the discussions prompted by members of the Frankfurt Institute for Social Research during their exile in America, and in a period of general uncertainty, on the nature of National Socialism.

Let us go back to Horkheimer. As has been seen, immediately after reading Pollock's essay, he did not hesitate to underline precisely its strength in providing an 'ideal type', flipping Adorno's judgement (with his reference to Husserl), as well as the formally analogous ones which would follow immediately afterwards, almost word for word:

---

28 Pollock 1978, pp. 71–2.

> The essay [by Pollock], to use an expression of old Husserl, allows us to go back to the things themselves. The thesis is convincing: economic development everywhere is showing a tendency towards state capitalism. The totalitarian form is just one of its possible forms. Let us define its essence, its structural core, and ask ourselves if it is fundamentally able to take capitalism beyond the difficulties of its private phase.[29]

On this basis, it comes as no surprise that it was again Horkheimer who defended Pollock's concept against the 'positivistic' criticisms levelled at him (as Adorno had foreseen) from Franz Neumann. The author of *Behemoth*, a work which would occupy a fundamental place in the historiography of the Third Reich,[30] had criticised Pollock's concept, calling it an 'abstract ideal type'. Taken aback, Pollock commented thus in a letter to Horkheimer: 'Our positivist friends, such as Neumann, evidently cannot accept that in the empirical world some things look different'.[31] Intervening in defence of Pollock's approach, Horkheimer again lets it be known that he used the concept built by Pollock as a measure to gauge what was happening and imposing itself in all parts of society at the time:

> Ideal types, in my view, should perform exactly the function that they have in the essay [by Pollock] …. They create utopias, wonderful or hateful, against which reality is measured … So, in the sense of the ideal-type method, [Pollock] is entitled to compare the contemporary social forms with his construction. This can be important to judge historical processes.[32]

And once again, in response to the 'collapsist' Henryk Grossmann who berated Pollock not only for proceeding with abstract categories but also for ending up painting a pessimistic picture, with no room for alternative prospects, Horkheimer writes: 'In the current circumstances, the only clearly logical prognosis that can be made is this: domination [*Herrschaft*] and always only domination and not its overcoming' [*die Herrschaft und immer nur die Herrschaft und nicht ihre Überwindung*].[33]

---

29 Letter from Max Horkheimer to Friedrich Pollock, 1 July 1941, in Horkheimer 1985–96, vol. 17, p. 90, own translation.
30 See Neumann 1966.
31 Letter from Friedrich Pollock to Max Horkheimer, 11 June 1941, in Max Horkheimer Archiv 31.VI, quoted by Campani 1992, p. 221, own translation.
32 Letter from Max Horkheimer to Franz Neumann, 2 August 1941, in Horkheimer 1985–96, vol. 17, pp. 115–16, own translation.
33 Horkheimer 1985–96, vol. 17, p. 118, own translation.

As can be seen, the 'anti-positivistic' speculative possibility left open by Pollock's generic or abstract manner could have an interesting upshot. Indeed, it seemed to enable the incorporation of 'totalitarian state capitalism' and 'democratic state capitalism', *phenomena* defined as opposites, into a sort of single form, or their retracing to a shared historical-economic root. As a result, it offered the tool to *deconstruct* the alleged absoluteness of this opposition and the historical impossibility of breaking it down.

As a figure of this 'state capitalism' (of a mainly totalitarian origin), the democratic variant also risked becoming entangled (according to that *Verflochtenheit* dear to Horkheimer), in its own ways and in ways still being formed, in the reproduction of a society of *domination*. Only the possibility and capability to exercise control over political choices seemed able to preserve the difference between the two extreme forms. But then who could guarantee, even where there was the possibility of exercising 'democratic' control, that this and its subjects might not have been socially and psychologically *conditioned* beforehand, in such an efficient and decisive way as to reduce and eliminate their capacity of discernment, control and freedom? At first, it was precisely the way in which Horkheimer and shortly afterwards also Adorno himself took possession of Pollock's semi-ideal type and used it, in a certain sense as a *fetish*, to draw up their critical diagnosis of late-modern *domination*. The dedication to Pollock at the start of *Dialectic of Enlightenment* should also be read in this sense, as a sign of a 'structural' debt towards Pollock.[34] The concern expressed by the latter regarding the inopportuneness of allowing the masses access to this truth – lacking any historicistic or dialectical consolation – was to be read in this light too. But already a few years earlier, the dystopian *Brave New World* imagined by Huxley was interpreted, in a text by Adorno from 1942, as the figurative representation of 'state capitalism' *as such*. Instead of looking more closely at what made it stand out, the democratic variant (as a principle and on several occasions recognised and distinguished by Pollock) seems to be absorbed and dissolve under the weight of a 'state capitalism' identified *tout court* in Adorno's text as an 'Americanism', apparently necessarily and exclusively realisable – in this, Huxley's novel, with its continual references to genetics and conditioning, is truly eloquent – in

---

34 The credit for highlighting this structural debt towards Pollock goes to Helmut Dubiel and Giacomo Marramao. In the reading I am proposing here, I would like to add that Adorno and Horkheimer's appropriation tended to halve Pollock's picture, albeit in a productive manner, by not paying too much attention to the specific differences inherent in the democratic variant of state capitalism.

terms of absolute bio-political *domination* alone.[35] On his part, in his essay 'The Authoritarian State' from 1940, Horkheimer demonstrated that he was not unaware of the theoretical possibility of a democratic variant of 'state capitalism'. However, the prime aim of his only mention of this was to not make any concessions to the Soviet attempt. The disastrous Soviet case – which in this essay from 1941 he interpreted by expressing for the first time the reading already developed by Pollock in 1927[36] – seemed important to him in order to make a historical outline of the problem of the relationship between political regulation of the economy and the recognition of freedoms. 'The historical contradiction, of demanding at the same time both rational planning and freedom, emancipation and regulation, can be overcome; with the Maximalists nevertheless authority ultimately won out and performed miracles'.[37] But his criticism of this authoritarian state was made here by trying to somehow again recall the model of the 'democracy of the councils' and denounce its betrayal by post-Lenin 'statism' and its party and trade union representatives.

> The concept of a transitional revolutionary dictatorship was in no way intended to mean the monopoly of the means of production by some new elite. Such dangers can be countered by the energy and alertness of the people themselves. The revolution that ends domination is as far-reaching as the will of the liberated. Any resignation is already a regression into prehistory. After the old positions of power have been dissolved, society will either govern its affairs on the basis of free agreements, or else exploitation will continue.[38]

In other words, for Horkheimer it was not (yet) a model of *democratic* state capitalism, at least in theory capable of reconciling planning and freedom, that needed to be drawn up to outline an alternative to both the Soviet and the Nazi authoritarian states. Horkheimer was trapped on one hand between the *real* emergence of the authoritarian state – 'State capitalism is the authoritarian state of the present',[39] in reference to both to Nazi Germany and the Soviet situation – and on the other the ongoing dream of a democracy of councils. While not giving in, the only thing left for him to do was confess that '[t]heory has no

---

35   See Adorno 1983.
36   On this, see later in this chapter.
37   Horkheimer 1978b, p. 99.
38   Horkheimer 1978b, p. 104.
39   Horkheimer 1978b, p. 96.

program for the electoral campaign, or even for the reconstruction of Europe which the specialists will soon see to'.[40] Critical theory, he adds, '[d]espite all the urgency with which theory attempts to illuminate the movement of the social totality even in its smallest detail, ... is unable to prescribe to individuals an effective form of resistance to injustice'. Horkheimer did not consider that, in order not to renounce all historical-political projectuality, more attention had to be paid to those very differences and *democratic* potentials which, despite their difficulties and failures, were nevertheless appearing on the horizon of state capitalism at that time. Thus, he concludes that: '[t]hought itself is already a sign of resistance, the effort to keep oneself from being deceived any longer'.[41] However noble, he was prospecting an intellectual resistance entrusted to single *virtuous* individuals. For him, it was only through them that somehow '[t]he era of the authoritarian state can be broken ... These attempts, which by their very nature tolerate no bureaucracies, can come only from the isolated'.[42] But then, to these same non-conformist *aristoi*, almost no space remained for resistance. As Horkheimer realistically recognised, in the Third International, 'even the enemies of the authoritarian state can no longer conceive of freedom'. In other words, at that unitarily (and unilaterally) defined point in history, the intentionality of thought itself seemed to be essentially under threat:

> Sociological and psychological concepts are too superficial to express what has happened to revolutionaries in the last few decades: their will toward freedom has been damaged, without which neither understanding nor solidarity nor a correct relation between leader and group is conceivable.[43]

No different historical or political hypothesis hence seemed to be able to offer at least a potential alternative to that condition of closure within the authoritarian state, homogeneous epiphenomenon of a distinction-free state capitalism. All that Horkheimer could do to try to deal with this was to appeal to a generic *moral* humanism, and his call for 'the intervention of men' outside every historicist schema was without doubt noble, but also aporetic in the face of the eclipse of the possibility of freedom that his same prognosis of the era had revealed.

---

40 Horkheimer 1978b, p. 116.
41 Ibid.
42 Horkheimer 1978b, p. 111.
43 Horkheimer 1978b, p. 117.

Effectively, already in Pollock, the hypostatisation of the concept of 'state capitalism' to some extent risked preventing the individuation of the at least in part *specific* character of the political, social and economic systems making up the single new realities of intervention or political control of the economy. This was at the same time both its limit but also its strength, at least up to a certain point. It resulted in the capacity to grasp possible entanglements and ambiguities (the *Verflochtenheit* and *Zweideutigkeit* encouraged by Horkheimer) between the two variants. But then might the differences in degree between these forms not refer to a difference in kind hidden beneath the single essence of 'state capitalism'? In short, did these differences in degree only have a relative relevance, with an exclusively phenomenal and exoteric meaning? In sum, already from Pollock's ideal-typical picture, the *relevance of the different manners of legitimation* that in effect accompanied the different manifestations of the configuration of the regulatory state, also with its *social state* aspects, risked not emerging strongly enough. Of course, these could lead to some 'grey areas', areas of overlap – first of all of an 'economic' kind – between the 'totalitarian' and 'democratic' forms. However, criticism of these overlaps, confusions or analogies should not lose sight of the fact that, in the case of *totalitarianisms*, planning, interventionism and the connected social policies fitted into a design for a *warfare state* which essentially enclosed the lives of the *populations* in the circle of the production of death.[44] On the other hand, in the case of the democratic attempts such as the New Deal and later on the Beveridge Plan and its various European variants, it was a matter of preserving or rather of confirming and strengthening the *constitutional state* with the social state, and with regulation and economic planning.[45] Now, in spite of everything – the suspension of judgement and the aporia that he did not manage to overcome in 1941 while trying to fully define democratic state capitalism, and his seeming, even later on, to put the difference in forms down to an exoteric level communicable in the face of a homogeneous esoteric-noumenal truth – Pollock is not at all insensitive to this difference that depends on the 'political ends' of the different types of 'social state'. In a later contribution, 'Is National Socialism a New Social Order?', he moves in an empirically more circumspect manner to his more famous philosopher friends, showing that he tends to have a clearer conception of the difference between the totalitarian and the democratic form of state capitalism. He understands that the

---

44 For a discussion on this differentiation, see Foucault 2003 in particular pp. 258–61; in this connection see Rapini 2012.
45 See in general Ritter 1989.

totalitarian form achieves 'the integration of society' by subjecting the individual to a 'mobilization ... without limits', and by devastating all remaining personal space. In other words, it implements a 'total brutalization of society' which is at the same time compensated and somehow instrumentally redressed with forms of security and relative well-being reserved solely for *Aryans*. The full employment policy, accompanied by tax measures favouring Germans alone (in particular of the middle to lower classes) and 'social' insurance institutions, constituted the organicist and social face of a *brutalisation* that expressed itself both in a predatory foreign policy and in violent internal discriminations. Among the new rules that National Socialism introduced to replace the ones of laissez-faire attitude, the 'iron necessity of full employment' immediately became of central importance. And indeed, as Pollock observes,

> [t]he totalitarian state is in a position to guarantee one single right to all its 'racial comrades', a right which no democratic state so far has been able to grant to its citizens: *economic security*. This security, it is true, is bought at the expense of a total brutalization of society. Still, the integrative function of full employment in this era of ever more threatening general economic insecurity can hardly be overestimated. It probably counts for more in the minds of most people than their standard of living (provided that this standard is not desperately low and has a tendency to improve), it probably counts for more to the small business man than the loss of independence, or to the worker than the loss of his own organization.[46]

With these observations, almost in real time Pollock understood the precise reasons for the *mass consensus* that National Socialism managed to collect. It was a consensus and a 'social integration' built not only through terror, but also through a fundamentally racist-authoritarian variant of the *social state* for a refounded national 'political body'.

> Political domination is achieved by organized terror and overwhelming propaganda on the one side, on the other by full employment and an adequate standard of living for all key groups, the promise of security and a more abundant life for every subject who submits voluntarily and completely. This system is far from being based upon rude force alone. In

---

46 Pollock 1941, p. 452, italics mine.

that it provides many 'real' satisfactions for its subjects, it exists partly with the consent of the governed.[47]

Hence, these analyses contain elements that seem to anticipate the outcomes of some important historiographical works dedicated recently to *Hitler's Willing Executioners* and in particular to the *Nazi Welfare State* and its means of producing Aryan community strength through joy (NS-Gemeinschaft Kraft durch Freude was the name of the organisation created in 1939 by the National Socialists to manage free time).[48]

In light of his analytical contributions, that is, his diary of the crisis, we can also specify – as I will show later on – that hereafter, in the same way as he arrived at a *different assessment of John M. Keynes's economic and political outlooks,* he sought to recognise and increasingly distinguish the different historical-political meanings of the opposing forms of the regulatory state. Highly critical in 1936 of a Keynesian perspective that all in all seemed to him to simply save the classist structure of society, in 1942 he would end another essay by returning to this same topic. It became clear to Pollock that the opposition of the 'democratic', non-totalitarian world to the closure of the 'new order' of totalitarian state capitalisms was the historically decisive stake at play. It was a stake that in the resisting 'democratic' forms, in the long term in particular, could be resolved and decided by jointly realising economic security and recognising freedoms.

Hence the prognosis or hope, in turn not lacking a certain ambivalence, with which Pollock rounds off the 1941 essay:

> If the democracies can show that economic security must not be tied up with the loss of liberty but can be achieved under democratic conditions, then I dare forecast that the new order of National Socialism will be followed in Germany and elsewhere by an infinitely superior democratic new order.[49]

To complete his position, Pollock latched onto his earlier discourse with this explicit vision of a possible overcoming or destruction of totalitarian state capitalism in favour of the affirmation of an 'infinitely superior' democratic social state. Already attentive to the theoretical possibility of democratic state capi-

---

47 Pollock 1978, p. 92.
48 See Goldhagen 1996; Aly 2016; and the already quoted Ginsborg 2014, pp. 371 ff.; and see again Foucault 2003.
49 Pollock 1941, p. 455.

talism, he added basic elements brought up in the US political debate by Alvin H. Hansen, one of the major interpreters of Keynes's lesson. It is the same Pollock who points out in an endnote that:

> An attempt to outline an economic program for such a democratic 'new order' was recently made by Alvin H. Hansen in a pamphlet issued by the National Resources Planning Board, After the War-Full Employment, Washington, D.C., 1942. Hansen formulates the problem as follows: 'If the victorious democracies muddle through another decade of economic frustration and mass unemployment, we may expect social disintegration and, sooner or later, another international conflagration. A positive program of post-war economic expansion and full employment, boldly conceived and vigorously pursued, is imperative. Democracies, if they are going to lead the world out of chaos and insecurity, must first and foremost offer their people opportunity, employment, and a rising standard of living'.[50]

With this discourse and this reference to Alvin H. Hansen, Pollock himself seems to invite us to almost take a step *beyond* the dystopian abstraction of his concept of 'state capitalism' and understand that the realisation of the democratic 'version' could actually aim to politically achieve something *new*, a '*new democratic order*' capable of *reconciling economic and social security and guaranteeing individual rights*. And so, even after providing the critical tools, Pollock showed that he no longer wanted to unilaterally dwell on deconstructing a 'state capitalism' abstractly *dystopianised* on the basis of an absolutisation of its totalitarian variant. Instead, he demonstrated that he wanted at least to carefully consider asserting an overall and mature idea of social security as a political end, reaching out beyond the criticism of *Herrschaft* developed by his friends Horkheimer and Adorno, while adopting, but only in part and with a radical esoteric spirit, its same lesson.

As such, one might say that while a greater knowledge and appreciation of Roosevelt's policy[51] – in particular I am thinking here of the famous Social

---

50 Pollock's words in the last note of his text (1941, p. 455) on the new order. Alvin H. Hansen is a well-known personality in the sphere of US political-economic history, often called one of the biggest Keynesian scholars of the period, and author, among other things, of *A Guide to Keynes* (Hansen 1953).

51 Pollock also had the opportunity to make a personal visit to Roosevelt, at the White House, on 5 February 1943, as evidenced in his letters from 23 January 1943 and 5 February 1943. However, to be true, it would seem he returned with some sense of disappointment.

Security Act of 1935 – presumably lay behind his abandonment of the maximalist judgement expressed on Keynes in 1936, before him lay the encounter with post-war Europe's orientation towards democratic welfare, with its disappointments and critical tensions, particularly in Germany. In any case, at that point, namely in the first half of the 1940s, Pollock's hope must have been that a virtuous balance could be achieved in that *new democratic order* between *justice, sociality and freedom*, capable of going beyond 'state capitalism' and achieving its democratic dimension. In other words, he hoped that the *era of state capitalism* would leave room to a *new era*, in which '[e]veryone, as a member of society, has the right to social security and is entitled to realization, through national effort and international co-operation and in accordance with the organization and resources of each State, of the economic, social and cultural rights indispensable for his dignity and the free development of his personality'.[52] It is precisely in this same direction that his inseparable friend Horkheimer would seek to question the post-war era and reposition critical theory and its political implications during his return to Germany and not least during their successive and joint retirement to Switzerland, a move which hence received a sort of justification, if not a theoretical foundation.

The prognosis on the continuing duration of domination – 'domination [*Herrschaft*] and always only domination and not its overcoming' – remains in the background. However, it is accompanied, in Horkheimer too, by increasing openness towards a not-just-exoteric retrieval of the liberal-democratic dimension within a 'democratic' state capitalism which, furthermore, also seemed increasingly threatened by endogenous factors leading up to an entirely administered society.

This evolution can also help us understand their ever greater perception of the Soviet reality, then resisting incarnation as 'totalitarian state capitalism', not just as a threat but also as a sort of uncanny double and authoritarian temptation for the fragile and ambivalent western democratic state capitalism.

2.2   Between Domination and Welfare

With regard to his analytical contributions, which, as has been said, constitute the genetic context from which Pollock extrapolated his critical ideal type, the following, by no means exhaustive observations nevertheless need to be made.

---

52   Article 22 of the 1948 United Nations' Universal Declaration of Human Rights.

a) Pollock had already dealt with the topic of *planning* in 1927 by directly studying the *Soviet case*. A few years later, in 1929, he published the results of what he had been able to study 'on the ground' on occasion of his pioneering stay in Moscow under the title *Die Planwirtschaftliche Versuche in der Sowjetunion [Experiments in Economic Planning in the Soviet Union]*. As a member of the Frankfurt Institute for Social Research, then directed by Carl Grünberg and not yet by Horkheimer, he was invited to Moscow on occasion of the ten-year anniversary of the October Revolution. The Frankfurt Institute entertained various ties with the Marx-Engels Institute in Moscow, directed by David Rjazanov, and it seems that relations with Rjazanov (at that time a prestigious USSR intellectual, holding similar views to Trotsky and, like him, then eliminated by Stalin) were very close and friendly.[53] Following some conversations with Pollock in Montagnola in March 1969, Martin Jay notes that:

> Through Ryazanov's friendship, Pollock was able to speak with members of the dwindling opposition within the Bolshevik Party during his trip, in addition to his actual field studies of Soviet planning. The impressions he brought back to Frankfurt after several months were thus not entirely favorable. His book carefully avoided commenting on the political consequences of the Revolution and the forced collectivizations of the 1920's. On the central question he treated – the transition from a market to a planned economy – Pollock was less the enthusiastic supporter than the detached and prudent analyst unwilling to pass judgments prematurely. Here, too, he and Grossmann had cause for disagreement.[54]

I think that on this point, so many years later, we need to be more explicit than Jay. In the pages that resulted from that trip to the USSR, Pollock immediately highlighted the aporias, the *fatal contradictions* even, that burdened the Bolshevik attempt to overcome the 'capitalistic' division between a political and economic organisation of society.[55] As he immediately understood, the forced step in the period of so-called war communism towards the abolition of the market and centralised planning would prove a 'violent utopia', owing

---

53 Geninazzi 1997, p. 247.
54 Jay 1996, p. 35; on the trip to Moscow and *Die Planwirtschaft* see also Campani 1992, pp. 88 ff. for whom 'at the historiographical level Pollock can be credited with sifting through a huge amount of material, providing an extremely informed and unbiased report in a moment when all the publications on the USSR – with the sole exception of the work by Dobb – fell into the category of political propaganda' (p. 94, own translation).
55 Pollock 1929, p. 98.

to the lack of the very historical and *technical* presuppositions for its realisation. As Pollock promptly observed:

> Even if we were to acknowledge that, for the Bolsheviks, abolishing the market was politically indispensable in order to keep a hold on power, from the purely economic point of view, it was an utter utopia to want to build a centralised economic administration, on a natural basis, in an economically backward, agricultural country, moreover exhausted by the war effort and civil war. 'In the fever of the civil war', the Bolsheviks did not realise this, otherwise at the start of 1920 they would have given their economic policy a different form and thus might have avoided enormous losses of human lives and material resources. The experience of 1919 and 1920 demonstrated that a country with an economy based on over 20 million smallholdings was lacking all conditions for an immediate passage to a market-less economy ... Only in such an economically backward country as Russia could bureaucracy experience a similar degeneration to that which in the end made the economy of war communism fall flat.[56]

Pollock's diagnosis recognised that a planned economy could only be proposed where the biggest economic weight had been shifted onto the big factories and giant companies in industry, trade and banking, and where a drastic simplification was underway in the field of state administration operations thanks to the development of new technical devices. Socialist planning could only be attempted in these conditions of production and administration techniques. Otherwise, as he observed, instead of a classless society they would generate a bureaucratic explosion, taking the 'bureaucratism of war communism beyond the very worst expectations'.[57] 'Instead of keeping the promise to establish a "cheap government", the Bolsheviks created such an immense and inefficient bureaucratic machine that it even put tsarist bureaucracy in the shade'.[58] It was unlikely that the failure of the historical-dialectical hopes, the denunciation of their 'degeneration' instead of their realisation, could have assumed more disenchanted and radical tones.

It can be seen that the members of the Institute with more direct political involvement, the communists Karl A. Wittfogel and Franz Borkenau, remained

---

56 Pollock 1929, pp. 102–3, own translation.
57 Pollock 1929, p. 110, own translation.
58 Pollock 1929, p. 104, own translation.

closer to Grossmann, while Horkheimer moved, albeit very cautiously, in Pollock's disenchanted wake. On this, Martin Jay is totally clear:

> Heated sub rosa discussions of Pollock's findings did take place, but never broke into print. In fact, after his book was published in 1929, the Institut maintained an almost complete official silence about events in the USSR ... It was really not until a decade later, after the Moscow purge trials, that Horkheimer and the others, with the sole exception of the obdurate Grossmann, completely abandoned their hope for the Soviet Union.[59]

Even in light of this anticipatory historical awareness, we have to go back to question the potential alternative between the totalitarian and democratic form of state capitalism left open by Pollock in 1941. It is evident that what he had already diagnosed concerning 'Soviet bureaucratism' then extended into the ideal-typical epochal model that he subsequently developed. In this light, while also thinking of the topics brilliantly taken up later on by Adorno and Horkheimer in *Dialectic of Enlightenment*, it is worth once again making use of Martin Jay's summary, based upon Pollock's direct testimony, giving it not just interpretative but documentary value. After the emigration, in the debate on the meaning of Nazism, Jay notes:

> The older members of the Institut's inner circle, on the other hand, followed the lead of its associate director, Friedrich Pollock, who, despite his administrative duties, found time to devote to scholarly pursuits. The centerpiece of Pollock's work was his theory of *state capitalism*, with which he described *the prevailing trends of modern societies*. In large measure, the theory was an extrapolation of his earlier analysis of the Soviet economic experiment. Pollock ... did not feel that Russia had succeeded in introducing a truly socialist planned economy. In fact, one of the reasons for the Institut's relative silence on Soviet affairs was its belief that the Russian economy, despite its unique qualities, was a variant of state capitalism.[60]

---

59   Jay 1996, p. 35. Despite also bearing in mind what appears to him Pollock's early 'enthusiasm' for the Soviet experiment, Campani once again proceeds in a very analytical manner to speak of his 'ambivalent judgement' on the USSR. In any case, Campani expresses his strong disagreement with the simplification made by Wiggershaus (1994), who limits himself to presenting a dogmatically pro-Soviet (!) Pollock. See Campani 1992, pp. 121–6. For the criticism of Wiggershaus, see Campani 1992, p. 119, note 26.
60   Jay 1996, p. 88, italics mine.

His timely observations found an echo and extension in Horkheimer's text, 'The Authoritarian State', published 13 years after Pollock's work. Here, state socialism is interpreted as the most complete form of totalitarian state capitalism: 'Integral statism or state socialism is the most consistent form of the authoritarian state which has freed itself from any dependence on private capital. ... The fascist countries create a mixed form'.[61]

> Whether revolutionaries pursue power as one pursues loot or criminals, is revealed in the course of action. Instead of dissolving in the end into the democracy of the councils, the group can maintain itself as a leadership. Work, discipline and order can save the republic and tidy up the revolution.

And even more radically he asserts: 'Even though the abolition of the state was written on its banner, that party transfigured its industrially backward fatherland into the secret vision of those industrial powers which were growing sick on their parliamentarism and could no longer live without fascism'.[62] Yet, already in 1927, Pollock had had the opportunity to directly study this process of heterogeneity of ends and degenerative upset which had led from the promise of a slimmed-down state and 'cheap government' to 'the bureaucratism of communism beyond the very worst expectations'. The sentences just quoted from Horkheimer's 1942 text must therefore also be listened to as a sort of resumption and meticulous re-elaboration of what Pollock had been able to recognise 'on the ground' 13 years earlier: 'Instead of keeping the promise to establish a "cheap government", the Bolsheviks created such an immense and inefficient bureaucratic machine that it even put tsarist bureaucracy in the shade.'[63]

What is more, in his analysis, Pollock was already aware that the very same technical production and administration conditions needed to achieve the planned economy would necessarily be bound to a process of complete rationalisation, the implication being a drastically efficient transformation denying the specificity of all social relations.

On outlining his ideal type, that is, generic state capitalism, in 1941 Pollock indeed observed that not only in all fields of state activity but also in social spheres,

---

61 Horkheimer 1978b, pp. 101–2.
62 Horkheimer 1978b, p. 99.
63 Pollock 1929, p. 104, own translation; but see also p. 110.

guesswork and improvisation give place to the principles of scientific management. This rule is in conformity with state capitalism's basic conception of society as an integrated unit comparable to one of the modern giants in steel, chemical or motorcar production. ... But once this principle of 'rationalization' has become mandatory for all public activities, it will be applied in spheres which previously were the sanctuary of guesswork, routine and muddling through: military preparedness, the conduct of war, behavior towards public opinion, application of the coercive power of the state, foreign trade and foreign policy, etc.[64]

Hence, to remove the aporias and authoritarian-bureaucratic drifts of the Soviet model, it would not be sufficient to avail of other technical production and administration tools. Indeed, transforming the whole of society into a sort of large, systemic 'integrated unit' after the model of giant production machines would have enabled any margins of freedom and autonomy to be eliminated; that same space where, through its control, the democratic variant of state capitalism should have been activated.

b) Some time after publishing the text on the Soviet Union, in 1932 Pollock described 'The Present Situation of Capitalism' as being characterised by a *structural* alteration to the liberal mode, at this point just an abstract theory, based on the idea of the market as the sphere of free and perfect competition. This 'entrepreneurial' idea of the market was only proving functional for the limited development of the production forces, while their economic and technical transformation towards concentration in 'large units' was leading to the demise of the very presuppositions for the market to function, linked to the stage of competitive or private capitalism. Starting from observations empirically documented in German and American sources,[65] Pollock observed that 'the ruins of these premises remain': capitalism was assuming more and more of an *oligo-monopolistic* structure. Diametrically confuting the liberalistic idealisation of the model of perfect competition, the historic-economic situation and the connected development of technology and production were imposing an economic picture dominated by a radically imperfect competition in which just a few 'large economic units [fought] to dominate the market' and were doing so by combining for their own purpose *technical development* – for example, unheard-of mechanisation and technicalisation of agriculture – and protectionist political interventions (for example, high customs barriers) to

---

64 Pollock 1978, p. 79.
65 See Pollock 1975, 'Die gegenwärtige Lage des Kapitalismus' ['The Present Situation of Capitalism']. The reference to the USA is on p. 21, and to the Germans on pp. 20–1.

favour monopolist prices. As Pollock affirmed in 1932, 'the time of free trade has passed, once and for all', announcing a strong tendency towards the increased rigidity or withdrawal of individual freedoms of initiative together with the historic obsolescence of the market. And it is in these words that the Frankfurt School's diagnosis of 'late capitalism' and/or post-liberal societies finds a sort of *point of no return*, a basic and shared premise, no matter how implicit. As Max Horkheimer writes in the same year, following in Pollock's footsteps: 'The economy is in large measure dominated by monopolies, and yet on the world scale it is disorganized and chaotic, richer than ever yet unable to eliminate human wretchedness'.[66] It is again Pollock, in reply, who defines the contradiction that had thus come into being as 'tragic' since 'right at the time when telecommunications and transport technology is making a fully unfolded world economy possible for the first time,[67] the economically stronger countries are progressively cutting themselves off' so as to protect the interests of their respective dominant economic groups. Instead of being developed in socially emancipatory and 'rational' terms, the contrast between preserving the relations of production and developing the productive forces is *blocked* at both the economic and political level, creating an entanglement in which the two spheres of power mix and blend together. This reordering was indeed happening, in the form of a more *stabilised* and rigid society. Pollock felt that this 'stabilisation of the situation of economic crisis' could be achieved not just thanks to a socialist planned economy (on whose problems and risks of bureaucratic-authoritarian drifts he had moreover already focussed in the case of the USSR), but rather (as highlighted by Helmut Dubiel) also through 'fascist reorganisation of the economy, indeed at the price of brutal social discipline and reordering production in an almost autarchic and military fashion even in peace time'.[68]

c) On this basis, Pollock would already introduce the concept of 'state capitalism' in his essay 'Bemerkungen zur Wirtschaftskrise' ['Remarks on the Economic Crisis'], published in the second issue of the Institute of Social Research's *Zeitschrift*, not by chance in the *annus horribilis* of 1933. With even more tragic radicality, he now diagnoses the structural transformation in the direction of monopolistic capitalism as 'irrevocable':

> The liberalistic economic mechanism, which arose on the basis of other presuppositions and hitherto worked relatively well, is no longer equal to

---

66 Horkheimer 2002a, p. 8.
67 Pollock 1975, p. 25, own translation.
68 Dubiel 1975, p. 14, own translation.

its tasks. All the clues suggest that it would be a waste of effort to seek to restore the technical, economic and social-psychological presuppositions for a free market economy.[69]

These 'structural transformations', in which 'the development of modern technology' has to be recognised as 'one of the most disruptive' forces,[70] at the same time make the whole system 'more susceptible to crisis'.[71] In the face of this contradiction between permanent overproduction and structural unemployment[72] which seems to generate ever new and more frequent economic and social crises, making them not just chronic but almost *permanent*, Pollock clearly distances himself from the orthodox Marxist *collapse* hypotheses and warns that *'the possibilities of the capitalist system to adapt to the changed conditions are far from being exhausted'*.[73] Passing through the economic crisis that had been raging in the USA since the end of 1929 and Roosevelt's New Deal to a prognosis on the German situation, he observes that:

> Like in other regions, here [in Germany] too capitalism has shown an unexpected ability to resist and adapt.
>
> In the end, however varied they may seem, these processes of adaptation can be reduced to the *same denominator*: they equate to a more or less far-reaching limitation to the power of the single owner of the production means to autocratically decide the way and direction of his economic activity. The fundamental rights of the liberalistic economic constitution are to a large degree relinquished to the advantage of the large economic units or the state itself. Corresponding to these limitations, at least for the large economic subjects, is a non-juridical but factual entitlement to state aid in difficult situations.[74]

The characteristic of the movements underway is further highlighted through the invitation to observe in them the transformations of the political sphere under the pressure of the large economic units. More than this, however, the attention is drawn to the transformations and surveillance of the economic

---

69 Pollock 1975, p. 50, own translation.
70 Pollock 1975, p. 49, own translation.
71 Ibid., own translation.
72 See ibid.
73 Pollock 1975, p. 55, own translation, italics mine.
74 Pollock 1975, p. 63, own translation, italics mine.

structures and their management (investments and directions), requested and directed by a new kind of state political intervention:

> Even more drastic transformations are produced by the state's rapidly increasing inference in the whole of economic life. The state already served as midwife in the early phase of capitalism, it was then thrust to one side, and today in its growing difficulties it again comes to its aid. ... While state interventions played a certain role in the past too, conscious economic measures, in the variety and intensity in which they have been appearing recently, constitute a phase of 'state capitalist interventions'. They are a symptom of the fact that the hitherto existing 'automatism' can in part be replaced, although with uncertain success, with new methods, without thereby affecting the basic structure of the existing order.[75]

Pollock was by no means wrong to centre these 'observations on the economic crisis' around the topic of state intervention and *economic and social stabilisation* as the underlying theme and 'common denominator' of the historic-economic situation. It is without doubt less risky in hindsight than it was then to recognise the 'regulated market' and 'planning' as the leitmotif – regardless of the different forms – of the right-wing, left-wing and also democratic policies.[76] But to draw up this diagnosis and prognosis, which, while not totally pessimistic, was nevertheless reserved and very much heterodox to the 'collapsist' vision when the situation was still in the making, was a sign of an out-of-the-ordinary capacity of analysis and quite rare perspicacity.[77] Capitalism,

---

75 Pollock 1975, pp. 64–5, own translation.
76 For an interpretation of twentieth-century economic history in this sense, see Judt 2010, 'The Regulated Market', pp. 55 ff.
77 A comparison with the analyses made more or less in the same period by Karl Polanyi could prove to be interesting. The Hungarian scholar, during his exile in the USA, also observed: 'the economic concept of society would disappear together with the dichotomy between politics and economy that it reflected ... It is the dividing line between liberalism on the one hand, fascism and socialism on the other. The difference between these two is not primarily economic. ... Even where they profess identical economics, they are not only different but are, indeed, embodiments of opposite principles. And the ultimate on which they separate is again freedom. ... is freedom an empty word, a temptation, designed to ruin man and his works ...?', 'Freedom in a Complex Society', in Polanyi 2001, p. 267 (translator's note: while found in the Italian version, please note the first sentence of the quote is missing from the English text); by Polanyi see also the collection of texts written between 1922 and 1960 and collected by Alfredo Salsano in *La libertà in una società complessa* (Polanyi 1987).

Pollock invited us to think, could and would deal with the crisis, but it would do so by hiving off a new phase or a new stage in its history, by assuming the brand new and in some ways paradoxical shape of 'state capitalism'. It would extend into this form, giving a new shape to the private ownership of means of production, which are preserved but in a *mediated*, politically mediated form. Pollock's analysis certainly did not fail to question the specific difference of the state political subjects and institutional spheres called upon to perform this mediation. But it developed progressively, increasingly bringing about a sort of correction to or reflection on his assessment and causing a sort of shift from the Marxist conception of the state to a Keynesian and Social Democratic perspective (see part 2.1). At this point, it must be properly underlined that at first the critical comparison with Marxism took on the shape of a comparison with the '*collapsist*' perspectives. To grasp the reach and fecundity of Pollock's theses, it must be specified that these essays from the 1930s were set against a background of the most important debate on economic theory developed in the Frankfurt School's *Zeitschrift*. The whole debate revolved around the 'collapse of the capitalist system', pivoting around the work of Henryk Grossmann, author in 1927 of the prodigious *The Law of Accumulation and Collapse of the Capitalist System*.[78]

In the face of the 1929 crisis Grossmann, who, like Pollock, had been assistant to Carl Grünberg and had then made a name for himself as the most important economist in the group, did not intend to diagnose the necessity for a practically 'automatic' collapse of the capitalist system. However, by taking up Marxian orthodoxy and hinging on the 'law of the tendency of the rate of profit to fall', he suggested that the only way out of the crisis would be to break up the capitalist puzzle and build the new society thanks to the class struggle as the factor of an authentic historical-dialectical negation-overcoming.[79] Although the attribution to Grossmann of an 'automatic' vision of the collapse of capitalism is presumably the result of a forced or even prejudiced interpretation,[80] in his case he undeniably thought of the exit from competitive capitalism through the strong paradigm of *collapse*, that is, the *Zusammenbruchgesetz*, entwined with and strengthened by a theory of dialectical action of the collective subject engaged in actively demolishing what was nevertheless already wobbly for

---

78 Grossmann 1992. See also Wiggershaus 1994, p. 30; Campani 1992, pp. 29, 30 and 61. On Grossman and his relations with Grünberg, to whom he was also assistant, and with the Institute until 1940, see Jay 1996, pp. 32 ff.
79 See Marramao 1973, pp. 23 and 19; see also p. 24 for the comparison proposed between Grossmann and Lukács 1971. On Grossmann's 'orthodox Marxism', see again Jay 1996, p. 34.
80 Marramao 1973, pp. 22–3.

reasons of its own. 'No economic system, however weak it may be, collapses "automatically"; it must nevertheless be demolished'. And then:

> As a dialectical Marxist I obviously know that both sides of the process, the objective and subjective elements, influence each other. These factors blend in the class struggle. ... My collapse theory does not aim to exclude this active intervention, but rather proposes to show in which conditions such a given revolutionary situation can and does objectively arise.[81]

And yet, in the debate around these theories, with these same heterodox essays by Pollock, it started to come to light that capitalism could instead exit the crisis. Yes, it would have to abandon its competitive-liberal phase, but at the same time it would be reordered with *state interventions*, with forms of *'planned reordering'* which would not lead to the collapse and dialectical reversal of the system but instead to its indefinite and *polymorphous* extension. Whereas Grossmann concluded his work by radically affirming that 'it is impossible to regulate production on the basis of the existing economic order', Pollock responded: 'Without doubt it may be established that this crisis can be overcome with capitalistic means and that "monopolistic" capitalism can continue to exist for a currently incalculable period of time'.[82]

So, what characterised Pollock's prognosis was no longer the collapse brought to completion with the revolutionary movement. That said, in itself it was not a somehow positive and *historicistically consoling* exit from the crisis either.

With planning on a monopolistic basis, the 'costs' and 'destructions' – *destructions* and not euphemistically 'frictions', underlines Pollock – caused by capitalism towards the *whole* of society, would become *systemic* and as such would extend *indefinitely* in time:

> Many things suggest that in controlled capitalism the depressions will be longer, the phases of expansion shorter and sharper and the crises more deleterious than in the times of 'free competition'; but its 'automatic' collapse is not to be expected. From the economic point of view, there is no peremptory force urging its replacement with another system.[83]

---

81 Letter from Henryk Grossmann to Paul Mattick, 21 June 1931, quoted by Marramao 1973, p. 23, own translation.
82 Pollock 1975, 'Die gegenwärtige Lage des Kapitalismus', p. 28, own translation.
83 Ibid., own translation.

As far as the social and cultural aspects involved in this transition to the *post-liberal* phase are concerned too, with his 'Bemerkungen' in 1933 the prognosis offered by Pollock was already anything but optimistic. Quite the opposite, it was harshly realistic. In the face of the affirmation in the dominating position of an 'increasingly small group of economic feudatories, and their supreme officials, who will be the true beneficiaries of the capitalistic order'[84] and the concentration of power in their hands, at the same time we will see both the proletarianisation of the middle classes and intellectual workers and the overall '*annihilation of the working class's capacity to resist*'.[85] It must also be highlighted that the reference for this diagnosis by Pollock does not seem to be either exclusively or primarily Germany, but the awareness of the relationship of more and more radical interdependence between the development of technology and the organisation of society:

> The systematic use of all technical resources in the workshop as well as in the office, the draw towards an increasingly capital-based mode of production, the clear tendency towards a person-free workspace or at least with a scant human presence, lead to the 'structural' unemployment of numerous 'hands' and heads, and at the same time to a clear differentiation between the employed people themselves.[86]

Where the concept of working class should have emerged, Pollock observes, analysis must increasingly note a differentiation between a social group of highly qualified forces and on the other hand a mass of 'semi-skilled or unskilled persons who – in the same way as some goods – are "fungible", that is, they can be replaced at will by the army of the unemployed'.[87]

Also on the basis of this lack of homogeneity, but not due to this alone,

> [t]he very will of the great masses to fight will be broken, both through the modern methods of mass conditioning and through the development of a functionalisation that today already appears clear. Ever more evidently, a relatively regular job is becoming more and more of a privilege and like the role of official it must be acquired over and over again not just through a faultless performance but also through a 'reliable' attitude. ... The annihilation of the working class's capacity to resist is therefore completed

---

84   Pollock 1975, 'Bemerkungen zur Wirtschaftskrise', p. 69, own translation.
85   Pollock 1975, p. 70, own translation.
86   Pollock 1975, pp. 69–70, own translation.
87   Pollock 1975, p. 70, own translation.

through this differentiation among the unemployed, between those who can still hope for a job and the 'unreliable elements' who are temporarily or constantly denied this privilege.[88]

'State capitalism', here still without distinction in Pollock too, hence tends intrinsically towards the authoritarian state. It also tends to combine the exoneration or marginalisation of parliamentarism (the executive was strengthened everywhere in those years) and the monopoly of a new type of strength, that of the *psychic* domination of totality:

> Owing to the liberation from the conditioning of parliamentarism and the disposal of the entire apparatus of psychic domination over the masses, the governments of this era seem to be independent from classes and stand impartially above society. A sociological analysis of the new state form is indeed a task which still needs performing; the economic problems dealt with earlier are the key to its understanding.[89]

Pollock closes his 'Bemerkungen' with this programmatic finale. Published in 1933, it is a text whose specific importance in the genesis of the Frankfurt School's *Weltanschauung* seems to me difficult to overestimate; it opportunely signalled the 'first setting out' of that thesis which constitutes 'a real constant in the parable of critical theory up to *Dialektik der Aufklärung*'.[90] Besides, this theory has recently been summed up in the very sharp observation that:

> In the reflection of critical theory in the 1930s, the idea – which would come to completion in Adorno's post-war reflections – had already fully taken root that the countless phenomenal variations of the foundation do not dissolve the basic core, even though they may jeopardise the operativity and transparency: harness its effects by way of the countertendential cement of institutionalised violence. The context formed by the latency of the catastrophic trend and by the constant rationalisation and automatisation of institutional control thus comes to form a single mechanism, the cogency of whose logic is such as to suppress every margin of autonomy of the 'civil' and 'private', the prerogative of individual emancipation of the bourgeois subject. It is reproduced through a domination that depoliticises the masses beforehand, with the help of the mass media

---

88 Ibid., own translation.
89 Pollock 1975, p. 71, own translation.
90 Campani 1992, p. 186, own translation.

and techniques of manipulation, guaranteeing their loyalty to the imperatives of accumulation and valorisation. More than an increase in the coefficient of integration between 'state' and 'civil society', for the Frankfurt School theoreticians the new authoritarian order represents the utter deprivation and removal of the second term.[91]

Within the vision opened by Pollock's analysis, a wholly disenchanted, or even tragically *ironic* picture of the philosophy of history already seemed to be forming compared to both the revolutionary and historicist dialectical one.[92] And this also needs to be affirmed in the light of the further thematic focus developed throughout his reflection, concerning the relationship existing between the assertion of monopolistic tendencies and the development of increasingly powerful and totalising production and administration techniques, applicable not only to the traditional economic spheres but also to the whole political sphere of propaganda and persuasion, and even beyond this, to the sphere of *psychology* and *food production*. It was a thread that Pollock came back to many times, providing fundamental elements for the formation of the (Frankfurt) critique of biopower, and which after the war would bring him to deal with the great topic of *automation* and its social and anthropological consequences.

d) In 1936 Pollock directly dealt with both the *Keynesian* diagnosis and attempt at a response to the crisis. In the essay 'Keynes' Revision der liberalistischen Nationalökonomie' ['Keynes' Revision of Liberalistic Economics'], written together with Kurt Mandelbaum and published in the *Zeitschrift* in 1936, Pollock underlines how the pathogenic dimension of liberalistic ideology had now clearly been acknowledged in the liberal sphere too.[93] To him it seemed that Keynes's work could at least be credited with this, that is, with recognising the deadly illness that weighed upon the self-regulated market and led to posing the problem of 'how long an economic system could be kept alive whose regular functioning depends on the need for more gold and earthquakes or wars to create more possibilities of work'.[94] But the Keynesian answer, its attempt to 'indicate methods to heal from the illness while maintaining the advantages of the current system, that is, *efficiency* and *freedom*', did not seem at all satisfying to Pollock at the time. To him it looked like a simple 'revi-

---

91 Marramao 2013, p. 135, own translation.
92 On the ironic ['*beffardo*'] and reversed outcome, with particular attention to Adorno, see again Marramao 1973, pp. 41 ff.
93 Baumann (pseudonym of Pollock) 1936, pp. 384 ff.
94 Baumann 1936, p. 387, own translation.

sion', as such not addressed to the social structure of the system. Hence, it was not able to refer to a better outlook but only to a 'dark future'.[95] Not without some radicalism (or a certain maximalism), in 1936 while sharing and quoting a theory expressed by Marcuse, Pollock wrote: 'what has previously been written in this journal on the struggle of the totalitarian authoritarian states against free trade is also valid for the Keynesian struggle against "classical theory". His struggle is not directed against the social structure of liberalism, he widely accepts this fundamental structure'.[96] And hence he drew his 'dark' prognosis.

While he may have agreed with the diagnosis, which can be summed up by the formula the *end of laissez-faire*, the same cannot be said of his relationship with the Keynesian perspective of limiting the contradictions of the free market without radically changing its structure and relations. However, he was forced to come back to this point. As we saw in the previous paragraph, the question of how, in a technologically advanced society, to preserve economic security and freedom, that is, how to avoid market crises without sacrificing democratic freedoms, would become the question underlying his successive writings. Evidently, with his negative judgements, in the 1936 text Pollock missed the social and political importance – which then proved historically decisive – of wanting to *preserve* freedom and individual interest within a movement to cure the liberalistic aporias, in the same perspective as Keynes and in general as the nascent movement towards a welfare-based regulation of the economy. In turn, the ironic reversal of collapsism into state capitalism was not to be seen as entirely necessary. What his perspective implied and prepared was not the symmetrical replacement of one authoritarian deterministic model with another. In Pollock's following essays, in his *questioning of the possibility of a democratic form of state capitalism*, it is hence necessary to read the start of a sort of self-criticism of any (positive or reversed) historicist perspective. In addition, and above all, it should be seen as a critical questioning of their critical Marxism – a critical interrogation inaugurated by Pollock on the terrain of economic theory and picked up and developed later on by Horkheimer when he dealt with critical theory 'past and present'.

e) The relationship between the *planning principle* and *modification of individual existence and activity* is a much more central theme in Pollock's two

---

95   Baumann 1936, p. 403, own translation.
96   Baumann 1936, p. 402, own translation. The reference is to the previous work by Marcuse, 'Der Kampf gegen den Liberalismus in der totalitären Staats Auffassung' (1934), English translation, 'The Struggle Against Liberalism in the Totalitarian View of the State' in Marcuse 2009.

essays from 1941, on *state capitalism* and the *new order*, which I dwelled on earlier. The first text speaks of the strict subordination of 'all other special interests ... to the general plan'[97] and denounces the forced sacrifice of every individual interest to a 'general plan' instrumentally brandished in reality to assert 'the interest of the ruling group'.[98] Moreover, it relates the subordination of the individual both to the affirmation of a totalising rationalisation and the affirmation of an era in which political domination replaces economic relations.[99] In the second text 'Is National Socialism a New Order?', on the other hand, Pollock would make use of the terms '*command economy*' and '*command society*' to take a closer and more specific look at this discourse. In an ever more acute way, Pollock thus goes on to lay down that social relations are no longer mediated by the market. He observes that however ideological, the very idea of a free economic subject is now annulled and substituted by the intervention of an authoritarian political mediation, which tends to command, put into hierarchies and purify all social relations so as to proclaim and perpetuate a *political power* which thus becomes total by also superimposing itself and presiding over the sphere of production and, in short, the whole of civil society.[100] Notice that this diagnosis is expressed very clearly in the first essay from 1941 too, but significantly here he refers to 'state capitalism' *tout court*, with a reference to the whole scope of the ideal type.

> The replacement of the economic means by political means as the last guarantee for the reproduction of economic life, changes the character of the whole historic period. It signifies the transition from a predominantly economic to an essentially political era.
>
> Under private capitalism, all social relations are mediated by the market; men meet each other as agents of the exchange process, as buyers or sellers. The source of one's income, the size of one's property are decisive for one's social position. The profit motive keeps the economic mechanism of society moving. Under state capitalism men meet each other as commander or commanded; the extent to which one can command or has to obey depends in the first place upon one's position in the political set-up and only in a secondary way upon the extent of one's property. Labor is appropriated directly instead of by the 'roundabout' way of the

---

97 Pollock 1978, p. 76.
98 Ibid.
99 Pollock 1978, p. 78.
100 Ibid.

market. Another aspect of the changed situation under state capitalism is that the profit motive is superseded by the power motive.[101]

Now this same diagnosis is taken up again and looked into more deeply in the second text from the same year, the one on the *new order*, but significantly in this the reference is explicitly and specifically restricted to National Socialist totalitarian capitalism. Here the definition of 'command economy' and 'command society' also resolutely appears for the first time. Now Pollock seems to consider this concept more suitable and precise than his first formula:

> Is it useful to label the new order 'State Capitalism'? Serious objections may be raised against this term. There are already grave doubts as to whether it makes sense to call the National Socialist system a state. ... Many other labels have been offered in recent discussions, such as controlled economy, state organized monopoly capitalism, totalitarian state economy, neo-mercantilism, bureaucratic collectivism. I believe the term 'Command Economy' best expresses the meaning of the new system. This word was first used by a Nazi writer in an article in which he asserts that 'competition, monopoly and command, these basic elements of every economic theory, equal each other today in scope as well as in power. But gradually the weight turns in favor of command'. What strikes me in the concept 'Command Economy' is that it essentially counterposes itself to the concept 'Exchange Economy'. It suggests an economy which is based upon command in a similar sense as the liberal economy is based upon exchange. It leads logically to describing the new society as a 'Command Society' in contrast with the 'Exchange Society' of bygone days.[102]

The specification of the reference is not only interesting because it shows that the ideal type in reality already displayed the strong imprint (as highlighted on several occasions earlier) of the totalitarian variant. It is also interesting because, in reference to the German situation, Pollock's discourse on the new centrality of the 'political' dimension becomes more penetrating. It allows for an explanation of the *political-economic* basis of the 'consent' built by the regime as well as the 'structural' role of the strategies of exclusion, purification and terror that it developed.

---

101   Ibid.
102   Pollock 1941, p. 450.

Now both essays from 1941 openly declared that it was 'necessary' to work on an analytical definition of authoritarian state capitalism for all those who intended to keep alive '*the values of western civilization*', and who hence had to be able to 'show in what way the democratic values can be maintained under the changing conditions'.[103] If this is what could be read in the opening to 'State Capitalism', we cannot neglect to again remember and underline the closing sentence of the subsequent essay on the *new order*: 'If the democracies can show that economic security must not be tied up with the loss of liberty but can be achieved under democratic conditions, then I dare forecast that the new order of National Socialism will be followed in Germany and elsewhere by an infinitely superior *democratic new order*'.[104]

On this basis, we must observe that the issue researched and debated by Pollock, the same presupposition that gives sense to his otherwise prevalently analytical approach, can be expressed as the issue of the possible morphologies and genesis of what after 1945 it became usual to call the democratic social state.

It was an *issue* – and here I want to underline this term, picking up on an indication-concern of Adorno – recognised in its historical relevance, but, for this same reason, Pollock never simply or ideologically celebrated it. Instead, he questioned/dealt with/criticised it by also highlighting the potentially ruinous aporias linked to the necessary belonging of the democratic variant of state capitalism to the *era of technology* too.[105]

Here we can make out a fundamental aporia, which Pollock had been aware of since the 1930s, but which in 1941 it probably did not seem right to fully express, for evident reasons of opportuneness in the historical and political situation (remaining of this opinion until the 1960s, when he tackled *Dialectic of Enlightenment* and proposed to cut out the parts that 'were not suitable for the public').[106] But would that 'new democratic order' of Keynesian imprint, based on economic expansion and full employment but also on maintaining and strengthening freedoms, which he looked towards with hope, not also have had to suffer from this political aporia of the technological era? If economic expansion and full employment were implemented by surrogating the whole of civil society into the big production model, would that not necessarily lead to a reduction of freedoms? How can opening the political universe be reconciled

---

103   Pollock 1978, p. 72.
104   Pollock 1941, p. 455, italics mine.
105   See in general Anders 1956; Galimberti 1999.
106   See earlier, letter from Friedrich Pollock to Max Horkheimer, 24 January 1961, in Horkheimer 1985–96, vol. 18, p. 502.

with closing the economic-social universe in the horizon of a 'one-dimensional' productivism? Pollock would not fail to deal with this aporia later on too, and he would do so in a precise way, in particular by dealing with the changes in the world of work due to the introduction of automation. It must nevertheless be added that the criticism of one-dimensional society and the closure of the political universe that it results in – a criticism brought to completion by Marcuse,[107] but also very present, right until the end, in Horkheimer too – without doubt gathered more than one seed from Pollock's texts. Capable of bringing aporias and antinomies to the surface, they were texts that nevertheless did not shirk from indicating those perspectives which may not have been historically exalting and decisive, but were at least in part exoterically feasible and not totally defeatist.

107 See Marcuse 1991.

CHAPTER 3

Expatriation, Disorientation, Islands

> ... Our life must be a testimony;
> to create utopia in even the smallest details.
> We want the other, the new, the unconditional.
> Our life is serious.
> Where we live, social laws must not apply. ...
>> 'Memorandum Friedrich Pollock-Max Horkheimer', 8 September 1951, own translation

∴

3.1   Leaving Germany (Eichmann Trial, Israel and the Atlantic Pact)

Despite Pollock's questioning overtures towards democratic welfare and the combined but more pessimistic ones by Horkheimer towards liberal democracies, the actual situation that they had to experience in the period of their return to Germany, that is, after 1949, presented more than a few highly perturbing elements.

Several years before the choice to go to Montagnola, at the start of the 1950s, Horkheimer and Pollock were *conscious* of going through a difficult phase, marked by a combination of objective adversities resulting from the historical configuration that 'the world' was taking on, as well as subjectively difficult and unhappy circumstances, in particular the emergence of a state of neurosis – obsessive-compulsive disorder ['*Zwangsneurose*'].[1] The latter risked 'crippling' and reducing theoretical and practical capabilities as well as weakening the 'imagination', one of the elements making up critical thought. Pollock's faculties seemed in particular to be subject to this condition, and, mindful of this, Horkheimer was again concerned.[2]

---

1   'Memorandum Friedrich Pollock-Max Horkheimer', 8 September 1951, in Horkheimer 1985–96, vol. 18, p. 219.
2   In the 1936 'Memorandum Notizen auf Beach Bluff' (referred to earlier), the most problematic traits of Pollock's character 'lack of warmth, sympathy and identification' and the 'inability to relate to others' are already interpreted in the following terms: 'It is probably neurotic [*neur-*

So, they were not unconscious victims of that state of unproductivity and inhibited thought and action of which the critics – from Habermas to Wiggershaus[3] – would then accuse them.

And again, for this very reason, Max and Fritz did not intend to give in and simply remain imprisoned in this situation. So they planned to achieve the different material as well as contextual conditions needed to set about their recovery and redeem their position. Despite their successes in the 'exterior' sphere, a few years after their return in 1948 to Germany, life had again led them into *psychic-political* suffering. It must be said that their reaction to seek other and better conditions did not make itself wait. Indeed, they set about their project to abandon Germany, where, moreover, they had only recently returned, at the beginning of the 1950s. Nevertheless, they only actually put their plan into practice a few years later, that is, almost at the end of the decade. This need to expatriate grew in line with their dissatisfaction with the way in which the Nazi past was being dealt with and resolved too casually by the newborn West Germany. For example, a law was voted in 1951, willed by the first German chancellor, Konrad Adenauer, to reintegrate a good number of employees who had occupied important posts in the Nazi regime in the new public administration. Hans Globke, a former Nazi party leader guilty of having written an official annotation to the Nuremburg race laws, was appointed under-secretary to the chancellery, and many trials against those stained by evident crimes under National Socialism were suspended and somehow dropped, in a climate of amnesty and rehabilitation of the past that did not bode well for the future. It was a policy to foster the integration of German society and enable Germany to become functional and economically independent again, but – as also said by historians who dealt with the question decades later – 'the creeping rehabilitation of former Nazis meant that West Germany laid itself open to accusations that it was a "renazified" state'.[4]

Horkheimer and Pollock immediately perceived the dangers linked to this drift, the threats of a new clouding of the moral conscience and the advent of a new type of 'democratic' totalitarianism, or 'false democracy'. Proof thereof, even before some aphorisms from *Späne* and the *Notizen*, can again be found in their 'private' writings. Their 'Memorandum' dated 8 September 1951 is already most eloquent on the matter. It shows that their project to dissolve their bonds and ties with Frankfurt was *already* taking shape *then*, in the face of that dif-

---

otische] behaviour, which is not willed and depends on complexes towards X (that is, Max)', Horkheimer 1985–96, vol. 15, p. 609, own translation.
3 See Habermas 1991, p. 93; Wiggershaus 1994.
4 Thomaneck and Niven 2000, p. 59.

ficult context. They were engaging all their forces to quickly conclude their appointments in Germany and cast the bases for a different future life. According to this 'Memorandum', as far as possible, Horkheimer was to withdraw from all things and events of the *extérieur*, while Pollock was tasked with making sure that their lives would then unfold under more positive and favourable conditions.[5] They were no longer pursuing their plan to share out their tasks more equally, set out beforehand to avoid 'tensions' and 'both becoming independent of their respective natures'.[6] Pollock consented to become, so to speak, the minister of the *extérieur* and Horkheimer of the *intérieur*. Nevertheless, the end purpose remained to manage to map out their being together as best possible. But where could they find these conditions? How could they establish and prepare them? Would they have to leave Frankfurt again? At that time there was no way of knowing and they would debate the identity of their new destination for years. But what they already felt to be urgent was the need to separate themselves from that form of reality, that form of totalising *exteriority* that seemed to be conspiring against their original wishes and pushing against them to make their '*critical behaviour*', their search for the other, resemble the identical, the homogeneous.

The incipit of their 'Memorandum' of 8 September 1951 is paradigmatic:

> Our life must be a *testimony*; to create utopia in even the smallest details. We want the other, the new, the unconditional. Our life is serious. Where we live, social laws must not apply. Now, so late in the day, we can no longer waste any time. We must create the conditions in which all our energies can be effective in our very own sense. Especially Max's talent and experience.[7]

Their life together aspired to take on the meaning of a *testimony* and in this sense it had to strive to create a 'little' *utopia*: in the name of the Other, the New, the Unconditional, at the same time it was, however, an essentially *concrete* heterotopia, down to the tiniest detail. There was no time to lose by passively complying with laws and social conventions. Other and different conditions to those in which they found themselves captive had to be actively sought and produced, conditions at last suited to developing and realising their own forces, in particular the intellectual [*geistliche*] abilities of Max.

---

5 Horkheimer 1985–96, vol. 18, p. 220.
6 See the discussion on this sharing of intellectual and administrative tasks in the *Memorandum* 'Notizen auf Beach Bluff', 1936, Horkheimer 1985–96, vol. 15, pp. 609 ff.
7 Horkheimer 1985–96, vol. 15, p. 218, own translation.

Hence, put in this light, it does not seem possible to attribute Horkheimer and Pollock's intention to leave Germany again in the 1950s to the search,[8] not unusual among German intellectuals, for a sort of hideaway close to Italy, blessed with the mild climate south of the Alps; a place where they could devote themselves to more or less nostalgically and 'resignedly' allowing their minds to wander, inevitably like Schopenhauer and/or Nietzsche. To grasp this fact, after the 'Memorandum' of 1951, we first of all also need to read the following note of self-reflection contained in the final section of *Späne*, written during the years in Montagnola, and given the title *Überlegungen aus dem Frühling 1960*:

Considerations from Spring 1960.

We are faced with the alternative of operating in Germany or withdrawing to the United States and undertaking to strive for knowledge and its formulation there. Can we reconcile our conscience with the fact of not doing anything, not raising our voice against all the atrocity that is again being prepared in Germany so long as we are still heard? Today we still have relative freedom of action.

Horkheimer refuses to lead the existence of a pensioner, like Mr von B. What is more, he finds a Jewish pensioner with a German passport in Ticino quite revolting.

Do we have to keep quiet if someone who is responsible for the death of 15,000 children still sits on the government? We must publish a new journal ['*eine neue Zeitschrift*'] to say what today has to be said and not leave this task to the publications in the East. Is it justifiable to stay silent while our task, as intellectuals, would be to shout out what is not right?[9]

Evidently, the reconciliatory way in which the accounts with the past had been settled in West Germany did not satisfy Horkheimer and Pollock in the slightest. Besides, the monopoly of criticism could not be left to Eastern bloc propaganda. A long aphorism in the *Notizen*, dated from the end of November 1960, is entitled 'Bewältigung der Vergangenheit' ['Coming to Terms with the Past']. It again loudly and explicitly denounces that 'in 1960 Germany was starting to "come to terms with" its Nazi past. At least at the start it was dealt with in a negative light'.[10] But in 1960, with the economic surge, the sentiment was already

---

8   See van de Moetter 1990, pp. 259 ff.
9   Horkheimer 1988, 'Überlegungen aus dem Frühling 1960', p. 544, own translation.
10 Horkheimer 1991, 'Bewältigung der Vergangenheit', p. 345, own translation.

making itself felt that they were not 'to be given lessons from anyone, [there was] a feeling of rebellion against the condemnation of the German past by "foreigners"' and hence there would be no delay in again 'proceeding against the individuals, emigrants, Jews, dubious elements, who have again muscled their way in'. 'For now', Horkheimer concluded, 'in Germany a collective sense of guilt and friendship for Israel is still somehow being expressed, but this will have to end too. Soon the slate will be wiped clean'.[11]

As other pages both in *Späne* and the *Notizen* show, this was the historical and political background that Horkheimer and Pollock wanted to leave behind them. They felt not only completely disappointed and disoriented, but also threatened (a concern that, as we will see, also at the immediately biographical level was not wholly lacking in foundation). In a page from 13 November 1966 dedicated to Federal Republic politics, Horkheimer did not refrain from denouncing the widespread presence in the nation of an in part unconscious and in part also conscious nostalgia for the period of extermination:

> Many sad considerations can be made about the Federal Republic's politics and the relationship of the masses with it. That all over Germany, not only in the NPD, if you call upon the strong man instead of recognising that, despite all the criticisms that can be levelled against him, Erhard at least has the advantage that he is not one who demonstrates an ineradicable tendency towards authoritarianism. While in other overdeveloped and underdeveloped countries where democracy appears more and more questionable, for very different reasons, calling upon force can only betray the obtuseness of future society, in Germany it means both unconscious and conscious nostalgia for the period of mass murder: *ein Volk, ein Reich, ein Führer*.[12]

It is also against this background that we must further highlight that the final aphorism of the *Notizen*, 'Für den Nonkonformismus', postulating the formation of *out-of-season collectives* aiming to intervene *critically* – remember the 'critical behaviour' of the 1937 text – against the process of affirmation of totality, was not a simple stock thought. The desire was for it to be linked to a new important initiative, the publication of a 'new journal to say what today has to be said'. Evidently, it was a matter of putting an end to that Nicodemist quietism and acts of appearance. An underlying correspondence must be pointed

---

11 Horkheimer 1991, pp. 345–6, own translation.
12 Horkheimer 1991, 'Zur Politik in der Bundesrepublik', p. 411, own translation.

out both with the 'Considerations from Spring 1960' in *Späne* and with the project for a real utopia and radical *testimony* expressed in the 1951 'Memorandum'. The truest task at that time was to shout out/passionately manifest 'what is not right', while remembering that, beyond subtle theoretical aporias, there can be no justifiable silence, or resignation, or conformism, before crimes against humanity. It is in a piece from 1961–2, contained in the *Notizen* under the title 'Täuschung' ['Deceit'], that historical denunciation and autobiographical *decision* become inextricably tangled, offering a portrait not without a dramatic restlessness, quite different from that – 'critical ornament ... established overnight!' – painted by Wiggershaus in his most famous work.[13] It is worth recalling Horkheimer's denunciation of the German deceit in full:

> It can be explained why Nazism took hold of power in Germany, even though what it did is inconceivable. The Jew who has come back to contribute so that it might not happen again is a madman who has remained loyal to certain Germans who gave their lives to combat the terror. But that he stays there, when he has seen how post-war Germany simply does political and commercial deals on mountains of corpses; how, depending on the circumstances, first it silences the so-called past, and then tacitly uses it to promote its exports; how those responsible for massacres sit again on high, or receive their pensions; how the instigators and beneficiaries again draw their profits – that he sees these things and does not shout until his mouth is closed, maybe forever, but still collaborates, is an attitude worthy of utmost contempt. Those who just do business can at least say that they would have more difficulty earning money elsewhere. They make no mystery of their motivations. The worst are the so-called intellectuals. These gentlemen, whose profession should be the truth, with their science strengthen the moral prestige of the country of killers in the world, that is, with their critical tone they add to it the hypocritical ornament of freedom, until the next economic crisis or some other occasion arises to remove the liberal frills. The Jewish intellectual who takes part in this operation denies the martyrs with his every word, since the deceit that a Jew who associates with the killers, without them crucifying him, can change something, is as evident as the evil tendency of this people. In all the world, I do not know a more hardened people. And they have their prisons and their abattoirs, their millionaires and their army, their churches and their secret service, just as if nothing had happened.[14]

---

13   See Wiggershaus 1994, ch. 6, 'Critical Ornament of a Restoration Society', p. 431.
14   Horkheimer 1991, 'Täuschung', pp. 361–2, own translation; on 'wiping the slate clean' of

This page is one of the most *staggering* since what is thematised and strongly criticised is not just the political inclination of some German sectors to rehabilitate the past, but it is also and explicitly the behaviour of the intellectuals, in particular the same 'Jewish intellectuals'. Is there an autobiographical aspect? A self-critical element? A sort of dramatic confession-conversion? Was the testimony to wash away the danger of the exoteric *lie*? Perhaps Horkheimer felt he had run this danger. Nor did he fail to realise that he had appeared to be inclined to compromise in some circumstances (as Habermas and Wiggershaus would later reproach him for or throw in his face).[15] But he did not remain inert and 'established', he reacted and evidently again undertook to mark his (and their) difference. And the one cited is by no means their only thought that deals with the relationship between executioners and victims and places it in a problematic light. Another aphorism, entitled 'Unter Gleichen' ['Among Equals'], denounces the appearance of a *homogeneous space* where executioners and victims end up resembling each other, almost proving their likeness:

> Today the German millionaires shake the hand of the Jewish notables, and the latter have forgiven. The friendly wink means that nothing will happen to the notables. They have money and a passport in their pockets. If their equals had been victims of a misfortune in the past, it was an oversight. The notables and the millionaires understand each other; their understanding is a tautology, they are the same thing, even if the notables make their fortune with radical art and critical theory. What harm can it do? Everyone knows that it is just a façade; the serious thing is the income. The memory of those killed a joke.[16]

The reasoning is totally *disturbing*, not just because of the bitter autobiographical reference, but also because Horkheimer has it emerge that there is no humanity anywhere that remains human when faced with a part that has already shown itself to be essentially inhuman. For example, no religious belonging exists that guarantees the humanity of its followers. At least in part, this is already said in *Dialectic of Enlightenment*, in the observation that:

---

the Nazi past see also 'Bewältigung der Vergangenheit', Horkheimer 1991, pp. 345–6, written at the end of November 1960.
15 See 'Critical Ornament of a Restoration Society' in Wiggershaus 1994, pp. 431 ff.
16 Horkheimer 1991, 'Unter Gleichen', p. 294, own translation.

> Rage is vented on those who are both conspicuous and unprotected. And just as, depending on the constellation, the victims are interchangeable: vagrants, Jews, Protestants, Catholics, so each of them can replace the murderer, in the same blind lust for killing, as soon as he feels the power of representing the norm. There is no authentic anti-Semitism, and certainly no born anti-Semite.[17]

It seems that there can no longer be a philosophical perspective, a 'critical theory' capable of providing this guarantee. The boundary between inhuman and human does not seem able to resist, all barriers prove relative and tragically mobile and ambiguous. What is belied is 'the spirit which recognizes the world for what it is: the perpetuation of suppression' as Horkheimer writes in another aphorism entitled 'All Are Criminal',[18] which ends by stating: 'Only a reprobate can live as a realist'. Recognising and distinguishing evil from good: this possibility seems to have vanished. And if this annihilation of moral consciousness affirmed itself with Nazism – on observing it what first comes to mind is the *grey zone* that Primo Levi spoke of, but also some pages of Hannah Arendt, prior to her *The Banality of Evil*[19] – with its end, this mortal crisis of moral consciousness does not seem to have been reined in or stopped at all. This crisis concerns humankind as such, and hence not even the Jew (and the intellectual even less so) can assume *a priori* protection or exemption. Horkheimer and Pollock are dramatically aware of this. A new type of human being was forming in the 'grey zone' into which the differences had precipitated, where there was no longer any distinction between good and evil. Historically destined to have good fortune, this human being would be the cynical and functional-acting type required by the automated and totally administered societies that were forming both in the West and East. As such, in one of Horkheimer's darkest aphorisms, Eichmann – the Nazi criminal guilty of a number of victims that could vary from 750,000 to 5 million, who was captured in Argentina in 1961 by the Israeli secret services and then put to trial and finally hung, this criminal who, during the long trial in which he acted as witness, declared on several occasions that he felt no guilt, that he was just doing a job – becomes the terrible *symbol of the future type of humankind*.

---

17 Horkheimer and Adorno 2007, p. 140.
18 Horkheimer 1978a, 'All Are Criminal', p. 201.
19 See Arendt 2005, which reads 'We need not specially mention the sorry reports about Latvians, Lithuanians, or even Jews who have participated in Himmler's murder organization in order to show that it requires no particular national character in order to supply this new type of functionary'. p. 129. For Primo Levi, instead, see Agamben 1999.

> In this period of the decline of democracy, that is, in the present and near future, states need more and more individuals who staunchly obey and are driven by a good dose of not sublimated sadism. In the Victorian classic bourgeois period, sadism expressed itself in the form of trade rivalry, obedience took on the shape of adaptation to the market. The more society transforms into a military bastion, the more characteristic becomes the type of thin-lipped, youthful under-commander. Oh, how enviable are the peoples where they are many Eichmanns! The impression is that they embody the future. And the poor Jerusalem state prosecutor should be drawing the spirit of the world onto his side![20]

On reading this dark forecast by Horkheimer, it is a good idea to remember that while following Eichmann's trial in Jerusalem, Hannah Arendt had already focussed on the frightening 'normality' of the Eichmann-type, the embodiment of a historically widespread, if not hegemonic type of subjectivity now totally incapable of distinguishing good from evil.

> The trouble with Eichmann was precisely that so many were like him, and that the many were neither perverted nor sadistic, that they were, and still are, terribly and terrifyingly normal. From the viewpoint of our legal institutions and of our moral standards of judgment this normality was much more terrifying than all the atrocities put together for it implied – as had been said at Nuremberg over and over again by the defendants and their counsels – that this new type of criminal, who is in actual act *hostis generis humani*, commits his crimes under circumstances that make it well-nigh impossible for him to know or to feel that he is doing wrong.[21]

And yet, in truth, in his prognosis Horkheimer goes even further than this assessment by Hannah Arendt. He stares into the abyss while taking the *Eichmann-type* to be the symbol of humankind 'of the present and the near future', a future marked by the further evolution of that 'decline of democracy' already underway at that time.

This evidently means that the 'ability to distinguish good from evil' seems to be compromised not only at the individual but also at the social and institutional level: it emerges as the core problem of the sense of affluent society, that is, also of the one might say cynical-democratic variant of state capitalism.

---

20 Horkheimer 1991, 'Zu Eichmann', p. 364, own translation.
21 Arendt 2006, p. 129; to be read while also taking into account what Arendt's 1945 text, cited above, adds about the 'international' phenomenon of the mass man capable of brutal acts.

Besides, Horkheimer tended to extend this critical diagnosis of his to include not only a) Israeli politics, whose instrumental action in the Eichmann case (as Arendt also observed) appeared exceedingly criticisable, but also b) the policy of the entire Atlantic Pact.

a) Specifically considering the Eichmann case, his capture and trial in Israel, in December 1960 Horkheimer already formulated his truly radical opposition to the action of the Israeli tribunal, denouncing in no uncertain terms what seemed to him to be its illegitimacy:

> The Israeli politicians are not only short of intelligence but also of heart. They neither know nor feel what they are doing. I plead the incompetence of the tribunal and for the return of Eichmann to the country from which he was taken. Nothing good will come of this trial, neither for the security and position of Jews in the world, nor for their self-consciousness. The trial is a repetition: Eichmann will do harm a second time.[22]

Indefensible from the formal point of view (as again Arendt had also denounced), the State of Israel's manner of proceeding risked being the precursor of ruinous consequences, both at the political-institutional level, and at the level of political self-consciousness. In his opinion, the nation was slipping up extremely badly, to the point that its manners resembled those of the totalitarian killers:

> If the court in Israel wants to be just, it will disqualify itself. The formal grounds for the trial are obviously untenable. Eichmann did not murder in Israel, nor can Israel wish that the seizure of political criminals in the asylum they should or should not have found become the general rule. ... Whatever may happen to him in Israel will prove the impotence, not the power of Jews conscious of themselves and their right, the arrogance, not the customary conduct of governmental authority in Israel. Everyone knows that it is with an eye to New York that the Israelis' totalitarian airs, which are reminiscent of Mussolini and the Russians, were let pass once more.[23]

As if what we have just read were not sufficient or extreme enough, Horkheimer draws an even stronger rebuke from this important event. It is a rebuke inten-

---

22 Horkheimer 1978a, 'On the Capture of Eichmann', p. 196.
23 Horkheimer 1978a, p. 194.

ded to denounce all undue political concessions to the worst instrumental reason and instead to seek to reconnect the threads between public and moral consciousness: 'Criminal trials based on political calculation are part of the arsenal of anti-Semitism, not of Jewry. The resistance of the good against the destructive powers will be paralyzed if it must avail itself of weapons which the enemy uses as a matter of course'.[24]

This also led to his very critical questions concerning Zionism (which I will also deal with later on), the suspicion that by being transformed into a state, Judaism was being compelled to take up weapons and 'values' that were evidently not solely spiritual but indistinguishable from those of the 'arsenal of anti-Semitism'.

b) The scene of international politics, marked by compromises and meetings between presumed opposites, always sealed in the name of the affirmation of one's own interest alone, was absolutely revealing of the loss of all respect for 'objective values' pursued in themselves and for themselves. In short, it expressed the decline of all endeavour to realise a rational universality.

Horkheimer now denounces this by also laying bare the opportunism of the 'North Atlantic Pact', which, far from continuing to fight 'anti-democracy' and 'totalitarian aggression', as the Allies had effectively done during the war, was now making 'alliances with the most reactionary governments in the world' and formulating 'offers of friendship to the totalitarian gentlemen on the opposing side'.

Because of its significance, here it is worth relaying the whole of this long note from 1959–60, which is also important in relation to the underlying question of the future of democracy. It is also significant to assess the political position assumed by Horkheimer during his return to Germany in a more balanced light. As can be seen here, his position proves to be a lot less conciliatory than he was reproached for not only 'in the heat' of the student protests, but also in the criticism of the advocates of communicative action:

> *North Atlantic Pact.* In the Second World War, England and America were still fighting anti-democracy, totalitarian aggression as such. They allied themselves with Russia when it was attacked by fascism although with his infallible instinct, Stalin had initially recognized his affinity with Hitler. Like the Russians, the Germans were newcomers, though older ones, and that's why both were nationalists from rancor. Today, when the Germans have been defeated, the Anglo-Saxons no longer confront just the

---

24   Horkheimer 1978a, pp. 194–5.

awakening Teutons but two awakening continents. They can no longer afford hostility toward anti-democracy but must join up with the authoritarian states on the right in order to resist Asiatics. The alliances with the most reactionary governments in the world, the invitations and offers of friendship to the totalitarian gentlemen on the opposing side the moment they make a friendly face, make it abundantly clear that the slogan 'war against totalitarian barbarism' has become the rationalization of very tangible interests. The mass murderers are patted and embraced, and it now takes a massive insult before one will walk out on them at a conference, and even then one does it reluctantly. A reign of terror no longer means that one will not hobnob with the tyrant unless his own people drive him out. Battista, a friend until just recently, is no longer welcome, and Khrushchev would certainly be shown no hospitality if he had to flee across the border, like the former. Dictators are not judged by their acts, but their fate. That is one of the indications that the objective contents to which the so-called free world is pledged, are disappearing with dizzying speed. The sense for them is about to become extinct – it is extinct. That is the result of the years since the end of the Second World War, the fifteen years during which the Anglo-Saxon world moved from the struggle against National Socialism or, rather, the German danger to England and America, to alliances with its like all the world over. That development was foreshadowed in the politics of Chamberlain and his ilk: they had no objections to Hitler's concentration camps, his designs on Russia. Today, they would help him. The unique Roosevelt is no more – and would have no chance to be elected in any event. That's over and done with.[25]

3.2 Free from the Coercion of the Reality Principle (Switzerland)

Not in Germany, not in the North Atlantic Pact, not, obviously, following the judgements of Pollock in 1927 and of Horkheimer in 'The Authoritarian State', in the Warsaw Pact: at this point, Switzerland almost seemed the obliged destination.

Horkheimer and Pollock had already had the chance to acquaint themselves with the southern part of Switzerland several years before they settled in Montagnola, as can be seen from the words of appreciation for Locarno in

---

25 Horkheimer 1978a, 'North Atlantic Pact', pp. 186–7.

this letter from Horkheimer to Leo Löwenthal on 29 October 1955 (that is, a few months after the 'incident' of the research commissioned by the Mannesmann factories):[26]

> Dear Leo,
>
> Since I was in Switzerland anyway, I went to Locarno over the weekend. I like Locarno – and still have a heavy heart. How time flies! Maidon is in Frankfurt, and Fritz is probably coming for a day. I want to spend as little time in Frankfurt as possible this semester, a so-called sabbatical, in order to avoid an abrupt transition. I'll finally have to give things some thought. Whether it will be Switzerland or America depends on many factors. You know what they are. If things go as I hope – who can say? – I will soon be retired and emeritus, even if it involves sacrifice.[27]

The alternation between the United States or Switzerland as the destination to settle down in, while bidding farewell to Germany for good, returns as a sort of leitmotif in no few letters and documents from the middle of the 1950s. In a 'Memorandum' dated 23 November 1955, considering that they had been discussing their long-term residence once they had left Frankfurt for over a year, Horkheimer and Pollock decide to opt for Switzerland.[28] But in another 'Memorandum', from the end of the same month, they reopen the discussion and the option reappears of moving back to the USA for good. The choice of Switzerland, they observed then, presented some important risks, especially if the German and/or international situation worsened as quickly as Max predicted and feared. They see the choice between the two possible destinations as a '*Würfelspiel*', a game of dice, as it did not really seem possible to establish which of the two destinations could offer the greatest guarantees. In any case, the presupposition for the discussion was their shared conviction that, seeing the German situation, it would have been rash and unsustainable to remain in Germany for the rest of their lives. So, it was worth somehow seeking to leave both possibilities open, while seeing on one hand if the question of living in America came to a favourable outcome and on the other hand acting, not wasting time, so that they could potentially build a new house in Montagnola.

---

26   See Wiggershaus 1994, pp. 478 ff.
27   Letter from Max Horkheimer to Leo Löwenthal, 29 October 1955, in Horkheimer 2007, p. 297.
28   See 'Memorandum Friedrich Pollock-Max Horkheimer', 23 November 1955, in Horkheimer 1985–96, vol. 18, p. 326.

> Since we have already been struggling with this decision for a year, and it would be irresponsible to stretch it out further in expectation of a miracle, we have decided, after again considering the main arguments, to go to the USA if the bill in House is accepted by 15 March 1956, and if not, to go to Montagnola. In order to not waste any time on a possible new build in Montagnola, we will immediately commission Brivio to draw up the plans, even if the costs for this were to be lost.[29]

Not only from a general historical point of view but also from a more specifically political one, there was no doubt that the choice for the USA, with the possession and maintenance of US citizenship, seemed to offer them greater security. Besides, during those same months, between the end of 1955 and the beginning of 1956, Horkheimer was developing a most gloomy vision of the contemporary condition in Europe. During the stay in Locarno that he wrote to Löwenthal about, Horkheimer went to Milan to take part in a conference, 'Avvenire della libertà' ['The Coming of Freedom'], during which, as he wrote to his friend, he was able to show how his thinking was not at all in line with the *Zeitgeist*. And a few weeks later, again from the Canton Ticino, but this time from Lugano, Horkheimer wrote to Löwenthal again, defining his *out-of-season* and now *pessimistic* diagnosis of that nevertheless economically prosperous time, and explaining the origin of the necessity to leave Germany no matter what and prepare a retreat, whether in the USA, or in Switzerland:

> The world doesn't look beautiful. One sees this quite clearly in Europe. It's evident that the affinity of National Socialism to the Russian system, as it was expressed in Ribbentrop's pact with Stalin, which was not yet completely in keeping with the reality of that time, corresponds to a tendency that in the meantime has greatly intensified. If I see things correctly, Poujade's election victory in France and Otto Strasser's intention to establish a party in Germany are to be understood in this sense. Even more important is the convergence of the collective anti-Western unconscious in many sections of society with quite sober considerations in certain elite groups (even more important, the development of modern technology). The groundwork being laid there is nothing good, and I believe it is more powerful than the Hitler movement. A dictatorship of the Right in a pact with the Russians. You recall that my words at the Milan congress

---

29   Horkheimer 1985–96, vol. 18, p. 328, own translation.

'Avvenire della Libertà' [The Coming of Freedom, 1955] already pointed in this direction. It looks like my foreboding will become reality even more precisely than I feared.[30]

The need to leave Germany can therefore also be understood in light of this gloomy and extremely alarmed diagnosis on the threat of renewed global totalitarian domination – a diagnosis in which, as well as the USSR, the topic of technology also makes an appearance. State capitalism seemed to be heading towards realisation without distinction, with just a small, temporary space potentially left over for the democratic variant. Hence, their choice for Switzerland also stemmed from this, although other reasons to economic ones and the urgency dictated by the overall picture of the Cold War were also involved.

The Frankfurt scholars had already had the chance to get to know the small nation that had remained 'neutral' during their providential exile at the start of Nazism. As is known, Geneva was the first city where they were able to take shelter and at least temporarily transfer the activities of the Institut für Sozialforschung. And Horkheimer would show a strong attachment to Switzerland, and Geneva in particular, on several occasions, not seldomly hailing it as a rare *island of freedom* in the European context after the 1930s. Having arrived in the United States, in October 1934 he would send a very heartfelt letter written in French to Mme Gertrude Isch, who had been his secretary during the short but important period in Geneva:

> Today I decided to send you at least a few lines to thank you and tell you that I miss Geneva. I hope that my health will allow me to stay here long enough to be able to get this branch, for which we must thank the generosity of Columbia University, off to '*a good start*'. Moreover, every day brings more proof of the sympathy for our work, and never before had I known such a favourable atmosphere for sociological research of our kind as in this country. Here not only the intellectual world but also the well-educated individual is interested in the progress of science and takes it seriously. It seems to me that Europe must also have known such an era at the end of the nineteenth century; it was then that the great works on history and society were able to come into being and develop in the midst of general sympathy. But this era is so far away for Europe! I'm not saying for Switzerland, since it is there that the finest spirits, which have been

---

30 Letter from Max Horkheimer to Leo Löwenthal, Lugano, 20 January 1956, in Horkheimer 2007, p. 302.

> able to preserve something of the great scientific tradition, always find exile and, under the powerful protection of Messrs Häberlin, Schüpbach and other friends of philosophy, are free to serve the truth, which is pursued and hunted down in every other country in Europe.
>
> Forgive me if I am a bit bitter; it is just that my love for your dear town makes me sad ...[31]

His attachment to Switzerland and Geneva in particular would be expressed again, if possible in an even more explicit manner, when Horkheimer had already been settled in the United States for several years. In 1937, in a letter again addressed to his Genevan employee, he writes:

> Do not think that I've abandoned my plan to come to spend a year in Switzerland. Nothing has changed in my desire to come and write a book opposite Mont Blanc. But the atmosphere, instead of brightening up, seems to be getting more and more adverse to this type of project. The European spirit no longer has much sense for its once very well-tended creature: philosophy. It has flown off to the new world, for a time whose duration is still unsure.[32]

In 1939 he finally managed to organise the flight of his parents, who had been ill for some time, to Switzerland. Until then they had not wanted to hear of leaving Germany, despite the pressing appeals that their son had made to them, even before 1933. His father – reasoning in the same way shared by a good deal of other German Jews – had objected that their family had lived in Germany for much longer than that Mr Hitler ... hence it was not them who had to leave! But in 1939, ten days after the outbreak of the Second World War, Max's organisational efforts paid off and his parents managed to migrate to Switzerland, where they then remained until their death and burial in the Jewish cemetery in Bern.[33]

Concerning Horkheimer's relations with Switzerland, the letters he exchanged with Hans Honegger, a Swiss economist who had met Walter Benjamin

---

31   Letter from Max Horkheimer to Gertrude Isch, 13 October 1934, in Horkheimer 1985–96, vol. 15, p. 241, own translation. The reference is to Heinrich Häberlin, Swiss jurist and federal councillor in 1926 and President of the Confederation in 1931; Hermann Schüpbach, president of the liberal-radical party, president of the national council in 1933–4.
32   Letter from Max Horkheimer to Gertrude Isch, 2 July 1937, in Horkheimer 1985–96, vol. 16, pp. 189–90, own translation from the French.
33   See Horkheimer 1975, pp. 27 ff.

in Berlin as a youth and, after that, still a student, met Horkheimer in Frankfurt and worked for the *Zeitschrift*, are also significant. Horkheimer remained in contact with Honegger for many years, also when in the second half of the 1930s he lived in the Canton Ticino, in that same small village of Montagnola where Horkheimer and Pollock would live many years later. In his correspondence with Honegger, distributed over a large time span, from 1926 to 1946, we find thoughts that concern in particular not only Switzerland, but also the Canton Ticino.

In any case, in 1940, after the successful expatriation of his parents, it is Horkheimer who addresses Honegger in these terms:

> You write that you love Switzerland. I can empathize. I don't know if I ever told you that there is no place for which I was more homesick than Geneva. The joy of sitting in the Perle du Lac [Pearl of the Lake, a public park in Geneva], with the lake on the left, the old city rising up on the right, the shore with white villas on delicate hills on the other side, and behind that the crown of Mont Blanc – this is among the greatest pleasures that life has to offer us. It's most beautiful in the fall when the light is more intense than at other times in the year. I hope it will be my lot that my wife and I will be able to sit there once again with you over a glass of golden Neuchâtel and look with a more encouraging gaze into the future than is possible today.[34]

The *Stimmung* that could be experienced in that Lake Geneva landscape should have somehow enabled the resurgence of a more encouraging vision of the future than what the reality principle was imposing almost everywhere in the world in the early 1940s. That landscape was also evoked as the figure of a *different* political and civil reality to the effectively dominant one, otherwise characterised, writes Horkheimer to his interlocutor, by a basic contradiction, a rent in the soul of contemporary human beings, reduced by the powers-that-be to slavery in their behaviours and yet, as subjects of the twentieth century, also already in possession of radically different potentialities, albeit now repressed and removed. The beautiful vision of the landscape that he and his Swiss friend could maybe share again sometime in the future, while drinking a glass of wine, in short almost constituted the symbol of a hope of which only a weakish trace remained. Besides, the reality suggested very different reflections between the

---

34   Letter from Max Heidegger to Hans Honegger, 12 January 1940, in Horkheimer 2007, pp. 162–3.

exterior and the interior space, echoing dully owing to the loss of all positive historical presuppositions. Looking at the landscape of another place, Lake Placid near New York, a few years earlier Horkheimer had noted:

> A small lake surrounded by small mountains with some relatively young trees. Once there were probably virgin forests with majestic trees. But since then there have been repeated fires, and now the trees seem to be afraid of becoming too big. It's not worth it.
> Humans should effectively wonder if it's worth it too ...[35]

The letter continued thus:

> In any case, old age is tough. My mother, who is 68, as you perhaps know, recently had a stroke. The part of the brain that controls language is damaged. She pitifully tries to find the words, but she can't. My father is totally confused and doesn't know how to take it. All of this is very sad and makes me suffer a lot. Nevertheless, you have to try to do the best you can during the years that you are healthy. People have to do good, evil comes of its own accord.

Needing highlighting, also because we will find it at the centre of Horkheimer's later reflection – on this point very close to Benjamin's thought – is the implicit tie established here between nature and language, or rather between wounded nature and the loss of maternal language. Evil comes of its own accord and the prognosis in the historical context that it would become radically strong and widespread is what, on observing those dumbstruck trees, Horkheimer was forced to acknowledge. 'I only see further decline ahead for the next few decades', Horkheimer also wrote in his letter to Honegger, brusquely returning from landscape to history, from imagination to reality principle.[36]

The economist's answer was not long in coming. It arrived at the end of that same month, January 1940. It contained some interesting observations on the international political situation, history and the Swiss soul, and then on a book about economics and sociology that he was working on. As far as the historical situation was concerned, Honegger wrote that he had more faith in the force of liberalism than Horkheimer did with his black outlook.

---

35 Letter from Max Horkheimer to Gertrude Isch, 2 July 1937, in Horkheimer 1985–96, vol. 16, pp. 189–90, own translation from the French.
36 Letter from Max Horkheimer to Hans Honegger, 12 January 1940, in Horkheimer 2007, p. 162.

In his opinion, the speeches of Churchill had to be given the right importance. Of course, one had to be highly concerned over the situation of the small states, who were then struggling to remain free from war. In this connection, Honegger invited Horkheimer to observe, frankly, that Belgium, Holland and the Scandinavian states were in more danger than Switzerland. Then, as far as Horkheimer's observation on the liberal potentials of humankind in the twentieth century were concerned, according to which, as a principle, it no longer seemed possible to 'enslave' or dominate, his interlocutor did not hide his perplexities, and reprimanded the Frankfurtian philosopher for actually being too optimistic. His argument on the subject was set out as a sort of geopolitical *excursus* on the situation in Switzerland. As he understood it, due to the history of the various cantons, marked by more or less subjection to the bordering powers, one had to be able to distinguish quite different sociological types: from the Grisons, seen as truly free people, who had almost always been that way, to the inhabitants of the 'vassal cantons' such as Valais, Thurgau and Ticino. Their inhabitants really did not seem to be free, that is, also inwardly free, and with regard to the Canton Ticino, Honegger underlined that its inhabitants actually seemed even less free than the others.[37] So, and this was the underlying sense of the observation, it was necessary to be prudent with philosophical generalisations and unilaterally pessimistic prognoses, and pay more attention to the actual, historically layered and nonlinear circumstances. Now, it would not seem arbitrary to hypothesise that, in truth, with these observations Honegger was also and perhaps above all arguing with himself, expressing a sort of self-criticism. A few years earlier he had in fact written a work called *Das Geistige Gepräge der Schweiz* [*The Spiritual Imprint of Switzerland*], whose aim was to bring out the difference in the Swiss spirit [*Geist*] and its 'imprints' from the German one. He was convinced that he had completed the most systematic work ever written on the nation, at the same time a 'sociology' and a 'philosophy' of Switzerland. And somehow, he thought that this book would become a great success, like that, as he wrote not without a touch of irony, of Spengler's *Decline* in Germany.[38] Despite Honegger's dreams and requests, this book on the imprint of the Swiss spirit was presumably never published, in the same way as the essay entitled 'Sozia-

---

37   Letter from Hans Honegger to Max Horkheimer, in Horkheimer 1985–96, vol. 16, p. 701.
38   Letter from Hans Honegger to Max Horkheimer, Montagnola, 9 May 1936, in Horkheimer 1985–96, vol. 15, pp. 519 ff. On that unpublished text of his, Honegger adds that he had received a splendid verdict from Ernst Steinmann, then secretary of the Swiss Freisinnig-Liberaldemokratischen Partei, and he was about to try to ask Katia Mann if her husband Thomas Mann could help him find a publisher.

lökonomik. Das Wesen dieser Wissenschaft' ['Social Economics. The Nature of this Science'], which he proposed to Horkheimer again in this letter – bearing the words 'Montagnola (Tessin)' above the date of 9 May 1936 – was never published in the *Zeitschrift* either. It was to this same address in Montagnola that some time before Pollock had sent a letter to Honegger from the Institute in Geneva, entrusting the Swiss economist with putting together two reviews for the *Zeitschrift*, then actually written in Montagnola and published in the Frankfurt School's official publication. Hence, it was with this exchange of letters that Horkheimer and Pollock first came across the name of that tiny place in the Canton Ticino, Montagnola, where they would live, but almost twenty years later, seeking shelter from the new totalitarian regression that they deemed to be happening again in Europe. It also needs to be added that, despite the somewhat servile nature attributed to the people of Ticino, in Honegger's words, he did not find life in that isolated and semi-rural place too favourable:

> I don't want to grant the Philistines the pleasure of having knocked me down, as we Swiss say. – Obviously, I've already gone back onto the *Veronal* again. – I'm often in a bad mood: I haven't left Montagnola for the whole week; this evening (Saturday), however, I want to see people again, at the gala ball, down in Lugano at Huguenin's, and spend the night in a hotel there. – I got the radio back yesterday, which I'd sent to get mended. You can't imagine the solitude in Montagnola! – It takes a lot to keep going (at least when the weather is bad and without an attractive woman!)[39]

So, was it the search for solitude and isolation that pointed the Frankfurtian scholars, almost 20 years after this exchange, in the direction of this same place (see Figure 1)? Was it the appreciation of the Ticino landscape expressed in the letter to Löwenthal? The combination of these two factors may certainly have favoured the choice of that place, in their effort to create that little *utopia* already expressed in their 'Memorandum' in 1951. But this search could not be understood, or misunderstood, as simply seeking an escape. The 1946 Nobel prize winner Hermann Hesse had lived in the same small Swiss village, not far from Horkheimer, since as far back as 1919 and then for just one more year after their move. As Alfred von Martin, author of a work on *Nietzsche*

---

39   Ibid., own translation.

und Burckhardt who had been in contact with Horkheimer since the end of the 1940s, wrote in a letter from 28 November 1964: 'I see that you have moved to Ticino: where Hermann Hesse lived at length. An enviable place to go to enjoy your retirement!'[40]

In his reply from 30 November, Horkheimer said absolutely nothing to this prompt; he dropped it completely, sharing no thoughts with him on the matter.[41] This silence of Horkheimer, two years after the death of Hermann Hesse, bestowed honorary citizenship of Montagnola in 1962, an extraordinary event in that semi-rural context, can perhaps be interpreted as a symptom of a lack of concern, or even of a certain dislike. In any case, Horkheimer did not see Montagnola simply as an *Alterssitz* [retirement home]. What we read in the 'Considerations from Spring 1960' about his 'refusal to lead the life of a pensioner' and the 'revolting' image of a Jewish pensioner with a German passport in Ticino,[42] is continually confirmed in the letters and materials from those years. 'Suffering the suffering of the world' had to remain part of their experience and testimony even on the Swiss *island*, and even on that island in the island that the village was to be. On a strictly biographical level, the first attempts made by Horkheimer to move to Switzerland with Pollock and find their oasis – if not the once longed-for *île heureuse* ... – where he could finally devote himself to philosophy once more, were nevertheless also entwined with the memory of his parents, who in the meantime had been buried in Bern, and with his desire to be hosted in the same Jewish cemetery there. The desire for this *proximity* in death is expressed by Horkheimer in a letter sent on 2 October 1955 to the president of the Israeli cemetery commission in Bern. In this letter, he expresses the further biographical motives leading to his decision to move to Switzerland. But what surfaces above all is the emotional and ambivalent existential intonation that accompanied that decision, and which should have been borne in mind, at least in part, even when he was accused of philosophical inhibitions and theoretical aporias:

---

40 Letter from Alfred von Martin to Max Horkheimer, 28 November 1964, in Horkheimer 1985–96, vol. 18: Briefwechseln 1949–1973, p. 583, own translation. It must be added that Collina d'Oro was moreover very popular with German citizens, also thanks to the presence of the Sanctuary of Agra not far from Montagnola, built between 1912 and 1914 following the plans of Edwin Wipf and nicknamed the 'Deutsches Haus'. See Fuselli 2009.
41 Horkheimer 1985–96, vol. 18, p. 584.
42 See earlier, p. 120.

Dear Mr. Weill:

… Since I am now over sixty years old, I intend to disencumber myself as quickly as possible of my various positions, among which is also the directorship of the Institute of Social Research, and to live in retirement working exclusively on philosophical books. I would like to buy or build a house in Switzerland, and negotiations are already pending. I am attached to Switzerland not only because of its beautiful landscape and venerable institutions but because, shortly before the outbreak of war in 1939, it took in my parents, the industrialist Moritz Horkheimer and his wife. Both are buried in the Jewish cemetery in Bern, and because of this I have visited it many times since my return to Europe.

My wife and I have the sincere desire also to be buried in this same cemetery. I don't know if the fact that my wife, who was raised a Protestant (she was born in England), never officially converted to Judaism is an obstacle to this. Yet we have been together for more than three decades, and she has shared my Jewish fate in every respect, and it is now her serious intent to rest in peace with me in the cemetery in Bern. We have no children.

I would now like to ask whether I can acquire a grave site for us in the cemetery and, should that be the case, ask you what the price would be.[43]

Effectively, as moreover decided and formalised in the 'Memorandum' from November 1955 (quoted earlier), in that autumn of 1955 Horkheimer was undeniably already taking some steps to settle down in the Canton Ticino, together with Fritz Pollock. Indeed, already in December of that same year, 1955, from his studio in Piazza Fontana in Locarno, the young architect from Ticino, Peppo Brivio,[44] sent the first proposal [Grundrisskizze] to Herrn Prof. Dr. Horkheimer, Westendstrasse 79, Frankfurt am Main for his and Pollock's homes in Montagnola.

---

43   Letter from Max Horkheimer to Eugen Weill-Strauss, 2 October 1955, in Horkheimer 2007, p. 296. Another factor that perhaps affected the choice of the Canton Ticino was the presence in Comano of Oscar Gans, famous dermatologist who succeeded Horkheimer as the rector in Frankfurt between 1953 and 1954. Gans also felt the need to leave Germany owing to the anti-Semitism (he emigrated in 1934 and while in exile in India was very involved in the Jewish communities) and returned to Frankfurt in 1949.

44   Peppo Brivio would then become a leading name in Swiss architecture. 'Born in Lombardy in 1923, after attending high school and the Polytechnic of Milan, he obtained a diploma in architecture from the Federal Polytechnic of Zurich. From 1969 to 1989 he was professor at the University of Geneva School of Architecture. He worked alongside archi-

And already from this first contact it appears that Fritz Pollock assumed a precise role, also because he could communicate with the architect more directly, in Italian, on the definition of the project for the houses in Montagnola. What is more, the instructions from the two clients must have been conceived of as a single project right from the start.

Going by the official documents, it moreover appears that the Pollocks already took residence in Montagnola in 1954,[45] while US citizen Max Horkheimer and his wife Rose Christine became residents in Montagnola on 27 August 1958. Rose Christine née Riecker, whom Max married in 1926 and to whom he had always given the nickname Maidon – intending to celebrate her as a 'gift' to him[46] – remained in the Swiss town until her death in October 1969; the philosopher would then remain in Montagnola as a widower until the end of 1972, before going to Stuttgart to spend the last months of his life, which came to an end in July 1973. Maidon had been linked to Horkheimer since 1916. She was the personal secretary of his father, eight years older than Max, Christian, and the daughter of hoteliers who had fallen into economic disgrace. For Max, the union with her was also to be 'a kind of symbolic marriage with the world of the downgraded and the workers .... His friend lost her job as secretary

---

tects Franco Ponti (1949–59), René Pedrazzini (1949–56), Rino Tami (1953–6) and Vittorio Gregotti (1963–4), developing a strict modernist style. Among his most significant works, in addition to the design for the 13th Milan Triennale (1964), the detached houses in Savosa (1958), Caprino (1963) and Bironico (1969), the apartment blocks in Massagno (1956) and Chiasso (1960) and the bank building in Chiasso (1967)'. As detailed by Cattaneo 2003. To my understanding, no reference had ever been made to the plans for the houses of Horkheimer and Pollock prior to my research. See Martinoli 2011.

In Conconi and Zannone 2013, may I point out a dossier dedicated to 'Casa Albairone di Peppo Brivio'. Among the contributions, see in particular the one by Vittorio Gregotti, 'Un architetto intellettuale. Brivio e la cultura milanese', pp. 62–3, in which the Milanese architect uses words of great esteem for his colleague and friend Brivio ('I still owe the best moments of my work to the influence of Brivio'). Having met at the start of the 1960s through Enrico Filippini, Vittorio Gregotti and Peppo Brivio's main work together was on 'fitting out the international introductory section at the 13th Milan Triennale, 12 June to 27 September 1964 ("A manifesto Triennale where the form of languages has a directly political value"), which Umberto Eco was responsible for organising together with Vittorio Gregotti'. A whole range of prominent figures took part in Gregotti and Brivio's overall project, 'from Luciano Berio to Umberto Eco, from Cathy Berberian to Lucio Fontana, from Tinto Brass to Achille Perilli and Nanni Balestrini' (ibid.).

45 Inhabitants control office document. Municipality of Montagnola-Collina d'Oro, Switzerland.

46 '... Maid, the English for *Mädchen*, and *don*, gift', Horkheimer makes a play on words in a letter to Eva G. Reichmann, 3 October 1970, in Horkheimer 1985–96, vol. 15, p. 17, note 1, own translation.

and a conflict between father and son began that was set to last for decades'.[47] Friedrich Pollock, still a German citizen, would live in Montagnola with Carlota Weil, whom he had married in 1946 in New York, and would live there until his death in December 1970. Carlota – as already mentioned – was the cousin of that Felix Weil who was the son of the first patron of the Frankfurt Institute of Social Research. Author of studies on the pedagogy of art and its significance for the social rehabilitation of young outcasts from society,[48] Carlota would be the last survivor of that small community of Frankfurtian intellectuals in Ticino; she would only leave Montagnola in 1975, alternating periods of extreme unhappiness and hospitalisation in the Viarnetto psychiatric clinic in Lugano-Pregassona.

The Pollocks and Horkheimers, respectively Fritz and Carlota, Max and Maidon, therefore settled down in that tiny village, and commissioned two beautiful homes to be built on a single plot of land which remained their shared garden forever (see the images in the Appendix to this book).

Unlike what had happened in Pacific Palisades, with the almost casual vicinity between the homes of Horkheimer and Thomas Mann,[49] in this case, the vicinity between Max and Fritz was evidently not casual at all but planned down to the tiniest detail over the years. Freedom from the 'coercion brought to us by the reality principle', to go back 'to dreaming, to the forbidden, to one's own original truth', to overcome 'habitual ways of thinking' and even 'death itself': these were the fundamental elements of this project, begun decades earlier, aimed more at the existential and intellectual than the practical aspect of living. Paradigmatic significance must be given to a page of *Späne* from September 1955, which hence, also from a chronological point of view, proves to be intertwined with the maturation of the project for the construction of the twin houses in Montagnola. Entitled 'Unsere Beziehungen' ['Our Relationships'], this page is highly autobiographical and at the same time has a remarkable philosophical meaning. It brings to maturity the motives present in the intimate documents written between the friends Pollock and Horkheimer both in more recent and distant years, and in the years to come. The text is found with the autobiographically themed writings in the appendix of *Späne*, immediately after a fragment entitled 'Das Geheimnis' ['The Secret'], in which the topic of relationships with other people in general is the subject of reflection. Here Max asks Fritz to transcribe:

---

47   Gumnior and Ringguth 1997, p. 18, own translation.
48   See note 134.
49   See Horkheimer's reminiscence in dialogue with Helmut Gumnior in Horkheimer 1975, p. 28.

I truly await the salvific word [*das erlösende Wort*], in the company of every person, but especially the people of the people [*Volk*]. What I talk to them about is serious, even when it sounds light-hearted. The others look like tormented and cursed people, as I am myself, but they might be able to help me. ...

Without this seriousness, without this sudden transport around the decisive, the spiritual, the true, courtesy, there is no authentic human relationship.

The need for authentic and immediate human relations has taken flight in a smile (insofar as it is authentic and is not reduced to a mere *keep smiling*).

What I am dealing with here does not let itself show or be grasped conceptually. Nevertheless, it is what is decisive, what gives sense to life.

Among my relationships with people [*Beziehungen zu Menschen*], there are some only oriented towards obtaining services, for example, sexual services. But for me, in most of them there is something serious, even though I may seem to talk to others about things of little importance.

When I do something good to a person, it goes beyond the intellect, it involves fundamental principles [*Grundsätzen*] and is linked to the experience [*Erlebnis*] of being *à la recherche du saveur*. But this happens with almost every student I talk to.[50]

After this reflection on the *secret*, on the longing to go beyond one's self inherent in human relationships in general, on their character that goes beyond the objectivisation of the intellect as well as sexual instrumentality as an end unto itself, the reflection of Max and Fritz is oriented towards considering their personal relationships, that is, *Unsere Beziehungen*. And what is expressed here, more radically, is the endeavour to overcome 'habitual ways of thinking' and to free 'from the coercion of the reality principle', so as to go back 'to dreaming, to the forbidden, to one's own original truth', beyond the principle of individuation. Owing to its significance, I here relate this joint reflection of Max and Fred from September 1955 in full:

---

50   Horkheimer 1988, 'Das Geheimnis', August 1955, p. 542, own translation.

Our relationships.

The common basis of these relationships is suffering the suffering of the world and our will to discover what we can do about it. This will must be perceptible in all the details of our lives. It expresses the seriousness with which we devote ourselves to problems and take care to make them further known.

The aim of our intellectual work is to do away with socially determined suffering. However, this means also understanding as socially determined the suffering deriving from the fact that we do not dominate nature as we might think. Taken to the extreme consequence, this means that through the solution to these problems we can overcome death itself. As socially determined as this problem may also be, there is no sociological resolution to the consequent questions. The way to approach a solution leads through shared forms of reaction that in the end are nothing but the condensation of theoretical reflections. But this does not concern the intellect alone. It must be possible to reproduce the gesture of thought [*gedankliche Gestik*]. Every true recording of a message is based on imitation [*Mimetik*]. The difficulty lies in the fact that many things become wrong when we say them out loud. The story of God on the cross comes very close to the truth, but it is spoilt because it is expressed in a coarse manner, because God dies in a coarse allegory.

Thought refers to the fact that habitual ways of thinking can be overcome. Therein we can see the task of philosophy in freeing us from the coercion brought by the reality principle: to go back to dreaming, to the forbidden, to one's own original truth. It is so close to the most important things to long for, to dream of the country where the exchange principle no longer applies. During their lives, most people are thrown back onto themselves and a primitive narcissism.[51]

Radically expanding the original anti-positivism of critical theory, these topics of self-analysis and the task of philosophy meant in terms of freedom from the coercion of the reality principle are carried on throughout these pages, written when the authors at this point had passed the age of 60.

Furthermore, this reflection on 'our relationships' from 1955 was not the only one, but it was in some way presupposed and pursued afterwards too.

---

51 Horkheimer 1988, 'Unsere Beziehungen', p. 543, own translation.

For example, in the 1936 'Memorandum', in which they once again criticised each other's characters:

> Y: laziness, dependence on comforts and the good life, great fear (political, financial, health).
> Z: Negativism, that is, his libido only deals with negative things. There is a wall between the conscious will, action and libidinal structure.[52]

And further examining the character of X in these terms:

> If one asked him who he really is then he would like to respond: a German Jew who lives in America and escaped the concentration camps. Everything that he thinks and writes comes from the experience [*Erlebnis*] of the camps. Aversion against everything that is called German today. He likes a good wine more than an art exhibition. Wine leads to an *embrace* (meant in a double sense), instead in a museum he finds nothing in common [*nichts Gemeinsames*].[53]

Again in 1963, in Montagnola Max and Fritz return to an exercise of 'self-analysis' and among other things note:

> Decisive trait: hate against all oppression, and thereby also against its apparatus and agents (laws, bans, bureaucrats, judges ...). Formulated positively: suffering together [*das Mitleid*] with the oppressed and those who suffer. ...
> Another decisive trait: love for pleasure [*der Genuss*].
> Learnt from mother: the hope that a complete condition will come to be (messianic hope).
> This is not achieved with love, but by loving love [*die Liebe zu lieben*].[54]

Thereby the self-analysis leads straight from the intimate and autobiographical to what is deemed to be *the task of philosophy*. The diary combines in a maybe fragmentary, but for this very reason also decidedly interesting way, *instinctual life, philosophical Eros and messianic hope*, according to a movement indicated

---

52   Horkheimer 1988, 'Stichworte zur Beurteilung von zwei Charakteren', December 1963, p. 547, own translation.
53   Horkheimer 1988, 'Zur Charakteristik von X', January 1962, p. 545, own translation.
54   Horkheimer 1988, 'Selbstanalyse', August 1963, p. 546, own translation.

here – not without a Platonic touch – in all as *loving love*. Again in *Späne*, this task ('Aufgabe der Philosophie') is further thought of in these terms:

> *Task of Philosophy*.
> 1. Schopenhauer is wrong on one point: in that he sees the objective [*das Ziel*] as something purely negative.
> 2. It is reconciliation [*Versöhnung*]. The key to everything is love, identification, saying yes even to the blade of grass that wants to come to light in the driest of soil, the love for everything that wants to come to light.
> 3. What is happiness? Is it enjoying the moment, is it the joy of birdsong, of the wind whistling, of feeling, seeing, hearing?
> 4. The task of philosophy consists of seeking the truth around the right life, appropriate life. But this task cannot be fulfilled without imparting [*verleihen*] language to that which is silent.[55]

Listening to, freeing *was stumm ist*, redeeming 'that which is silent' is seen here as the primary task of critical philosophy, a consciously *'messianic'* task, which implies listening to and redeeming the uniqueness of every being, even of that defiant and almost last blade of grass.

'To philosophize is not to exercise a specialist science, but to relate to things with the objective of finding the truth and becoming just with them'.[56]

> The truth lies on another level to that of the natural laws that can be written on the blackboard.
> The truth needs the 'inner voice', but this is not a faculty established by an authority, instead it is the mystical, spontaneous, active element that is also a part of the truth. It must be recognised that there is no truth without enthusiasm.[57]

Hence, openly, there is also 'a mythical element [*das Mystisch*] of truth' which critical thought seems to take the risk of remembering in these late and solitary years. On one hand, it is opposed to the horizon of instrumental reason that reduces all sense to the level of pragmatism and self-affirmative interest, but at the same time it is also opposed to a merely intellectualist outlook: to become just with things, save them, make sure that the 'inner voice' enters into 'mystic'

---

55 Horkheimer 1988, 'Aufgabe der Philosophie', p. 236, own translation.
56 Horkheimer 1988, 'Philosophie [1]', p. 222, own translation.
57 Horkheimer 1988, 'Das mystische Element der Wahrheit (Hegel)', p. 230, own translation.

resonance with what has been reduced to silence. The 'risk' that is a characteristic of this position, aware of its presuppositions, includes the search for a 'reconciliation [*Versöhnung*]', whose key is 'love, identification, saying yes even to the blade of grass that wants to come to light in the driest of soil, the love for everything that wants to come to light'. Like 'loving love', here philosophy seems to go back to being 'remembrance of nature within the subject', 'nature made audible in its estrangement', or revelation of the 'unrecognized truth of all culture'.[58] The movement of truth seems to coincide with the messianic movement with which alterity is emancipated from the oppression-repression exercised by the same objectivising reason, and the without-voice retrieves its voice, reacquires its character, its face, its name. Against the pragmatic insensitivity and the blinding of the identity of subjectivist-instrumental rationality, 'objective reason' here implies more and more accommodation and listening, tends to raise the alterity from the coercion of the object, welcoming it as a subject and partner of communication. 'Objective' reason shows that it presupposes and alludes to a dialogical-communicative relationship, and in the meantime, inside and outside itself, encounters nature as the text of the other, or even the other text, a text that has to be read in the *right* way, by listening to its suffering. 'Instrumentalized subjective reason either eulogizes nature as pure vitality or disparages it as brute force, instead of treating it as a text to be interpreted by philosophy that, if rightly read, will unfold a tale of infinite suffering'.[59] 'Once it was the endeavor of art, literature, and philosophy to express the meaning of things and of life, to be the voice of all that is dumb, to endow nature with an organ for making known her sufferings, or, we might say, to call reality by its rightful name. Today nature's tongue is taken away'.[60] With these observations, never without a particular introspective dimension, Horkheimer is also very close to the conception expressed by Walter Benjamin in his essay 'On Language as Such and on the Language of Man'. Here the silence of nature already present in creation, to whose aid humankind was called by giving it its right name, revealing its own divine name, is also accompanied by another form of silence, the other muteness of nature, as Benjamin says, characterised by great sadness. Here, 'the sadness of nature makes her mute', and this sadness, as well as this silencing, is triggered or at least radicalised by 'overnaming', the excess of names relentlessly pursued by human languages after the fall.

---

58   Horkheimer and Adorno 2007, pp. 31–2.
59   Horkheimer 2004, p. 85.
60   Horkheimer 2004, p. 69.

'There is, in the relation of human languages to that of things, something that can be approximately described as "overnaming" – the deepest linguistic reason for all melancholy and (from the point of view of the thing) for all deliberate muteness'.[61]

In Horkheimer's words, overnaming is without doubt to be linked to the assertion of instrumental reason, pragmatically insensitive and *unjust* towards nature, because of whose coming 'today nature's tongue is taken away'.

Already in *Dialectic*, while alluding to Benjamin, Horkheimer observed that '[t]he work of art constantly reenacts the duplication by which the thing appeared as something spiritual, a manifestation of *mana*. That constitutes its aura'.[62] From this point of view, the loss of aura should not be ascribed, with ambivalent meaning, to the phenomenon of technical reproducibility but should instead be connected to the advent of instrumental rationality which does not take care to listen to the duality, the tension between the finite and infinite burdening every being. The insensitivity of instrumental reason towards nature and animality, and in short, all alterity and all, also inner duality, again bears witness to the complete transformation of the world into a world of means instead of *ends*. Where *reconciliation* speaks of a world in which every being, like every blade of grass, should be recognised as an end in itself, in the present day

> [e]very word or sentence that hints of relations other than pragmatic is suspect. When a man is asked to admire a thing, to respect a feeling or attitude, to love a person for his own sake, he smells sentimentality and suspects that someone is pulling his leg or trying to sell him something. Though people may not ask what the moon is supposed to advertise, they tend to think of it in terms of ballistics or aerial mileage.[63]

Under the yoke of instrumental reason, as Horkheimer highlights, the annihilation of contemplative reason is accompanied by the loss of the strong sense of the landscape:

> Less and less is anything done for its own sake. A hike that takes a man out of the city to the banks of a river or a mountain top would be irrational and idiotic, judged by utilitarian standards; he is devoting himself to a silly or destructive pastime. In the view of formalized reason, an activity

---

61   Benjamin 1996b, p. 73.
62   Horkheimer and Adorno 2007, p. 14.
63   Horkheimer 2004, p. 69.

is reasonable only if it serves another purpose, e.g., health or relaxation, which helps to replenish his working power. ...

The children may imitate the father who was addicted to long walks, but if the formalization of reason has progressed far enough, they will consider that they have done their duty by their bodies if they go through a set of gymnastics to the commands of a radio voice. No walk through the landscape is necessary any longer; and thus the very concept of landscape as experienced by a pedestrian becomes meaningless and arbitrary.[64]

And yet

> We cannot maintain that the pleasure a man gets from a landscape, let us say, would last long if he were convinced *a priori* that the forms and colors he sees are just forms and colors, that all structures in which they play a role are purely subjective and have no relation whatsoever to any meaningful order or totality, that they simply and necessarily express nothing.[65]

In other words, humankind's relationship of living with beauty and nature falls among the exclusively personal and psychological ways of being in appearance only. Ways of being and behaviours instead also refer to an 'objective' plan, to a symbolic-narrative content of mythological origin, to an 'absolute' meaning that involves, but does not depend on, the subject.

This *'other reality'*, which implies upsetting the world of means into a world of ends 'is accessible to him who takes upon himself the effort of dialectical thinking, or, identically, who is capable of *eros*'.[66]

Hence, in the same way not only critical theories, but also behaviours and life forms can tear meanings, ways of being and experiential spaces from the process of asserting instrumental reason.

'We cannot credit our enjoyment of a flower or of the atmosphere of a room to an autonomous esthetic instinct. Man's esthetic responsiveness relates in its prehistory to various forms of idolatry'.[67] And in the warmth inherent in every thing that is loved for itself and not as a means to obtain another one, we have to be able to recognise the expression of those 'old forms of life smoldering under the surface of modern civilization'. As seen, in its establishment, the latter gradually destroys all ties with 'objective' reason and with the traces of

---

64   Horkheimer 2004, pp. 25–6.
65   Ibid.
66   Horkheimer 2004, p. 8.
67   Horkheimer 2004, p. 25.

mythological and religious memory that nourish it. Subjective reason empties concepts of objective reason, and they become figures of mere functional calculating reason. It takes control of humanity's way of being to such a point that emotions, pleasures and enjoyments too seem forced to rid themselves of their tie with the objective world, while deprived of their dimension of mythological-metaphysical resonance and reduced to an empty, solely subjective life, as such with a totally relativistic meaning. Nevertheless, this was certainly not the original sense of beauty and its experience, the sense of that beauty which humankind experienced in nature no less than in art. Even before directly getting involved in the project for Montagnola, Horkheimer therefore saw the aesthetic dimension as a possibility of preserving a relationship with nature, recognised as a living landscape, essentially other to the one dominated by instrumentality. The pleasure of owning and looking after a garden, a pleasure which in Montagnola he then shared with Fritz, Maidon and Carlota, took on a telling meaning:

> These old forms of life smoldering under the surface of modern civilization still provide, in many cases, the warmth inherent in any delight, in any love of a thing for its own sake rather than for that of another thing. The pleasure of keeping a garden goes back to ancient times when gardens belonged to the gods and were cultivated for them. The sense of beauty in both nature and art is connected, by a thousand delicate threads, to these old superstitions. If, by either flouting or flaunting the threads, modern man cuts them, the pleasure may continue for a while but its inner life is extinguished.[68]

3.3 Beyond Instrumental Architecture (the Houses in Montagnola)

In Montagnola, they were clearly close to each other again, *neighbours*, Horkheimer (with Maidon), and Pollock (with Carlota). Now, as they had also planned in the text from 1955, Fritz and Max wanted to relaunch and actually realise their *decision*, their ethico-existential and properly 'philosophical' *Gemeinschaft*, where 'we can see the task of philosophy in freeing us from the coercion brought by the reality principle: to go back to dreaming, to the forbidden, to one's own original truth. It is so close to the most important things to long for,

---

68 Horkheimer 2004, pp. 24–5.

to dream of the country where the exchange principle no longer applies. During their lives, most people are thrown back onto themselves and a primitive narcissism'.

Apropos, while the plan for the twin houses was actually coming to life on their shared plot of land in Montagnola, they were still engaged in setting down some 'Memorandums', in continuation of what they had announced and already begun to plan in 1935. In the 'Memorandum' dated 11 May 1959, the two friends, considering 'what serious consequences the failure to observe this principle brings with it', decide to 'only separate for the shortest periods' as they agree that 'it is more necessary than ever to begin to lead a continuously shared life [*ein kontinuierliches gemeinsames Leben*] as quickly as possible, in order to achieve an adequate correspondence [*eine adäquate Übereinstimmung*] of thoughts and feelings'.[69] The historical and biographical context in which this 'Memorandum' was situated was objectively different to that accompanying the 1935 text – now Germany was being rebuilt and Horkheimer had returned with no few honours. But beyond the 'objective' appearances, it must be repeated that they were experiencing the context of post-war Germany with a strong sense of *disorientation* and frightening *Unheimlichkeit*. Hence, in point seven of the 1959 'Memorandum', they again state that 'taking up residence in the USA would mean salvation or a greater chance of salvation for the rest of our lives'.[70] And the conclusions of this document, signed 'Max and Fred', are not lacking a dramatic tone:

> WE DECIDE: We are emigrating (together) to the USA as soon as possible, should the political situation, contrary to expectations, not have changed so radically as to make Montagnola appear an acceptable permanent situation. Only a higher power, which our forces cannot objectively overcome, may change this decision.[71]

---

69   'Memorandum Friedrich Pollock-Max Horkheimer', 11 May 1959, in Horkheimer 1985–96, vol. 18, p. 453, own translation.
70   As we have already observed, the oscillation between the USA or Switzerland as the place to emigrate to is recorded in many documents. In 1957 in some letters Horkheimer expresses his great attachment to the USA, in particular to the landscape and houses of California (letter from Max Horkheimer to Friedrich Pollock, in Horkheimer 1985–96, vol. 18, p. 403), and Chicago and its lifestyle (letter from Max Horkheimer to Paul W. Freedman, 25 February 1957, in Horkheimer 2007, p. 307); see also the letters from Max Horkheimer to Helge Pross, 21 February 1957, in Horkheimer 1985–96, vol. 18, p. 381.
71   'Memorandum Friedrich Pollock-Max Horkheimer', 11 May 1959, in Horkheimer 1985–96, vol. 18, p. 453, own translation.

To again take up the concept guiding the 1935 'Memorandum', what appears is therefore that the *exterior*, the sphere of the actual historical *Gesellschaft*, was still giving the Frankfurt scholars much to think about, and that, for them, finding a safe place was no foregone conclusion. Moreover, it must not be ignored or kept quiet that in 1956, 'owing to repeated manifestations of anti-Jewish hate by a colleague' Horkheimer asked to be appointed professor emeritus in advance. The faculty head 'urged him not to go'. To make him stay, the head asked the Ministry of Public Education to grant Horkheimer a special position. Thus, until his 65th year, he was exonerated from teaching duties for half of the time while remaining on a full salary.[72] Those who have wanted to observe that he was being given an exceptional academic privilege – as it appears Wiggershaus wished to do – at least in part underestimate the climate of insecurity and fear that must have been linked to the not just subjective possibility of a return of anti-Semitism. The story of anti-Semitism, like that of the discrimination against different people in general, obviously had not completely come to an end. Indeed, in a direct and personal way, from 1956 to 1963, Horkheimer at length dealt with the case of Mr Gerhard S. and his daughter who was not granted any compensation despite the serious mental illness that had appeared following their deportation from the Krakow ghetto to a concentration camp. Horkheimer did not just pay attention to this case, defining it an 'especially crass epilogue to the story of the concentration camps',[73] he also reported it to Bruno Bettelheim in order to obtain real help for that victim in whom the deportation seemed to have taken on the form of a permanent exile beyond the margins of 'normality'. Horkheimer was appointed professor emeritus in 1959, and going off the 'Memorandums', it seems we can say that, from then on, he did not intend to remain in Germany any longer. It was a country which, despite his return in 1949, for him essentially remained *unheimlich*. In his opinion, the tendency was to completely *'wipe the slate clean'* by actively removing the Nazi past and 'proceed[ing] against the individuals, emigrants, Jews, dubious elements, who have again muscled their way in'.[74]

As Habermas recognised, 'despite all of the bourgeois honours, after returning from his emigration Horkheimer never again felt at home in a country which he thought might fall back into barbarity. For the rest of his life, this

---

72 Wiggershaus 1994, p. 467.
73 See the letter from Max Horkheimer to Bruno Bettelheim dated 12 June 1958, in Horkheimer 1985–96, vol. 18, p. 424, which narrates the whole sad story, from the Krakow ghetto to the concentration camp and the unacknowledged illness.
74 Horkheimer 1991, 'Bewältigung der Vergangenheit', p. 345, own translation.

country remained uncanny [unheimlich] for him'.[75] The 'uncertainties' and 'inhibited productivity' that characterised the years in Montagnola should therefore also be framed in the context of this situation, which was still marked by fear, mourning and the threat – imaginary but not exclusively so – of the return of totalitarian terror,[76] hence not only and not primarily by the 'theoretical aporia' of which we again read in Habermas. Besides, it is in a further 'Memorandum', probably dating from January 1961, that we see the explicit and painful thematisation of their being 'in a state of transition' and the resulting impediment to doing their 'true tasks' which their sense of responsibility would instead have asked of them.

> Considering that it is irresponsible to continue to live in a state of transition in which we must speak of *exterior* things instead of intensively dealing with our true tasks, and that for many reasons it is high time to act, *we decide*:
> 1.   once and for all we must establish whether we can find favourable enough living conditions in the USA;
> 2.   if this were not possible, a pied à terre must immediately be found, possibly in Connecticut, where M. has residence and where we could both temporarily withdraw to. So, our main residence remains – as long as it is sustainable – Montagnola.[77]

Montagnola therefore imposed itself as the best practicable solution in the face of a political situation that, with the McCarthy offensive, was not really the most favourable in the USA either. And in the rest of Europe life seemed to have transformed into a joyless experience, marked by sadness and melancholy everywhere. This, at least, was their impression. In a letter from Paris, the city that was the stage for their youthful experience of the *île heureuse*, Pollock writes:

> I do not meet many people here, but one cannot help but notice that smiles have disappeared. Almost everyone seems sad, dejected and full of anger inside. Germaine [Krull], whom I saw today, and who knows countless people here, confirms this impression. She adds that in conversations with leading Gaullists and intellectuals about future projects, the

---

75   Habermas 1991, p. 109.
76   Letter from Friedrich Pollock to Max Horkheimer, from Paris, 22 October 1960, in Horkheimer 1985–96, vol. 18, p. 489.
77   In Horkheimer 1985–96, vol. 18, p. 454, note 3, own translation.

reservation always recurs: *'pouron qu'on ne m'assassine pas'*. – This atmosphere is matched by the dark autumnal weather.⁷⁸

A reflection of theirs from those years, thematising the inner void of a humanity that 'worships WCs instead of God', also bears the title: 'Warum die Menschen so traurig sind' ['Why People are so Sad'].⁷⁹

In the meantime, in the first half of 1958, in Montagnola the two houses with the shared garden, which Horkheimer and Pollock must have started to think about realising in 1954, had been built up to roof level. In August of the same year, Horkheimer wrote to his philosopher colleague Wilhelm Weischedel, telling him to pass by to visit him if he was in the area, in his 'Häuschen' – his little house – close to Lugano.⁸⁰ The Frankfurtian scholars had followed the definition of the combined project and its realisation down to the smallest details. Not just Pollock, who always acted in any case as Horkheimer's *alter ego* in the relations with the architect, but also Horkheimer himself, who, despite academic engagements in Frankfurt and Chicago, managed to express himself on the project and enter a collaborative dialogue with the young Swiss architect (see Figures 3, 6, 9, 11–13). He would have liked to deal with it much more than his engagements permitted, as he wrote to the architect Peppo Brivio in August 1958:

> As you know, unfortunately, I have been able to deal personally with the construction very little; Mr Pollock has been so kind as to do so for me. During the work, I twice taught for one semester in Chicago and for the rest of the time I have been extremely busy teaching in Frankfurt. At the moment, I've got surveys, articles and conferences going around my head that I'll have to get done before I leave ...⁸¹

And yet, if we consider all of the correspondence maintained by the philosopher, both directly as well as indirectly (through Maidon or her secretary), with the architect from Ticino, it has to be said that, despite his lack of time, he dealt meticulously with the project and its realisation, and wanted to decide

---

78 Letter from Friedrich Pollock to Max Horkheimer, from Paris, 22 October 1960, in Horkheimer 1985–96, vol. 18, pp. 489–99, own translation.
79 Horkheimer 1988, p. 219, but see also 'Das WC gehört zum Überbau', pp. 208–9.
80 Letter from Max Horkheimer to Wilhelm Weischedel, 25 August 1958, in Horkheimer 2007, p. 309.
81 Letter from Max Horkheimer to Peppo Brivio, 7 August 1958, private archive, own translation.

not just some details but the actual layout of the rooms. In the meantime, it must have been arranged right from the start that the project was to be a joint one, and that the two new houses were to be erected within a shared plot of land, which was to be kept as such, conceiving of it as a single garden, with no boundaries. Moreover, as we have seen, this continuity was the fundamental and philosophical presupposition for their life project and, in particular, for this late phase of their lives. Initially, it was not at all clear to the two commissioners which of the two houses and which part of the plot would be whose. Of course, the 'reality principle', which in its architectural expression is called the 'site plan', made this division necessary. However, it had to be done without denying or preventing, but instead concretely realising that desire of theirs which oscillated between utopia and the project for a 'continuously shared life' as established in the 1959 'Memorandum'.

It was Max Horkheimer who wrote from Frankfurt, on 21 December 1955, to the architect:

> Dear Mr Brivio!
>
> I received your letters of 12 and 15 December, together with the floorplans and the designs. For now, I can't well imagine what the house will be like. It could be no other way, since we still don't even know which side will be the house for professor Pollock and which will be ours. I'll decide when I'm there, with professor Pollock.[82]

In the end, these expressions of indecision and potential exchange of the parts reflect the very essence of the relationship between Horkheimer and Pollock. What their ongoing dialogue in those years dynamised and mobilised was indeed not only the assignation of the physical place where they would live, but also the assignation of the theoretical place that they each occupied. In the end, it was their very dialogue on *state capitalism* that almost registered a sort of exchange of places and roles, in a movement in which Pollock ended up abandoning his overtures to welfare and democracy. Indeed, in his treatment of the impact of automation on subjectivities, he came to provide a prognosis on the *eclipse of democracy*, which for many aspects could already be read in Horkheimer. He, on the other hand, by increasingly opening critical theory to a social-democratic perspective, in turn seemed to be assuming Pollock's welfarist overtures.

---

82 Letter from Max Horkheimer to Peppo Brivio, 21 December 1955, private archive, own translation.

The indecision between the first proposed plan for a single building and the one, then adopted, for two distinct but twin houses with a shared garden (see Figures 2 and 3), almost brings their identity dilemma to a graphic expression.

At the end of the same letter from 1955 to Brivio, it was not without reason that Horkheimer repeated:

> I'm aware of the fact that the uncertainty as to which place will be mine and which professor Pollock's means that it is not very appropriate to make too precise plans; nevertheless, even in these conditions, the matters can be looked into in more depth than you have done.[83]

'*Look into the issues*': by using this expression, Horkheimer addresses the architect using the same expression, the same rigorous, even strict, admonition that he would use before a philosophical work: 'The issues can be looked into in more depth than you have done'. But what were these issues? Evidently, the level in question here must have much more directly regarded the design. And so once again Horkheimer shows that he is a very attentive and hands-on client, or potential co-designer even:

> As for the layout as a whole, we do not think it a good thing for the garage to be built right next to the house. From our experience, this can cause great disturbance as regards noise and above all smells. There has to be enough room in the garage not just for tools but also heavy suitcases and the odd bit of machinery. Even though we drive a European car at the moment, the garage should be designed for a large American model.[84]

The garage, as can be seen from Brivio's first plan, was not only right next to the house, but directly adjacent to Horkheimer's study and library, which in turn was also positioned badly with regard to the bedroom, something which most certainly did not escape the philosopher's attention:

> Among the things that seem evidently wrong to me is the position of the bedrooms. It is clear that the smaller one has to be immediately next to my library so that I don't disturb my wife if I go to the library during the night. In the plan, it's the other way around …[85]

---

83   Ibid.
84   Ibid.
85   Ibid.

Both of these criticisms, concerning the position of the garage and the internal sequence of the spaces were accepted by the young architect Brivio, and meticulously translated into the definitive plan. These important changes in the design hence also faithfully reflect Horkheimer's intervention, and were also in part drawn by him.

The philosopher, in dialogue with the architect, added:

> During my last stay in Locarno I had laid out our general necessities to you. For example, we discussed the details of the library and many other things at length. Now I need to have a better idea of what you will be proposing both for the library and for the other rooms, including the location of the wardrobes, the bathrooms, etc. I'd also like to know, more or less at least, how you imagine the doors, the terraces, the windows and the loggias. It would be best if I could know in good time, since I intend to come to Lugano in the first half of January and it would be a great help if I could already know what you are proposing then. You can even send me a list of questions, but possibly so that we don't waste any time.[86]

Evidently, the 'issues to look into' concerned the layout of the rooms and the spaces inside the house, which Horkheimer judged from his point of most interest, the large room for the library and study, where he would effectively go very often, also at night, to draw up the *Notizen* and discuss the topics of the *Späne* with Pollock.

In short, the house in Montagnola had to be thought out and designed so that they could work there intensely, also at night, according to an existential-spatial design that, from this point of view too, was difficult to reduce to an *Altersitz* for a resigned retirement.

The 'issues' therefore concerned the distribution of the rooms and spaces for getting around the house, as well as the size of the bookcases (which Brivio would design himself and have made by hand to obtain very deep shelves which could hold two rows of books). The 'issues' nevertheless also concerned aspects linked to the relationship of the *inside* and *outside*, the definition of the windows, doors, and in general the threshold areas.

The presupposed foundation of that combined project, that is, the desire to be able to create a 'continuously shared life' ('Memorandum' 1959) with Pollock was conceptualised by making use of the internal/external oppositional

---

86   Ibid.

pairing. Against the bad and falsifying exteriority of the *Gesellschaft*, it was a matter of making sure that 'the interior always goes before the exterior' and that 'in the conflict of interests between exterior and interior, the interior takes precedence by principle' ('Memorandum' 1935).

Evidently this non-synthetic dialectic between the internal and external, this dual, introflexed or 'romantic' (in the terms of Hegel's aesthetics) and no longer classically reconcilable conceptual-topological relationship was not to be contradicted by the building project. Indeed, it was being called upon to make their dream of *Gemeinschaft* and *Beisammensein* real.

Nevertheless, Horkheimer was very much aware that the difference between the *outside* and *inside* was historically being subjected to a process of erosion and overcoming in every sphere. Everything that before that era and its totalising logic had always been distinct and differentiated was exposed to a levelling that tended towards *resemblance in an indistinct totality*, in an immediate synthesis: family and State, civil society and State, the different phases of life, city and countryside areas, shadow and light, open and closed.

The advent of 'totally administered society', 'the passage from the still semi-liberal stage of the turn-of-the-century bourgeois order, to the phase of *all-pervading* industry' was decreeing in an increasingly direct and immediate manner that '*what is outside is inside*'. That which was historically becoming asserted and had asserted itself throughout with the totalitarianisms therefore was not a classical-idealistic conciliation or harmonisation between *intérieur* and *extérieur*, namely, between subject and society, between the private and public space, it was rather the coming domination of the exterior that tended to overflow and occupy every interior and devastate its possibility. At the beginning of *Dialectic of Enlightenment*, it is moreover argued that '[t]he wholly enlightened earth is radiant with triumphant calamity', specifying a little further on that

> [b]ourgeois society is ruled by *equivalence*. It makes dissimilar things comparable by reducing them to abstract quantities. For the Enlightenment, anything which cannot be resolved into numbers, and ultimately into *one*, is illusion; modern positivism consigns it to poetry. Unity remains the watchword from Parmenides to Russell. All gods and *qualities* must be destroyed.[87]

---

87   Horkheimer and Adorno 2007, p. 1 and pp. 4–5, italics mine.

Later, in the *Aspects of Sociology* the increasing pressure of the outside on the internal world is pointed out on several occasions which, also due to the crisis of the family, was increasingly finding itself lacking protection.[88]

Now, the tendency to 'level' the qualitative differences in the name of a total enlightenment-transparency had found an expression, and a particularly radical one, in the architectural sphere too. Horkheimer was not unaware of the several variants of *glass architecture* that at the start of the 1950s, from *Farnworth House* by Mies van der Rohe to the *Glass House* of Philip Johnson and the *Glass Building* built for the United Nations by Oscar Niemeyer, had become true posters for modernism. Evidently, these architectural proposals seemed to be missing the fundamental question of living, that is, *mediation*. Living requires a mediation capable of preserving the differences and specificities in the relationship, those of the *intérieur* no less than those of the *past*, that is, a mediation capable of preserving the sphere of personal freedom and responsibility in the context of an increasingly unilateral instrumental-functional society.

> The brightness that enters the room through the opened blinds, the view from the window in a still dusky interior, afford the experience of light. In the picture windows and glass houses, it is about to disappear, and even the talk of housing authorities that mankind needs building with air and light is tied to recollections, the memory of slums, although there it was not windows but toilets that were in short supply. Life continues through change but the course of progress which destroys present and future happiness is essentially nothing but this unending decline unless what is past is also preserved. The proverbial official in his dark office who looked out from behind his small window and closed it abruptly when the clock struck was an object of scorn and envy, and both with good reason. An object of scorn, because he dwelt in bureaucratic darkness; of envy, because he could shut out the world. Today, he and his like sit in the glass house, checked by all that pass, and the end of the working day is quietly respected by the public. Things have improved. The official sits in the light, and the people no longer have anything against him. But with the removal of the evil, something positive has also disappeared, the bliss of darkness, the freedom to lock up, the freedom to scold with a good conscience.[89]

---

88   See Frankfurt Institute for Social Research 1973, pp. 140 ff.
89   Horkheimer 1978a, 'Happiness and Consciousness', pp. 189–90.

Such are the musings of the client Horkheimer in a fragment from those years which seems to sum up the most famous pieces of modernist glass architecture, as if in a nightmare. And to think that for him and Pollock, the *intérieur*, that is 'unsere Gemeinschaft', should have 'by principle taken precedence over the exterior'.

These, therefore, were the by no means simple issues that the young architect should have been able to look into, Horkheimer *dixit*, 'in more depth'.

Brivio, the young architect who would then make a name for himself as a leading figure in Switzerland, did not disappoint that demanding client at all. Indeed, he managed to convince him in an incredibly short amount of time, by making the requested modifications and other revisions.

On 4 March 1956, not even two months after the first plans had been sent, Horkheimer expressed himself in these words:

> Dear Mr Brivio!
>
> After examining the plans and the other documents, I can now tell you that we fundamentally agree with the project. I attach the list of questions with the answers. Some trifles can still be changed, but it is just things that can be smoothed out later with no harm done. My wife and I are very happy now that things have got to this point and we hope that you will rapidly take the necessary provisions and that the work can soon begin.[90]

So how had Brivio's plan dealt with the issue of the relationship between the *inside* and *outside*? The solution that he came up with set out and counterbalanced extremely generous *openings*, distributed to the south, with equally as many *closures*, characterising what was actually the façade of the house, the entrance side. The result was effectively a reassuring complementarity. From this point of view, the study-library, where the *relationship* between inside and outside achieve an almost ideal balance of meaning, was exemplary of this (see Figure 9).

At least in part, perhaps directly under the influence of this planning experience, Horkheimer then also dedicated himself to further 'looking into' those same architectural issues from his own, namely philosophical, point of view.

---

90 Letter from Max Horkheimer to Peppo Brivio, 4 March 1956, private archive, own translation.

And to be true he also did so with Pollock, as can be seen from some passages of *Späne*, the work-diary also made possible by that rediscovered condition of contiguity.

Besides, reflection on art was not at all alien to Horkheimer. Suffice it to think once more of the chapter on the cultural industry in *Dialectic of Enlightenment* (despite it mainly being written by Adorno); or, to look back more radically, his important essay 'Art and Mass Culture', where we meet – as we have seen – interesting references to Picasso and above all to an art capable of making the interruption of communication its motif. Furthermore, once again *Dialectic of Enlightenment* was not short on meticulous observations on architecture, on the twilight of the possibility of living (a diagnosis very close to what we would then read in *Minima Moralia*). And Horkheimer had already written a letter to Pollock on grandiose and immense or even 'colossal' architecture, which not only lacked empathetic potentiality, but whose very purpose was to 'intimidate and crush' the visitor, in 1937. On visiting the International Exposition in Paris that year, Horkheimer had been able to come face to face with the most imposing creations presented there by the dictatorships, and, in disagreement with the prizes attributed to Albert Speer for Germany and Boris Iofan for the USSR, he had not failed to immediately note how '[t]he individual is meant to feel his insignificance in the face of all these colossal things'.[91]

But, as we have started to observe, it is above all in some fragments of the *Notizen* and *Späne*, written in Montagnola in that same library designed by Brivio, that Horkheimer and Pollock placed particular attention on thematising living and its transformation in a historical context marked by the domination of instrumental reason.

Also owing to the loss of the dialectical sense of light, the domestic space risked being turned from a place of experience of *resonance* where subjects could experience their own specificity, into one of assimilation and mortification. Through serial standardisation it risked becoming a place where the sentence that 'what is individual must perish', which seemed to be weighing down on the whole era, could find expression and fulfilment:

> Architecture, the high rooms, the furniture intended for a particular person and to which memories could attach, had exalted him, albeit at the expense of the masses, for they seemed to make what were means, house, chair, bed or rug, into ends. Through them, through the way each in

---

[91] See letter from Max Horkheimer to Friedrich Pollock, from Geneva, 25 August 1937, in Horkheimer 2007, p. 114.

its particularity could enter the long days of childhood, the individual discovered his uniqueness, to which they belonged. Today, everything becomes instrumental in turn, and nothing remains to exalt the subject one is, neither food nor dress nor ornament through which to recover oneself as distinct. The subject becomes the object of a process of production it does not control.[92]

Evidently, despite their other commitments, the care with which Horkheimer and Pollock devoted themselves to thinking out the plan for the houses and defining the materials must also be thought of starting from this diagnosis. Indeed here, while speaking of the *disappearance of the home no less than the person*,[93] the focus is on a particular aspect of the broader depersonalising picture outlined by the concept of 'state capitalism' and 'totally administered society'. On the cultural meaning of details, it is also worth remembering a brilliant page of Adorno's *Minima Moralia*, entitled 'Do Not Knock', which is particularly akin to what we are observing with regard to the friends from Frankfurt's attention to their houses in Montagnola:

> Technology is making gestures precise and brutal, and with them men. It expels from movements all hesitation, deliberation, civility. It subjects them to the implacable, as it were ahistorical demands of objects. Thus the ability is lost, for example, to close a door quietly and discreetly, yet firmly. Those of cars and refrigerators have to be slammed, others have the tendency to snap shut by themselves, imposing on those entering the bad manners of not looking behind them, not shielding the interior of the house which receives them. The new human type cannot be properly understood without awareness of what he is continuously exposed to from the world of things about him, even in his most secret innervations. What does it mean for the subject that there are no more casement windows to open, but only sliding frames to shove, no gentle latches but turnable handles, no forecourt, no doorstep before the street, no wall around the garden? And which driver is not tempted, merely by the power of his engine, to wipe out the vermin of the street, pedestrians, children and cyclists? The movements machines demand of their users already have the violent, hard-hitting, unresting jerkiness of Fascist maltreatment. Not least to blame for the withering of experience is the fact

---

92 Horkheimer 1978a, 'Function and Limits of Bourgeois Culture', p. 172.
93 'Schwund der Wohnung – und der Persönlichkeit': this is the title given to this fragment by the editors of the *Notizen* in Horkheimer 1988, p. 72.

that things, under the law of pure functionality, assume a form that limits contact with them to mere operation, and tolerates no surplus, either in freedom of conduct or in autonomy of things, which would survive as the core of experience, because it is not consumed by the moment of action.[94]

In the care reserved by Horkheimer and Pollock to the details and the materials wanted by the architect for their houses, from the decoration of the ceilings to the type of bricks used for the façades and the type of marble for the floors, we can see their attempt not to be transformed into 'objects of production'. Instead, they wish to assert themselves as clients and interlocutors in a project which endeavours to escape homogenisation and assert its aesthetic-artisanal dimension, its *heterotopic experiential surplus* in the face of anonymous reduction to functionalism, denounced as an expression of the domination of instrumental reason, annihilator of independence and dignity both *a parte subjecti* and *a parte objecti*. Since the vocation of architecture and artisan design in general is to 'make what were means into ends', they seem to be able to cause a break in the horizon of instrumentality and give a voice and auratic atmosphericity back to the world of forms, otherwise reduced to silence. Of course, it is nevertheless true that an intense page of *Späne*, which combines a thematisation of the functionalism of the *machine à habiter* with Pollock's original topic of automation, denounces that '*the victory of instrumental reason is unstoppable*'. They diagnose that

> [i]n the end, society will be organised in a strictly functional manner, cohabitation and economic processes will take place in an almost automatic way. The role of religion, morality and emphatic feelings will reveal itself to be a transitional phase between the instinctive action of animals and the automation of man. ... It is characteristic that the most modern architects occasionally call their apartment blocks *living machines*.
>
> Where this journey leads can be demonstrated through the history of abstract art. At the outset it was the expression of the struggle against a world increasingly stripped of sense. If, as happens today, this art no longer rebels, it becomes a senseless ornament.[95]

---

94   Adorno 2005a, p. 40.
95   Horkheimer 1988, 'Der Sieg der instrumentellen Vernunft', pp. 494–5, own translation, italics mine.

Not unlike what we have seen above, in this consideration too, modernism in architecture would seem in a 'characteristic' way to correspond to, or in other words, to almost immediately and fully obey, the unstoppable movement of the assertion of instrumental reason. Furthermore, it seemed to reflect what, in those years, while implicitly developing his discussion on the aporias of 'state capitalism', Pollock very radically defines as 'the era of automation'. In addition, on occasion of the funeral of Le Corbusier, in the house in Montagnola, during one of their night-time discussions Pollock and Horkheimer noted:

> *Modern Architecture*. Today architecture expresses more strongly than other arts that everything to do with feelings, love and loyalty, is useless frippery. To the extent that today architects do not make technically necessary constructions, they do it for love of representation or even for a tease. Le Corbusier did not go so far, but he pointed the way to this historically necessary course.[96]

And in confirmation of this diagnosis, again in *Späne* under the title 'Ästhetik und Erkenntis. Architektur' ['Aesthetics and Knowledge. Architecture'], we read: 'Mourning as a fundamental feeling. ... Architecture as the direct expression of the epoch. Difference with respect to music and painting: it cannot be critical'.[97]

Besides, upon reading the at the same time specific and very real observations that Horkheimer in particular addressed to their architect regarding the work in Montagnola, we are given the impression of the engagement on his part to assert that, in the end, not everything that has to do with feelings, the memory and in short subjectivity and desires, is to be disparaged and eliminated like some 'useless frippery'. Hence, his engagement to 'decide some details together with the architect, for example, the choice of marble for the floors' – decided upon as 'dark red tiles' – and his choice of a certain type of brick for all of the exterior areas, to avoid clashes with concrete parts:

> Brick number 1 is the one I like best. I suppose that the only visible parts of the house will be bricks and windows, as well as the terrace and columns of course. The concrete frames not at all, for example. The combination of bricks and concrete is what I don't like about a lot of buildings. I would

---

96   Horkheimer 1988, 'Moderne Architektur', p. 335, own translation. A reference is made in the note to *Laudatio funebris* by André Malraux, *Neue Zürcher Zeitung*, 2 September 1963.
97   Horkheimer 1988, 'Äesthetik und Erkenntis. Architektur', p. 285.

EXPATRIATION, DISORIENTATION, ISLANDS   163

be grateful if you could confirm this and send me a colour sketch of the prospect of the house shortly. As for Pollock's decision, we will send you a telegram.[98]

Fitting perfectly into this context of considerations, which then translate into the actual design of the details of the façades (see Figures 6 and 13), is the architect's proposal to make a decoration along the ceilings, intuitively touching on a topic that Horkheimer pays attention to in the *Notizen*. It comes as no surprise that the proposal is swiftly accepted and almost redrawn by the clients. In short, from the floors to the ceilings, those nevertheless modernist spaces were not to sacrifice the personal sense of the *intérieur*, the empathetic experience of resonance, even at the price of committing the *crime* – as Loos's modernist purism would have it – of frippery.

Dear Mr Brivio!

In response to your letter of 20 February I would like to observe that your proposal for the decoration of the ceilings, a small, two-centimetre-wide plaster seam along the walls, seems right to me. Nevertheless, it would be better if within this seam you could make a small groove or elevation at a distance of around ten centimetres. You know that we do not love plain ceilings, with no interruption. So, as regards your question no. 1): the ceilings in the living room and hall must be made with this fluting.

As far as the decoration of the ceiling in the bedroom is concerned, please have drawings done by someone whom we could consider hiring and have them sent here, or keep them ready for my arrival which is due to be in mid-March. At the moment, as you know, professor Horkheimer is in America, and I have no idea if he has been in contact with anyone about this. The simplest thing is if you commission someone local. As already said, I will be in Lugano in mid-March and then we could speak about everything else.[99]

This is what Maidon wrote from Frankfurt to the architect Mr Brivio on 23 February 1957, completing her letter with a drawing of the detail of the fluting. In the meantime, Horkheimer seemed to look into the same issue, completing some other high-quality aphorisms. While they were discussing making the

---

98   Letter from Max Horkheimer to Peppo Brivio, 3 June 1956, private archive, own translation.
99   Letter from Maidon to Peppo Brivio, 23 February 1957, private archive, own translation.

bookcases and the doors in Montagnola by hand and the decoration for the ceiling with that discreet and most unobtrusive moulding, the philosopher notes down in a page from 1956:

> *Handmade and manufactured goods*. Difference between handmade and manufactured goods: the latter satisfy wider needs, for both more people and purposes. But the ephemeral difference in the appearance of a piece of handmade furniture or a hand-bound book, the barely conceptually graspable, definable difference, is the margin in which the individual experiences and honours himself. It really means everything. The difference between the modern factory-made chair and the work of an old carpenter is the same as between the most delicate Chinese tea and Coca-Cola. But this is true also and first of all for language, which can live from and for the thinking man and for every shade of expression, every letter represents a question of conscience, and [on the other hand] for the ready-made jargons of the press and bestsellers.[100]

By opposing handmade objects and ready-made objects – and jargons – Horkheimer seemed to be applying the paradigmatic contrast between *objective reason* and *instrumental reason*, which he had already thematised some time before, to the sphere of things and communication. He grasped the sense of privation denounced, not without some irony, in Duchamp's practice of ready-made art, which, moreover, he had already extended to the sphere of architectural design, with all its critical, corrosive effects towards not only all aura of authorship, but also all remaining individuality.

But, unlike the great avant-gardist, Horkheimer evidently considered that the task and role of the thinking man could and should still be similar to that of the old carpenter and the bookbinder, a role capable of escaping serial assimilation and manifesting 'the margin in which the individual expresses and honours himself'. In effect, and not least in the jobs given to Brivio for the furniture of the house in Montagnola, Horkheimer contrasts ready-made design with artistic-artisan work and design, as the premise for a way of living in which people in their singularity can enter an empathetic relationship capable of stimulating their individuation.[101] In a not dissimilar manner, in another aphorism from the *Notizen*, dated 1957, Horkheimer contrasts Heinz beef soup as the figure of an abstract culture projected towards dematerialisation, in which

---

100 Horkheimer 1991, 'Handware und Fabrikware', pp. 231–2, own translation.
101 For a definition of craft as a form of work in which 'labor is not simply a means to another end', see Sennett 2009.

tinned food takes the place of real roast beef, with the experience and knowledge of 'when the mother went to the butcher and competently talked about the piece that she was buying'. And before the 'universal void' of the tin of industrial food – void insofar as the specific, that is the actual and succulent piece of roast, disappears into it – he concludes: 'Things are not so different for the idea of beauty'.[102] In this sarcasm we must not only see an ascertainment of the paradoxical capacity of Kant's reflective judgement or of the formalisation of reason in general.

In addition to this, the criticism of the era of the ready-made did not fail to touch on the pop demystification of seriality, perhaps even before its time. After Duchamp, a name to mention would be that of Warhol and his famous *Campbell's Soup* (1962). And again, Horkheimer seems to relate to this. His intention is not only to thematise, but above all to criticise, the privation of the objective, sensitive, concrete faculty. He sees this nihilistic outcome of overnaming standardisation as the aesthetic equivalent of the 'formalisation' of reason, which essentially debases subjectivity along with the memory, experience and knowledge, and objectivity.

In the end, to look into these 'issues' concerning living and 'taste' was to manage to call things by their *right name*, that is, to conceive of them in a truly fitting and coherent way – not without a touch of messianic endeavour – and develop them according to the law and the overall measure immanent to that entire project. In short, from this point of view, the artistic-artisan project showed more than the odd analogy with what Horkheimer deemed to be the critical-utopian task of philosophy, formulated here in the wake of Schopenhauer as well as Walter Benjamin:[103]

> Philosophy is at one with art in reflecting passion through language and thus transferring it to the sphere of experience and memory. If nature is given the opportunity to mirror itself in the realm of spirit, it gains a certain tranquillity by contemplating its own image. This process is at the heart of all culture, particularly of music and the plastic arts. Philosophy is the conscious effort to knit all our knowledge and insight into a linguistic structure in which things are called by their right names.[104]

Here too we can understand how the opposition to 'ready-made jargons', as last expressed by Horkheimer, presupposed positions that had been brought

---

102 Horkheimer 1991, 'Warenkunde', pp. 232–3, own translation.
103 See Benjamin 1996b, p. 65 and Schopenhauer 2014, in particular the Third Book.
104 Horkheimer 2004, p. 121.

to maturity a great deal earlier. This opposition, and its enunciation in defence of artistic-artisan rather than serial design, also expressed by contrasting 'the most delicate Chinese tea with Coca-Cola', refers back to *calling things by their right names* as the *revelatory* and ethical task of true culture. In other words, also for the *plastic arts*, it involves their relationship with the truth and its ethical-cultural implications. It is the same as what happens in the case of philosophy, where '[t]his concept of truth – the adequation of name and things – inherent in every genuine philosophy, enables thought to withstand if not to overcome the demoralizing and mutilating effects of formalized reason'.[105]

From this point of view, to resist *ready-made seriality* is to honour individuality, celebrate its uniqueness and assumption in contrast to the nihilistic privation inherent in the very idea of seriality and linked to the capitalistic headiness of creative destruction. The name we give to this storm is progress. Despite the piles of rubble it leaves behind, its advancement is dizzying; at the same time, it inevitably leads to regression. And what pays the price is the *faces of the cities* no less than the identities and 'addresses' of the inhabitants: 'The dizzying progress of society! We have just learnt the telephone numbers off by heart and they are already being changed – like the face of the cities'.[106]

As we have already read on another page of the *Notizen*, which it is a good idea to relay again:

> Architecture, the high rooms, the furniture intended for a particular person and to which memories could attach, had exalted him, albeit at the expense of the masses, for they seemed to make what were means, house, chair, bed or rug, into ends. Through them, through the way each in its particularity could enter the long days of childhood, the individual discovered his uniqueness, to which they belonged. Today, everything becomes instrumental in turn, and nothing remains to exalt the subject one is, neither food nor dress nor ornament through which to recover oneself as distinct. The subject becomes the object of a process of production it does not control ... [He] is lost in the mass ... In the absence of forward movement in the history of individuals and nations, regression sets in.[107]

Here, by taking the side of 'handmade goods' and mentioning the experience of these objects as an integral part of a process of authentic individuation and

---

105 Horkheimer 2004, p. 122.
106 Horkheimer 1991, 'Der Fortschritt', p. 235, own translation.
107 Horkheimer 1978a, 'Function and Limits of Bourgeois Culture', p. 172.

not paradoxical massification and conformism, it therefore appears difficult to deny that Horkheimer openly appears to criticise 'progress'. In the end, as far as the plastic arts and their objects are concerned, we could be brought to understand that his position lies in the long wake of the romantic reaction against industrialisation, comprising the lesson of Ruskin and his many successors. But remembering 'what is disappearing' actually exercises a critical function towards the present, by underlining its privative and negative character. As Benjamin had said when looking at Eugène Atget's photographs of an abandoned Paris, the image of the rubble and the urban remains removes the make-up from reality, sucks up its aura and therefore reveals the real in its misery.[108] In a similar way, Horkheimer writes on a later page of the *Notizen*:

> Descriptions of the decline of culture in mass society are readily criticized for being romantic. But actually the account of what is disappearing expresses what is negative in the present. It denotes the misery of things as they are too exclusively to also lay claim to setting forth the splendors of the past. Because they feel this, the reactionaries today are against the past. The roles have been transposed. To praise the old becomes suspect, and confidence in the future the conventional thing. The analysis of the suffering from which this new romanticism springs reveals the pressure of reality. As long as that pressure does not become the object of direct, unblinking reflection, accounts of mass society will be no more than a form of distraction. The misery in a remorseless industrial society is disguised as grief over culture. This is an alibi for those intellectuals who do not want to see that misery for what it is.[109]

Moreover, from the *Eclipse of Reason* onwards, Horkheimer shows he is aware of the risks linked to a solely aesthetic reaction to the affirmation of the modern jargons and ready-made forms. This reaction must be combined with critical analysis of the 'pressure' exercised by the dominant reality on the very idea of reason and planning. So, taking Heidegger's abstract anti-modernism to account, he went on to write that

> ontological revivals are among the means that aggravate the disease. Conservative thinkers who have described the negative aspects of enlightenment, mechanization, and mass culture have often tried to mitigate the

---

108 See Emery 2012, pp. 87 ff.; and in general Emery 2011.
109 Horkheimer 1978a, 'Transposed Roles', pp. 143–4.

consequences of civilization either by re-emphasizing old ideals or by pointing out new aims that could be pursued without the risk of revolution.[110]

Instead, the negative aspects of mechanisation were to be criticised as figures of the *unilateral* imposition of the instrumental attitude, made to *wipe out* all past meaning. This needed to be opposed by a dialectical, critical and hence also more complete attitude, capable of elaborating and developing the *memory* (like the relationship with nature) instead of cancelling it and then being subjected to its return in mythicised form. It is evident that this cancellation implies the violent devaluation of all that is different from the present. This attitude can be seen not only towards not yet entirely urbanised places, forms and landscapes, but also towards all different figures of culture, such as those linked to the peasant world.

> The bourgeois perceived man's nakedness, his rawness and stupidity in the peasant, he acquired his self-confidence as the town dweller who, though not of the nobility, was certainly not its underling. ... The successful businessman shrugs his shoulders at the little man, and even that insignificant gesture reveals the identification with his class, the detachment from the person who is not really part of town life. Like the peasant, the other is just a human being and therefore mere cattle.[111]

This shrugging of the shoulders towards the outmoded and/or anachronistic expresses the inability to make an authentic mediation with the other in time, society, culture or species. This other, inasmuch as it is not mediated but isolated and repressed, will then paradoxically have to return and cause its own irrational and mythicising-destructive nemesis of the no less nihilistic domination of civilisation.

> It is well known that the bourgeoisie became the victim of its own means: money, or of abstract power, purchasing power, that it generally understood all ends as rationalizations, ideologies for a hypostatized exchange value. The mechanism that plays the most important role here is the dwindling of memory. It manifests itself in the kind of mentality that is peculiar to the bourgeoisie, i.e., skepticism. The negated myth is not sub-

---

110 Horkheimer 2004, p. 111.
111 Horkheimer 1978a, 'Bourgeois and Peasant', p. 136.

lated but cancelled, liquidated, forgotten. Not having been surmounted, it survives in the lower regions, and finally the thoughtless victor becomes the victim.[112]

Hence it is not a matter either of wiping out or of mythicising the other forms, the past and its figures, for example that authentic-pastoral condition evoked by Heidegger and among others by Hermann Hesse and Karl Kerenyi,[113] in both cases by removing them from mediation. It is rather a matter of remembering and encountering these alterities with a view to a critical conciliation, while in the meantime requesting a slowdown and criticising the current domination of instrumentality.

Effectively, while also considering his personal relationship with the design for the house in Montagnola, it needs to be observed that Horkheimer's endeavour to take care of the artisan aspect never became a unilaterally anti-modernist position. The very choice of design with a flat roof – a very modern and in actual fact totally unique choice in what was still rural a context – attests to the fact that there was complementarity in his (and their) positions, an aesthetic of mediation that in reality referred to an ethic of mediation. Without wanting to overstretch the biographical side of things, we can perhaps also consider the images that portray the Frankfurtian scholars taking part in the folk festivals in the village of Collina d'Oro (see Figures 14 and 15) in the light of this philosophy of *critical mediation*. Rather unusual documents in the least of real, neither devaluating nor mimetic-mythicising participation, their relationship was definitely very different from that of Hermann Hesse with those same places and same countryfolk, whom he transfigured and mythicised on paper but in actual fact kept at arm's length!

In the end, in the case of the pair from Frankfurt, what was at work and being applied to the field of the design, as well as their local relations, remained that desire to *temper* instrumental and objective reason, and to encourage their mutual critique, as expressed in the conclusions of the *Eclipse of Reason*. From this point of view, there is again a particular isomorphism between the situation of latently communicative 'objective reason', and that of the plastic arts in their attempt to remove living from unreserved adaptation to the alienation of subject and object, which is instead what instrumental reason sets out to do.

---

112   Ibid.
113   Kerenyi also resided in the Canton Ticino for many years, not rarely transfiguring the places in a Dionysian key, see Kerenyi 1963; Kerenyi 1972. For a discussion, also with reference to Walter Benjamin's short stays in the Canton Ticino, see Emery 2013.

The present-day systems of objective reason, on the other hand, represent attempts to avoid the surrender of existence to contingency and blind hazard. But the proponents of objective reason are in danger of lagging behind industrial and scientific developments, of asserting meanings that prove to be an illusion, and of creating reactionary ideologies. Just as subjective reason tends to vulgar materialism, so objective reason displays an inclination to romanticism ... As vulgar materialism, subjective reason can hardly avoid falling into cynical nihilism; the traditional affirmative doctrines of objective reason have an affinity with ideology and lies. The two concepts of reason do not represent two separate and independent ways of the mind, although their opposition expresses a real antinomy.

The task of philosophy is not stubbornly to play the one against the other, but to foster a mutual critique and thus, if possible, to prepare in the intellectual realm the reconciliation of the two in reality.[114]

In the end, can these reflections not again be read as (involuntary) metaphors of the relationship with Pollock, as figures of the oscillation between the abjuration of totalitarian state capitalism and the attempt to build a figure of mediation, identified, despite it all, as democratic state capitalism?

114 Horkheimer 2004, p. 118.

CHAPTER 4

Automation and the Eclipse of Democracy

> Automation will be developed as far as is conceivable. But what consequences will this development have on the structure of people's brains?
>
> M. HORKHEIMER – F. POLLOCK, 'Späne', 1955–6, own translation

∴

The crisis of dialectical dynamism, diagnosed in the great essays of the early 1940s but prepared in even earlier contributions – especially those of Pollock, as we have seen, differing from the 'collapsist' hypothesis – makes up the backdrop for Horkheimer and Pollock's subsequent reflections, right until their last years. On the one hand, despite a certain insistence by the critics on the discontinuity between the 'past and present of critical theory', in particular with regard to the philosophy of history, it seems possible to discern a single underlying picture. On the other hand, also in this last period too, we cannot help but be struck by the renewed vicinity of the topics of the later Horkheimer with the later Pollock.

Their dialogue in search of a theory still draws a sort of isomorphism with what was highlighted in relation to the earlier period. Even now, with his soberly analytical gaze, in some ways Pollock seems to outline the so-to-speak structural elements giving rise to Horkheimer's parallel philosophical reflection. But it would not make much sense to want to see this relationship in terms of cause and effect and somehow mould it in a rigidly deterministic way. Whose place was whose? In the utopia of the new and permanent nonconformist theory, they almost ended up changing roles as they gave life to that continuative relationship, strongly sought after in real terms and expressed figuratively in the almost inextricable entanglement of their physical places.

4.1   Era of Automation and Crisis: Pollock's Prognosis

It must be observed that in Montagnola Friedrich Pollock immediately got to work on a new edition of his book *Automation. Materialen zur Beurteilung der ökonomischen und sozialen Folgen* [*Automation. A Study of its Economic and Social Consequences*]. It is evident that where in the book his considerations hinged around the 'social consequences' of automation in particular, he was dealing with the same thing that would then be found at the centre of Horkheimer's reflection, not least in the *Notizen*. In Montagnola, Pollock passed the proofs of the second edition of *Automation* for press. The first edition, which in turn expanded on a study published at the start of 1955 in the volume *Aspects of Sociology*, published by the Frankfurt Institute for Max Horkheimer's sixtieth birthday, had come out in 1956. The 1956 edition of Pollock's book was immediately translated into six languages. Urged to reprint it a few years later, at the start of the 1960s, he restructured the book, expanding and to a large extent rewriting it (see Figures 7 and 8).[1] This structural rehash of the book had become necessary owing to the very speed with which automation had proceeded in those years. Pollock affirms this right from the first lines of the preface to the new edition, dated 'Montagnola (Switzerland), June 1963':

> When the Europäische Verlagsanstalt proposed a new edition of my book on the economic and social consequences of automation, which had been published in 1956 and appeared in six different languages, it was evident that, in the face of the extraordinary development that this new production system had undergone in the six years since then, I could not take responsibility for an unchanged or barely integrated edition. Not that I was forced to review the considerations and theoretical analyses expressed in the first edition: on all the essential points, they have proven to be correct. But the rate and extent of the diffusion of the automation has surpassed all expectations, its technical and organisational possibilities to a large extent have crossed boundaries which until just a few years ago were considered insurmountable in the foreseeable future.[2]

Pollock's book set out to be one of the first investigations based on documents, statistics, empirical data – mainly referring to the USA, but in the second edition also to Europe and the Soviet Union – on automation as the new 'production system'.

---

1 Pollock 1964, preface. Translator's note: there is no English translation of the second edition of *Automation*, which, as said, was largely rewritten and therefore differs extensively from the first. However, where possible, I have taken the English version of the first edition (Pollock 1957) as the basis for the translation of the various passages quoted in this chapter. Nevertheless, all references given in this chapter are to the German second edition, rewritten in Montagnola.
2 Pollock 1964, preface.

In order to gather and update the technical literature on the matter, for the second edition, from Montagnola Pollock made use of the collaboration of his colleague Emil J. Walter, professor at the St Gallen faculty of economic and social sciences, with whom he had been in epistolary correspondence for years. Furthermore, he had additional help from a philosophy student, another indicator of the fact that Pollock's interests and research programme continued to straddle his discipline and that of Max.

Now, the edition of the book prepared in the early years in Montagnola opens with an important chapter dedicated to the definition of the concept of automation. In it, Pollock asserts that the word automation was increasingly being used to indicate a technical development that *replaces* manual labour in factories and offices with machines.[3] The field touched on by the concept '*from the factory to the office*' is very broad: the concept of automation outlines not so much a fact as a *method*, capable of reconfiguring both the production of material goods and that of services and intellectual or intangible goods. It goes beyond the classic distinction between the secondary and tertiary sector of the economy:

> By 'automation' we understand the use of certain methods in the current phase of technical development of automatically producing and processing goods (production); of producing and processing information for the business management (bookkeeping, stock-keeping, statistics of all kinds, calculation of alternatives, etc.).[4]

The specific difference of the *era of automation* compared to the era of industrialisation is that in the new technical development

> a large part of the functions that the worker still exercises in 'automatism', such as introducing the material, starting and stopping machinery, controlling both the volume and the quality of the output, the general supervision of the whole process and handling of non-automatic tools and single-purpose machines, can be done by prevalently electronic devices.
>
> The logical conclusion of automation is a *completely automatic working process*. This is technically already possible though it can in practice be achieved only in certain exceptional circumstances.[5]

---

3   Pollock 1964, p. 13.
4   Pollock 1964, p. 14.
5   Pollock 1964, pp. 15–16, own italics.

In other words, the outcome is a working process – specified as a *total continuous process* – in which the both physical and intellectual human workforce is completely *replaced* by machines working on the principle of 'feedback' and 'electronic calculators'.

> The *aims* and *methods* of automation may be provisionally defined as follows: the aim of automation as a production technique is to replace men by machines as far as possible in operating, directing and supervising machines as well as in controlling the products so that no human hand touches the product from the beginning to the end of the operating process. Its methods may be applied either to part of the manufacturing process or to the entire process of turning raw materials into finished products.[6]

War industry factories, atomic factories, oil refinement and automobile engine sectors, plants for manufacturing glass bottles, biscuits and cigarettes, are mentioned by Pollock as examples of factories that are already almost *completely* automated. But it is not only a question of factories and goods manufacturing processes, but also the reconfiguration of the tertiary sector:

> When automation is fully applied to office work in the broadest sense, all calculations, records, statistics and controls of the desired 'information', as well as many writing operations connected to these functions, are done by machines instead of men.[7]

On this basis, one can understand how the effects of automation do not only concern levels of employment and the strictly economic sphere, but affect the whole social and cultural and in particular communicative level. In his book, analytical and prudent as ever, as far as the strictly economic consequences are concerned, Pollock does not hide his fears of an increase in the risks of a *slump* due to automation.

To the optimism of the liberal advocates of economic harmony he objects that 'it is possible that mass unemployment might lead to a contraction of the market which would lead to a slump in a chain reaction'. As he has it, 'if the results of the "second industrial revolution" are met merely by improvisations and palliatives and left virtually to the "free play" of economic forces, then it is possible that destructive tendencies might develop of such force that no

---

6 Pollock 1964, p. 14.
7 Pollock 1964, p. 14.

"free" society would be strong enough to withstand them'.[8] In confirmation of this first thesis, Pollock does not only cite Arnold Toynbee (and it must be pointed out how close this quotation is to the late reflection of Horkheimer in Ticino), but he also quotes the speech given by Harold Wilson at the October 1963 Labour Party conference, highlighting the *correspondence* between his observation and the following ones by Wilson:

> technological progress left to the mechanism of private industry and private property can lead only to high profits for a few, a high rate of employment for a few, and to mass redundancies for the many ... [O]nly if technological progress becomes part of our national planning can that progress be directed to national ends.[9]

And evidently, Pollock thus once again felt the need to make a new comparison with that topic of planning and welfare which had intensely occupied him in his previous works, now belonging to a distant past.

The new methods of calculation and simulation, Pollock hoped, would be addressed to building a rational social order. But in order for this to happen, the least requirement would be the elimination of the 'automatic market'.[10]

Nevertheless, not without some disquiet and far-sightedness, the book rewritten in Montagnola did not restrict itself to highlighting the effects of automation in the economic sphere and the dangers of endemic crises that it involved. Among the problems that appeared with the replacement of people by machines were the *anthropological and social problems* linked to the new production system's requirement for people to be highly mobile and adaptable to new and unforeseen situations. Hence, educational and training requirements appeared that had not been envisaged before, such as the possibility of almost continuous 'training and re-training' for every worker in order not to lose 'the connection with technical development' and to be able to respond to future requests.[11] The increase in free time that should have accompanied the introduction of automation, as requested by the trade unions, would in actual fact receive a response that was anything but emancipatory for the workers. This is the second aporia that Pollock, critical theorist, analytical as ever, does not hide. According to some positions that were appearing in

---

8   Pollock 1964, p. 329.
9   Harold Wilson, Labour's Party Plan for Science, Scarborough 1963, quoted by Pollock 1964, p. 329.
10 Pollock 1964, p. 353.
11 Pollock 1964, pp. 333–6.

the USA, 'the hours thus earned must be partially or totally "confiscated" for the purpose of urgent further training tasks'. And those workers who did not want to be subjected to this *confiscation for retraining* would have to keep their former working hours: 'during the confiscated hours they would have to work or resign themselves to a corresponding deduction in their wages'.[12]

Before such influential positions, it is clear that Pollock too expresses no little scepticism towards the possibility of automation, without market regulation, *freeing up time that is effectively positive in terms of cultural and social emancipation*. As a total system, automation instead manages to immediately absorb those spaces and times that one might hope its advent would have '*freed*'. There is no longer any brake on the person's exoneration, *depersonalisation*. It continues and intensifies even where – in free time – it should in theory have been limited and reversed.

> The nineteenth-century hope that the eight-hour or even shorter working day would have sparked an unprecedented mass cultural evolution naturally gave way to a widespread scepticism. In the *administered world*, the use of so-called 'free time' has long been subject to manipulation and the strongest social pressure. Rapidly growing industries – of great importance to the economy – serve to supply the largely artificially created needs brought about by the increased leisure which follows the reduction of working hours. In the United States they are called 'leisure industries' and it is expected that they will be able to absorb a considerable proportion of the workers rendered redundant by automation.[13]

As can be seen, in Pollock's book, the topic of *automation* constantly follows the parallel track of cultural and anthropological *manipulation*. As a result, paradoxically, the *ironic* correspondence to Marx's definition of free time as the 'time for the full development of the individual', as 'idle time and time for higher activity', seems to be the forecast that 'the introduction of a four-day working week will simply mean one more day that the workers can waste watching westerns on the television'.[14]

Pollock is therefore perfectly aware of the fact that the '*era of automation*' tends to result in what he himself, in a passage quoted above, defines as the

---

12 Here Pollock is referring to the 'Hypothesis for a Partial Answer', presented at the Washington symposium by the directors of the 'Educational Implications of Automation' research project, see Pollock 1964, p. 336.
13 Pollock 1964, pp. 336–7, own italics.
14 Pollock 1964, p. 337.

totally administered world. To contrast the tendency of the mass media to manipulate the masses in the free time at their disposal, he calls for educational measures of all kinds, *countermeasures* in the sense already expressed by Georges Friedmann.[15] But on this point too, Pollock's view of automation and its consequences is rather disenchanted, and his radicalism seems to anticipate not only what Horkheimer was elaborating right there in Montagnola as he spoke of the 'death of singularity', but also Marcuse's criticism of the 'one-dimensional man'. Indeed, in the period of his lectures at the *École Pratique des Hautes Études* in Paris, prior to writing the *One-Dimensional Man* (a book which as we know would exercise immense influence in the 1960s), Herbert Marcuse often held epistolary debates with Pollock, speaking of the marginalisation of the social role of the workers and the entrepreneurs themselves (replaced by the technical figure of the manager) within the 'schema of a society organised under the domination of the automatic system of production'.[16]

Laconic, Pollock is no less radical than his much more famous philosopher friends: 'Man is "socialised" in an increasingly *total* way by social institutions. ... while encouraged and done with the best intentions, giving shape to free time in turn contributes to the process of *depersonalisation* already hastened by automation.'[17]

In short, as a 'system of general production' and essential form of the *era*, hence its specific and omnipresent trait, automation tends to *wholly govern the subjectivities*, or rather it tends to *produce them and govern their reactions and relations*. Moreover, automation is not just limited to the tertiary sector or the cultural industry, but it also totally affects the *world of politics* and its communication, which is reduced to surveying and propaganda strategies. And this is the third aporetic implication on which the Montagnola edition of *Automation* casts light, taking up the lesson of Norbert Wiener:

> Norbert Wiener was the first to clearly appreciate the social significance of automation. Even during the Second World War he recognised that the coming of automation heralded a new industrial revolution. He saw that despite its marvellous technical achievements automation carried with it a grave threat to humanity from many points of view. He saw mass unemployment looming ahead. He saw that many highly skilled occupations were doomed. He saw how the new methods could be put to the service

---

15   See Friedmann 1955 and 1978.
16   See some indications in Scafoglio 2009, pp. 13ff.
17   Pollock 1964, p. 338, own italics.

of an authoritarian administration. Like some American atomic scientists, he feared that modern technical achievements would be used in the wrong way and so do untold harm.[18]

'Computer simulation', explains Pollock, situating himself along this critical trajectory, to a large extent enables us to anticipate and forecast the behaviour of groups, who are understood, studied and manipulated as 'electors' in the same way as consumers. These techniques increasingly tend to be used by politics – Pollock writes while looking towards the USA in particular – in a fundamental reification of the social processes, in the same way as the processes of the natural sciences. The primary goals become 'to draw up methods that enable the domination of social processes according to the principle of least effort'. Instrumental action, unmindful of all political endeavour for 'the common good', thus becomes the same method with which to build the communication programmes and select the candidates' profiles, that is, their images:

> Like *non-human* nature, social processes cannot be arbitrarily subjected to the will of domination either. But the more we get to know their 'laws of movement', the more effectively we can use them to achieve the ends of the manipulating subject. When applied to the sphere of the political struggle, the further development of 'computer simulation' means a possible further *erosion of the sense* of democracy ...[19]

Pollock recognises that these computational techniques and practices of communication-manipulation can in theory be used by all parties. As a principle, this *'new domination machine'* remains at the disposal of any party, 'so long as it can meet the costs'.[20] But he once again invites us not to underestimate a very much threatening *totalitarian outlook*:

> However, it is not possible to ignore the danger that in the end it can be monopolised by a totalitarian group. It would no longer need an ingenious propaganda minister to perpetuate its domination; instead, by using strictly dosed scientific means, it could achieve its internal ends, and perhaps those of foreign policy too, with a degree of perfection that would even overshadow the world of Orwell's 'big brother'.[21]

---

18   Pollock 1964, p. 339.
19   Pollock 1964, p. 345, own italics.
20   Pollock 1964, p. 347.
21   Ibid.

Moreover, in a letter sent to Felix Weil in 1957, it is the same Pollock who asserts – not without dramatic concern – that the technocrats were now on the march everywhere, almost *the world over*. The link between state capitalism and automation is reflected and realised in the emergence of a single ruling group, on the march to conquer the whole planet: *'Die Technokraten sind auf den Marsch – all over the world'*.[22]

In this light, we can understand how Pollock's book can have a hidden dramatic tone. The final warnings that a planned welfare economy could manage to rationally dominate the problems arising from automation need to be read against a background of awareness that there now risked being no distance between automation and a totally administered world.

4.2 Is Critical Theory Antiquated?

'Marx heute' ['Marx Today'], an essay published by Horkheimer in Germany in 1968, opens with this quite resolute statement: 'History has proven different to what Marx thought. In the capitalism that he analysed, the impoverishment of the proletariat has not progressed, nor has the revolution he expected broken out ....'[23]

In the Frankfurt scholar's opinion, in short, the 'general social situation' no longer presented that violent contradiction between capital and labour which, according to Marx, would lead to the revolutionary struggle. Marked by a critical radicalism, the research and engagement of the early Institute for Social Research, under Horkheimer's directorship, had nevertheless been underpinned by the Marxist dialectical schema. Nor does Horkheimer deny this; in fact, on looking back on the path they had followed since the early years in Frankfurt, it is something he almost tends to underline:

> As amply expressed in the *Zeitschrift für Sozialforschung*, as is usually the case at the outset, our original critical theory was very critical, especially towards the dominant society since, as I have already said, it had brought about the horror of fascism and terrorist communism. It produced much pointless misery, and we hoped that the day would come when this society could be organised in view of the common good, as it would already be possible to do today. We were of the conviction that a central aspect

---

22 Letter from Friedrich Pollock to Felix Weil, 24 December 1957, in Horkheimer 1985–96, vol. 18, pp. 406 ff.
23 Horkheimer 1972b, p. 152, own translation.

in human relations and thinking consists of the fact that there are the rulers and the ruled, as became particularly evident in national socialism. Hence, at that time, we placed our hope in revolution, since, in Germany, after national socialism, the revolution could certainly not make things any worse. Once 'just society' had been implemented through the revolution of the ruled, as Marx had thought, the thinking would become more just too. Because it would no longer have depended on the conscious and unconscious struggle between the classes.[24]

The revolution had been understood as a negation of negation, a negation necessary to revitalise, if not to perfect, a positive form. While not explicitly recalling it, here Horkheimer also seems to be evoking the time when Grossmann's theory of the 'collapse of capitalism' was central in the *Zeitschrift*. No few of the aphorisms in his youthful text entitled *Dämmerung* [*Dawn*] were situated along this line:

> Most people are born into a prison, which is precisely why the present form of society, so-called individualism, is actually a society of standardization and mass culture. So called [*sic*] collectivism, i.e., socialism, on the other hand, is the development of individual talents and differences.[25]

But 30 years had passed since the critical theory of that very early period, and in those dramatic decades, marked not least by the early Soviet comedown, 'we understood that on many points Marx was wrong'.[26] A decisive role in the maturation of this critical awareness had been played by Pollock. Indeed, not only had he denounced the failure of Soviet authoritarianism and bureaucracy, he had also abandoned the collapsist-revolutionary paradigm and realised that the progressive historical dialectic had become stuck in the inverted forms of the dialectic of enlightenment and totally administered society.

The discourse set out by Horkheimer in 'Marx heute' continues and is expanded in some other texts from the end of the 1960s. One of these is the important conference 'La teoria critica ieri e oggi' ['Critical Theory Past and Present'] held by Horkheimer at the Cini Foundation in Venice on 19 and 20 September 1969.

---

24   Horkheimer 1972c, p. 164, own translation.
25   Horkheimer 1978a, p. 47.
26   Horkheimer 1972c, p. 165, own translation.

Horkheimer had been invited to speak by the director of the Fondazione Cini, Vittore Branca, at that time already in contact with Adorno who was to hold the inaugural lecture of the 'Corso Internazionale di alta cultura' [International Course of High Culture] for the Venetian foundation. In response to Branca's letters, the first from 23 December 1968, on 14 April 1969 Horkheimer wrote from Montagnola to specify his willingness to accept the offer, defining his topic as such: '... as a topic I propose LA TEORIA CRITICA IERI E OGGI [Critical Theory Past and Present]. I would talk about the theory that I formulated and its transformation up to the present day'.[27] The sudden death of Adorno on 6 August 1969, in Visp, Switzerland, then intervened to place Horkheimer's Venetian critical and self-critical stocktake in a more dramatic light. Speaking in Italian too, these were his starting words:

> I had hoped to meet my friend and colleague here, Theodor W. Adorno, and now, just a few weeks ago, he totally unexpectedly died. You can imagine how hard this hit me ... The personal things that I will say now are not irrelevant for critical theory.[28]

Moreover, Adorno's death was not to be the only event of mourning to affect him that year. Just a couple of months after the Venetian lecture, Maidon also died, and for Max, as can be seen from his letters from that period, it was an extremely difficult moment. Shortly afterwards, it would be Pollock's turn, after a long illness.[29] At the same time, it must also be added that the genesis of this Venetian lecture and philosophical testament was closely tied – also chronologically, as they dated respectively from 7 October 1968, 19 December 1968 and 1 February 1969 – to some interviews with Horkheimer made by Enzo Bettizza for the television of Italian-speaking Switzerland.

The topics of the Venetian lecture held in September 1969 were broadly anticipated in these interviews. Starting from that long farewell from revolutionary Marxism, as can be seen in Horkheimer's statements in the first interview:

> The thought of the growing poverty of the workers, who, according to Marx, were to be at the basis of the revolution, has become abstract and illusory. ... The employment contracts, which expressed a brutal oppres-

---

27 Letter from Max Horkheimer to Vittore Branca, 14 April 1969, in van de Moetter 1990, p. 193, own translation.
28 Horkheimer 1972c, p. 162, own translation.
29 On these biographical aspects, see also Chapter 5.1.

sion of the workers at the time of the *Communist Manifesto*, now constitute the basis for trade union claims, but no longer for revolutionary uprisings.³⁰

While his thought still took and recognised a critical-negative form, of Jewish origin, now, thanks to the 'free world' or even the 'world of bourgeois freedoms', it appeared possible to him that these contradictions could be limited or softened. It seemed that the trade unions could adjust them, at least at the quantitative level.

In these interventions, Horkheimer seems to avail himself of that welfarist democratic variant that Pollock had announced as a historical potentiality of 'state capitalism'.

In those years, against the background of the protest movements spreading in Europe which aimed to create an anti-capitalist alliance between students and workers, Horkheimer was pressed on this theme over and over again. With these public expressions, changing depending on the circumstances and occasion, the master of critical theory, the older companion or even master of that Marcuse who was taking his revolutionary word to thousands of students on US campuses, seemed to side with a prudent reformism, and in no uncertain terms condemn all prospects of revolt.

It was no coincidence that, resident moreover in Montagnola and able at least in part to converse in Italian, he was repeatedly questioned about this in the Italian-speaking area too.³¹

The second interview, lasting over an hour and put together in several sittings, was made for Swiss television by renowned *Corriere della Sera* journalist Enzo Bettizza (who would later become senator of the Italian Republic). In it, after diagnosing the changed condition of the current proletariat compared to the condition at the start of the nineteenth century, Horkheimer infers that overturning the system – that system which seemed to guarantee more and more widespread and continual *well-being* and to be able to avoid economic crises – was a goal that could no longer in any way be classified among the real interests of the proletariat. As a consequence, what would form between the 'revolutionary' students and the working class would not be an alliance, as the political avant-gardes of 1968 dreamed, but inevitably a contrast, antagonism.

---

30 'Enzo Bettizza a colloquio con Max Horkheimer' ['Enzo Bettizza in Conversation with Max Horkheimer'], 7 October 1968, now in van de Moettter 1990, p. 66, own translation.

31 Instead, the same cannot be said in the case of Pollock, whose presence was almost ignored by the Italian and Swiss-Italian press.

The young revolutionaries, therefore, would have to give up their dangerous illusions, which would not lead to emancipation and freedom, but, on the contrary, to results inevitably fraught with oppression.

Owing to its duality, state capitalism could once again veer towards its totalitarian variant. On this point, in his Ticino conversations of 1969, in truth Horkheimer was also somehow revising and backpedalling on what not even a year earlier, in 1968, he had maintained at the *Nürnberger Gespräche*. Then, in an intervention with the paradigmatic title, 'Zur Kritik der gegenwärtigen Gesellschaft' ['For a Critique of Present-Day Society'], he indeed deemed that he could conclude his discourse by observing that *'in a certain sense, everything that I have said is contained in the youth protests'*.[32]

But now, thanks to bourgeois democracy and trade union participation, since the existent seemed at least largely to have become the positive, the inevitable result of the revolution – as the negation of the positive and no longer the negation of negation – would be a threatening, tyrannical negative, a new authoritarian state. Bidding farewell to all revolutionary perspectives, Horkheimer's line of argument in his second lengthy Ticino interview with Bettizza went as follows:

> So, today, the students who rebel and want to overturn the system are separated from the proletariat since they want to radically change society, while the proletariat, it seems to me, have no interest in doing so. On the contrary, their concern is to have more free time and better salaries in order to manage to access well-being. Therefore, they are afraid of upheaval. The upshot is this: the relationship between the intelligent students and the proletariat has changed completely. In the end, today's students know they are alone in front of the proletariat. I believe it is important to point this out and also add that this implies a change in meaning of the Marxist theoretical structure. Once Marx was the hope for all those suffering in society, and not just the workers: think of National Socialism. Nazism came about in the 1920s and it was – as I see things – not absurd to expect that then if the manual workers, the office workers and all the other thinking people had come together, they would have been able to drive it out. If they had intervened in time, for example, at the start of the 1930s, with a strike and the determination not to want the dictatorship, they would have made Hitler's rule impossible. At that time, believing in Marxism still held some value, a meaning, while today

32   Horkheimer 1972a, p. 150, own translation.

we have to expect the opposite from a revolution. In Germany and other countries, not to speak of Switzerland, democracy exists, and if it was to be overturned, the result would be dictatorship. Overturning it would not prevent dictatorship, it would cause it.[33]

Instead of leading to that 'realm of freedom' which Marx had wanted to prophesise, the revolution would in fact inevitably and paradoxically arouse its opposite: a further form of domination. The existent – it now had to be recognised – seemed to attest to the fact that democracy had been realised, even in that Germany which he had done everything to abandon a second time.

By sustaining this, as well as by defending the 'free world' as the only 'island' that could save from the sea of totalitarianism, might Horkheimer have also intended to uphold that in the end the existent already corresponded to the kingdom of freedom? But whatever had happened to the longing not just for a simple life, but for a *happy* life? In its movements between past and present, had critical theory turned upside-down?

Now what had to be assumed as the first and foremost criterion in assessing society was not the concept of distributive justice for the construction of a more equal 'rational society', but instead the personalistic concept of freedom. Significantly, it is in the first interview made by Enzo Bettizza in Montagnola on 7 October 1968 that Horkheimer expresses himself in these terms:

> I believe that it is the right and obligation of every thinking human being to measure the free world with the concept of freedom that is at its basis, in the same way as to relate to it in a critical way. But at the same time, I think that this free world is an island in space and time. If it were to founder in the ocean of totalitarianism, it would also mark the end of culture, which is every person's supreme and most precious asset.[34]

While on one hand this review of the criterion of analysis had to lead to the relinquishment of the Marxist schema, on the other, it did not necessarily imply that the theory would have to be tied to the 'order of the facts', or critical theory shrugged off and reduced to the reifying and conformist positivism of 'traditional theory'. While the engagement to defend what remained of

---

33 'Intervista del giornalista Enzo Bettizza con il filosofo Max Horkheimer' ['Interview by journalist Enzo Bettizza with the philosopher Max Horkheimer'], 19 December 1968, 1 February 1969, now in van de Moetter 1990, pp. 70–9, own translation.

34 van de Moetter 1990, p. 66, own translation.

liberal-bourgeois civilisation, that is, for the reaffirmation of individual freedom in the context of a society striving for equality, was definitely a polemic against the revolutionary arguments then being waved around by the protest movements, it was nevertheless not an unquestioning surrender to state capitalism, but a concerted effort to enable its control. In the same way, however eminently outmoded in the context of the left-wing culture of those years, his pointing towards Schopenhauerian pessimism, increasingly intertwined with indications towards the tradition of the Other, could not be seen as a conformist surrender to the existent either. The lack of sympathy demonstrated by Horkheimer towards the 1968 student protests, as well as his opposition to the young Habermas, should not lead – so many years later, moreover – to perfunctory judgements which tend to ignore the specific and distinct traits of his position, however questionable it may have been.

Besides, on the socio-political level too, it appears that in his (and their) view, recognising the transformation of manual workers into office workers and their progressive integration evidently did not have to be accompanied by an 'elimination of critical self-reflective exercise'. Seeing the historical error inherent in the revolutionary paradigm did not mean that the theory – still the same *critical* theory, despite being renewed – no longer wanted to understand and criticise the social, historical and anthropological motifs expressed in those new contents, namely the integration and transformation of the working class. But in the era characterised by this integration and above all by the advent of automation, as well as politically inopportune, it seemed historically inadequate and senseless to go on crystallising the Marxist revolutionary paradigm. The technical era, Pollock's 'era of automation', together with the absolutely transversal concept of 'state capitalism', in short demanded other analyses and other critical responses. The traditional categories of politics, as well as its geopolitical maps, had to be unmasked, not only in light of the far-sighted *racket theory*, but also as variants objectively subordinated to the affirmation of a shared production ideology, expressions of the self-assertion of a single 'apparatus', that is, the global organisation of the technical era:

> *In the apparatus.* In the liberal period, the bourgeoisie was characterised by a relatively high number of autonomous existences. The economic process led to the concentration of power in the hands of monopolies and, today, in a number of rackets in the various industrial, professional and political classes, which, through a hierarchical structure, push towards strictly ordered administration, corresponding to automated society. In the West as well as the East, it now only depends on which racket sits at

> the helm. But even they have little freedom. The apparatus – regardless of the competing apparatus that has to be used – restricts the development of its own productivity.³⁵

The global apparatus had moreover already shown itself, in the West and the East, in its intrinsic biopolitical aspect. Hence, it was a matter of having the courage to recognise that today

> [t]he line of demarcation runs between respect and contempt for life, not between the so-called left and the so-called right, which is already an outdated bourgeois antithesis. Cliques may fight each other where their interests demand it. Their true enemies are individuals that are conscious of themselves.³⁶

The necessity of the final claim for nonconformism without doubt also originated from here. Of course, as can be seen, correcting Marx's 'historical error' involved no few consequences and crucial reconfigurations, but by no means implied renouncing self-reflection or falling into the positivist-conformist subalternity that was the order of the day. This outcome would be avoided not least by rediscovering the permanently negative knowledge of that hunchbacked dwarf of Jewish theology which Benjamin had already recognised as the origin and destiny of critical thought,³⁷ unwilling to infinitise and therefore celebrate or absolutise any form of the finite.

But in the first place, what were the presuppositions and implications that accompanied the transformation-integration of the working class and the lessening of the contradiction between workers and capital? What was the historical meaning of that integration marked by more and more widespread possibilities of *consumption*? While on one hand the lessening of the contradiction seemed to allow important spaces of freedom and potentialities specific to the '*freie Welt*', it has to be said that, for Horkheimer too, a critical understanding of this transformation nevertheless also had to grasp its ambivalent and anything but unilaterally *progressive* nature. On looking more closely, even when he moves on the level of meticulously analysing current affairs, Horkheimer highlights contradictions and aporias, he never simply 'gets comfortable' in the existent, he by no means tends towards circumstantial *gauchisme*, but assumes awkward positions. In a note from May 1966 entitled 'Amerika im Mai 1966'

---

35   Horkheimer 1991, 'Im Apparat', p. 409, own translation.
36   Horkheimer 1978a, 'The True Conservative', p. 230.
37   See Benjamin 1968, p. 253.

['America in May 1966'], he observes that the United States found themselves in an almost 'impossible' situation, marked by the war in Vietnam on one hand and on the other the simultaneous development of the civil rights movement. He strongly feared that this split would not only lead to an increase in inflation, an advance in nationalism and a desire for authoritarianism, but also the temptation to 'base foreign policy on lies'.[38]

Some months later, on occasion of the week of German-American friendship, which was the object of strong protests by the student movements, he held a speech at the *Amerikahaus* in Frankfurt. In that speech, he attempted to interpret the war effort in Vietnam by recalling the United States' general commitment to the defence of human rights, and in particular by remembering that without the intervention of the United States in the Second World War, Germany and the whole of Europe would have been dominated by Nazism and Fascism.[39]

Horkheimer's stance received a harsh reply from Marcuse, who wrote to him in a letter that he instead, and in contrast, saw America as the 'historical heir of fascism'.[40]

Perhaps for this reason too, in some further statements of his position on the topic, Horkheimer tended to clarify that he considered the situation of the USA in South Vietnam a drama, a calamity, a great misfortune [*ein grosses Unglück*], or even that he saw it in properly 'tragic' terms.

And looming against the background of that 'tragedy', he saw the global affirmation of Chinese totalitarian state capitalism, '*the hell of Chinese world domination*'.[41] Just like in a classical tragedy, the perspective of the American withdrawal – encouraged by the protest movements and 'intellectuals' – would not only have meant a frightening bloodbath in South Vietnam but would also have accelerated the Chinese route to conquering the West. What those intellects like Marcuse did not see, Horkheimer warned, was the horror of Chinese world domination, *die Hölle einer chinesischen Weltherrschaft*.[42]

And so in turn he accused these radical '*Intellektuellen*', whose behaviour reminded him of that of those 'Oxford students' before the Second World War, intent on proclaiming, in a totally abstract way, that they 'did not want to fight

---

38 Horkheimer 1988, 'Amerika im Mai 1966', p. 364, own translation.
39 See Wiggershaus 2013, pp. 218 ff.
40 Letter from Herbert Marcuse to Max Horkheimer, 17 June 1967, in Horkheimer 2007, p. 344.
41 Horkheimer 1988, 'South Vietnam und die Intellektuellen', pp. 360–1, own translation, with a note in which Horkheimer, referring to an article by Richard Löwenthal, speaks of the 'tragic situation' in which the USA seemed to be tied up.
42 Horkheimer 1988, p. 361, own italics.

for King and country'.⁴³ Hence, this is another reason for his defence of America's engagement, a defence that intertwined with the awareness of a historically 'tragic' condition. Of course, it can be debated whether his vision was not ideologically warped, but what must be observed is that it nevertheless did not translate into a simplistic apology of the existent.

In September 1966, under the title 'Für Amerika' ['For America'], Horkheimer notes:

> anyone in the West, and especially in the United States, that portrays the States as worse than other nations because of it [the war in Vietnam] or other painful, cruel events such as racial unrest, contradicts himself. That he is free to express himself without wasting away in a penitentiary, without being tortured to death, he owes to their [the United States'] existence, to the fact that they stood their ground. Without them, the world would long since have been divided up between eastern and western Hitlers. Such a person may want the better, the right society, but his criticism of the existing one requires devotion to freedom as a necessary ingredient. Freedom must be preserved and developed lest the violence he accuses become the unintended meaning of his talk.⁴⁴

In other words, the defence of the '*freie Welt*' was not to become a mere reconciliation with reality. Despite all the concessions, it was not to lead to a disregard for the great contradictions and aporias that risked undermining the very exercise of freedoms and democratic control formally recognised in democratic state capitalism, however preferable it may have been to totalitarian capitalism. A loyalty to freedom, meant as the effective possibility of criticism, hence led Horkheimer and Pollock on one hand to seek to defend the American model, and on the other, at the same time, to highlight its ruinous aporias linked to the advent of the technical era. Nor does Horkheimer deny the loss of sense of democracy, diagnosed by Pollock in *Automation* as an anything but far-off drift, in *Späne* either. Under the title of 'Kultur in USA' ['Culture in the USA'], one can read:

> Small talk and jokes are characteristic of every party. Topics of any seriousness are immediately veered away from. ... American civilisation can produce nothing new. It has no depth. Thought is powerless. ... Why is

---

43 Ibid., own translation.
44 Horkheimer 1978a, 'For America', p. 230.

thought powerless? Because it is not at the service of a specific interest. Nevertheless, the only thing alive in the USA is what is immediately directed towards interests. Great technical personal performances are characteristic of this. ...[45]

Yet, it was precisely towards this civilisation 'with no depth', whose cultural and anthropological change in connection to the technical era was decreeing the definitive decline of the thinking human being, that one had to look to seek to deal with the immediately totalitarian variant of state capitalism. Moreover, this decline of the role granted to critical intelligence and independent intellectuals was decreeing its victory on the immediately political level with the 'end of the Kennedy era' and the victory of Johnson, under whom the only important thing was to remain in power.[46]

Seeking to save the democratic variant of state capitalism was hence an aporetical task, dramatic even. However, for this same reason it was also in line with the recognition, already begun by Pollock and implicitly continued in *Dialectic of Enlightenment*, of the essentially dual nature of 'state capitalism' as such, full of potential overlaps and entanglements with its totalitarian variant.[47]

Hence, if the Marxist hypothesis was to be self-criticised as an illusion, the same ostentation of the island of the '*freie Welt*' was not to be simply absolutised and celebrated in the simplistic figure of open society. Indeed, this would be to fall into a no less illusionary conciliation with the existent, with a global reality that was being increasingly moulded by the development of technology, and its 'Copernican' consequences. From this point of view, in *Späne* the Chinese cultural revolution itself – beyond its specificities – is interpreted as a great symptom of the fact that, in exactly the same way as what was happening in the West and in the Soviet Union, in China too technical development [*die Entwicklung der Technik*] was now demanding a departure from the conceptual pictures and values linked to tradition. In this revolutionary movement of global significance, however paradoxical, the precise task of culture then seemed to be to make the autonomous individual lose all function, in order to ultimately permit 'the economy and society to "function" almost automatically [*quasi automatisch "funktionieren"*]'.[48] Hence, it was not only in China that the

---

45   Horkheimer 1988, 'Kultur in USA', p. 288, own translation.
46   See 'Johnson contra Kennedy', in Horkheimer 1988, p. 312.
47   See Chapter 2 of this book.
48   Horkheimer 1988, 'China und der Untergang der Kultur', 4 October 1966, pp. 367–8, own translation.

decline of culture was strongly evident. It was an epoch-making phenomenon, reducing humans to generic beings, heading towards an organisation similar to that of ants and bees. The short-sightedness of the traditional political and geopolitical divisions of the pre-technical world had to be replaced by a highly disenchanted gaze towards the future: 'the future of humankind: a corporation for exploiting nature and at the same time an anthill'.[49]

Despite the discrepancy between the past and present positions, during his late Venetian stocktake, Horkheimer repeats, 'critical theory has the task of expressing what is generally not expressed. It therefore has to point out *the costs of progress*, the danger that in its wake even the idea of the autonomous subject, the idea of the soul, will melt away, since in the face of the universe it appears futile ...'.[50]

In other words, the physiognomy of the labour-capital contradiction was changing owing to the immense increase in productivity, made possible by the technical transformation of the means of production. But in actual fact this transformation was taking place with an increase in *automation*, and critical intelligence certainly could not help but ask what the repercussions of automation and 'artificial intelligence' would be on subjectivity, freedom, on what after Kant the philosophers indicated as the *autonomy of practical reason*. Freedom is the criterion, the unit of measurement with which to approach and hail the '*freie Welt*'. But then the suspicion could arise – Pollock *docet!* – that the '*free world*' was being built on the transformation-negation of freedom, that is, in its own way *automated* society was intrinsically confiscating the free world and thereby disposing of both the form of personal subjectivity itself and the prerequisites of democracy. Such were Horkheimer's words, again in the interview with Bettizza:

> You have to read Marx while putting him in relation, in the right way, with the present. Let me make an example: Marx says that revolution is the passage into the realm of freedom. Now, however, we have to examine which conditions still exist in this *automated society* for what can be defined as the 'realm of freedom'. Indeed, we have to speak of this principle of freedom. Indeed, it runs the risk of becoming a slogan ...[51]

And in more radical and pessimistic terms, in the Venetian conference that same year:

---

49   Horkheimer 1988, 'Stichworte zur Lage', p. 364, own translation.
50   Horkheimer 1972c, p. 171, own translation.
51   'Intervista del giornalista Enzo Bettizza con il filosofo Max Horkheimer', 19 December 1968, 1 February 1969, now in van de Moetter 1990, p. 84, own translation.

> We have convinced ourselves that society will develop into a *totally administered world*. That everything will be regulated, absolutely everything! Just as we have got to the point that humans entirely dominate nature, that everyone has enough to eat, that there is no longer any need for one to live worse or better than the other, because now we can all live how we please, it no longer holds any meaning that one is a minister and the other only a secretary, so in the end everything is equal. Everything can be regulated automatically, whether it is state administration, traffic regulation or the regulation of consumption. It is a tendency immanent to the development of humankind ...[52]

Where the increase in the production forces, within a different logic of social distribution, promised emancipation and the realm of freedom, the radically threatening image of the 'totally administered' world reared its head. What appeared was an inexorable *iron cage*, also of the Weberian kind (but not exclusively so), in the place of the Marxian realm of freedom. 'The wholly enlightened earth', as we already read in *Dialectic of Enlightenment*, 'is radiant with triumphant calamity'.

As far as Horkheimer is concerned, his most interesting contribution on these topics is probably a long interview with Otmar Hersche made for Swiss radio in 1970, which was given the title 'Verwaltete Welt' ['Administered World'], in Italian 'Rivoluzione o Libertà?' ['Revolution or Freedom?'].[53]

However, once again, the alternative posed in the title – presumably given by the editors – is not lacking in instrumentality, as if there really were no other theoretical scenarios between the 'revolutionary' one and the one apologetically engaged in making the existent correspond to the realm of real freedom. And yet we have to recognise that despite the stances he effectively took as a 'foreground philosopher',[54] in this conversation Horkheimer relaunches the *need for a critical theory* in the face of the technical era coming about in that historical period. And Marx's teaching could not be simply expunged or cancelled from this critical theory.

The Marxian diagnosis on the contradictions of capitalism was proving to be wrong in terms of the immediate contents, but the fact remains that from a deeper point of view it needed to be resumed and reformulated. While Marx might have failed in diagnosing the 'fall in the rate of profit' and the workers' progressive impoverishment, he had nevertheless shown the way,

---

52 Horkheimer 1972c, p. 165, own translation.
53 Horkheimer 1970.
54 Schmidt 1974, p. xlvii.

not least again with the concept of *alienation*, to diagnose *another type of misery*, a misery capable of exceeding the directly economic one. And the later Horkheimer still teaches us to think that in the era of automation this other misery, this already enormously widespread *existential misery fraught with a fundamental, dehumanising loss of sense*, was destined to grow more and more, to the point that freedom and its effective spaces would become a wholly formal concept. Whereas diligent interpreters seemed to be committed to celebrating the progressive triumph of freedom, the philosopher responded – in his typically discreet manner of thought – that 'the inevitable result' instead risked being '*desperation*'.[55]

And despite it all, Horkheimer still recognises the memory of Marx in his (and their) diagnosis, as he thinks over his lesson in order to interpret the present and future:

> I could add that Marx's view, according to which in our society workers' misery would get worse and worse, is indeed not right. However, totally unconnected to this, there is a great deal of misery among lonely old people and in prisons, and in many other places. And it is this misery that should be removed. Critical theory has the task of pointing out these phenomena.[56]

In this interview, even though Horkheimer does not say so in so many words, in addition to the dialectical relationship with Marx, it is plain to see that the whole diagnosis of the present day that he proposes contains the 'structural' lesson, or rather, the inseparable proximity of Pollock.

This is also evident if we observe how on one hand, by explicitly remembering the essays from the 1930s, Horkheimer hinges on the problems deriving from the concentration of industry and its bonds with 'political control', and on the other how he slots the discourse on automation into this reflection.

> The immanent logic of the economic process is the tendency towards absolute control, that is, a situation in which everything is regulated, where everyone knows what they have to do in every situation, like an employee in a company who always has to resolve those same particular questions, or like someone who crosses the road. He reacts to the signs imposed by the central control and its mechanisms. Marx thought that

---

55 Horkheimer 1970, p. 25.
56 Ibid., own translation.

society was moving towards freedom. But he was doubly wrong. First of all, as I have already explained, because society is moving towards automation and not towards freedom; second, because the dialectic between justice and freedom completely escaped him.[57]

Instead of leading to the organisation of more human production relations and permitting people's emancipation from work, the development of the production forces therefore seemed to be leading not only and not so much towards negating freedom, depriving it of 'fantasy' and 'inventiveness'[58] as, even more dangerously, mummifying freedom and its forms and forgetting all about them:

> But individuals in the bourgeois world must learn that the formula: I am autonomous, I am free, my own end, is no less abstract, no less false than the claim of the Russians that their society is the true reality. ... The belief of the individual in himself has become sterile. It was a moment of the bourgeois process of emancipation and, as such, a moment of truth. Today, that doctrine prompts the answer that *the individual must die* without the possibility of an active absorption in a meaningful totality ... At the same tempo and to the same degree as bourgeois culture passes beyond the point where it can still become more than it is, it and everything in it become more false.[59]

Starting from here too, it comes as no surprise that at the centre of the *Notizen*, a 'nocturnal' book composed as we know in Montagnola, we find a diagnosis of contemporaneity, defined as an epoch characterised essentially by the '*decline of the individual*' and by the 'castration of inner life':

> That society, in its most advanced form, today mentally reduces individuals to the point of castrating the inner life and autonomy of its members, is ultimately due to the atrocious manner in which the self-domination of the human race imposes itself on nature. Killing the inner life is the price paid by humans for the total lack of regard they show towards exterior life, towards life outside themselves. They must necessarily do that violence towards the outside, called technology, to themselves, to their inner selves too. The wealth that grows thanks to apparatus, the violence of machinery, at the social level is turned into totalitarian domination,

---

57 Horkheimer 1970, pp. 29–30, own translation.
58 Horkheimer 1970, p. 20, own translation.
59 Horkheimer 1978a, 'Function and Limits of Bourgeois Culture', p. 171, italics mine.

while everywhere and on the psychological level it reduces spiritual life to pure astuteness aimed at individual self-preservation, in other words, poverty of thought.[60]

In the *Notizen* this diagnosis on the decline of the individual is accompanied by attentively sounding out the symptoms, wherein Horkheimer outlines a sort of micro-physics of 'instrumental reason' (not dissimilarly to Adorno's *Minima Moralia*).[61]

The symptoms that he criticises can to a large extent be traced back to the modification of experience, of the perceptive and natural space, arising from the modification of the production techniques and the 'suspension' of the historical dialectic that accompanied their appearance. As already observed, a large part of the symptoms onto which Horkheimer casts his gaze express the standardisation that seemed to be affecting the sphere of practical life to the point of emptying the personal dimension; in concrete terms, the decline of handmade objects, loss of the personal value of living, from furniture to taps, the uniformity of materials such as glass, medicine packages,[62] the transformation of food and flavours, and the loss of difference in the landscape with the disappearance of the difference between rural and urban. Hence, the whole horizon of 'culture' thereby proves to be threatened, and what remains of it in the magazines is but 'a pretext for advertising inserts', as the only thing that counts is 'selling' and hence 'hammering this conviction into all brains, modelling human beings according to this principle, transforming them completely into automatic devices that cry hallelujah and in reality react exclusively to money, to the motorbike, refrigerator and position, this is precisely their ideal'.[63] The thus diagnosed radical anthropological transformation also inevitably affects the sphere of language. Indeed, we have to see its semantic and syntactic impoverishment as the manifestation of a step back in the quality of its meaning and thereby in the very sense of the human. The decline of the individual and the reduction of language to a tool constitute the two simultaneous sides of the regression with which the technical era is fraught:

> Concurrently, the individual declines. The less typical the autonomous citizen, the individual, becomes of society, the less he has 'something to

---

60 Horkheimer 1991, 'Der Preis der Selbstbeherrschung', p. 285, own translation.
61 See Adorno 2005a.
62 Horkheimer 1991, 'Handware und Fabrikware', p. 231 and 'Warenkunde', p. 232. And also see 'Der Mensch in der Wandlung seit der Jahrhundertwende' in Horkheimer 1972.
63 Horkheimer 1991, 'Die Reklamekultur', p. 247, own translation.

say', be it reactionary or progressive, oppositional or conservative, the more the non-technical uses of language become mere show, recommendation for a career, for membership in groups, like clothing, table manners, habits. When people get together, there is small talk; the content is inconsequential. Those who hear or make declamations full of pathos or attend festivities, gatherings, religious services, also realize that substance is of no moment. What counts is observing customs. ... No one is so naïve as to consider what language says, let alone to take it literally, at least no one that is up to date. Children already *learn* language in this way, they do not understand that it could be different. They only know purposes, not meanings.[64]

It is no coincidence that the diagnosis expressed in *Späne* is very much the same. Here the references to contemporary culture – including technical and scientific culture – formulated with Pollock's help, become more direct and the diagnosis about the complete transformation of the human being into an 'automatic apparatus' even more crude.

Cybernetics and Biology (Theory of Biological Information)
([February] 1968)

Plant and animal seeds contain a programme that regulates their growth. They are so to speak programmed, in a similar way to a computer. The same goes for the organisms whose life processes are regulated by a programme. This is formed by amino acids that are combined together in long lines. Next, there is a genetic code in the genetic material, whose programme is however flexible and can adapt to the environmental conditions. Environmental stimuli can cause adaptations of the programme, which appear as illnesses. All the psychosomatic illnesses belong to these (gastric and intestinal ulcers, circulatory diseases, angina pectoris, etc.).

Through the change of environment, the easing of 'stressful' situations, new environmental stimuli, a chemical 'exchange of information' can take place, the programme can be changed. The old 'information proteins' disappear, and 'an inversion of the organism' occurs 'through chemical synthesis and degradation of the regulatory molecules'. Example: [Max] Bircher-Benner's 'order therapy'. Every life expression is 'regulated by information (programmed)'. It is a 'transferral of chemical-electrical-

---

64   Horkheimer 1978a, 'Small Talk', p. 155.

mechanical information'. Today we have therefore found a scientific formulation of the 'homme machine' (La Mettrie) and Driesch's entelechy.

This progress corresponds exactly to the tendency to liquidate the individual. We are already at the point that the machine is no longer explained through human beings, but human beings through machines.

Obviously, all mental processes are accompanied by biological processes. However, today a causal relationship which excludes the spiritual is made out of this very ancient insight. 'Programme', 'information' in the place of mental processes. This contributes to reducing the individual to an indifferent piece of nature and must influence self-awareness and self-conception in a decisive way. Indeed, language 'regulates' thought and in the end makes it superfluous.[65]

Hence, it appears that also for Pollock and Horkheimer, to use the well-known expression of Günther Anders, the human being was becoming *antiquated* [*antiquiert*].

It was around the criticism of this transformation that Fritz and Max laid down their last questions, for shared works to come.

As can be read in their 'Notes on Automation':

1. What does A[utomation] mean for the lives of human beings?
2. What will become of [human beings] if their own, that is, their intellectual functions [*geistigen Funktionen*], can be taken over by machines? If theoretical problems can be thought through better by computers than by the human brain? What remains [to them] to possess that is still distinct? Something of metaphysics? The constructor's role: they still need positive fantasy, to the point in time when machines will build other machines by themselves.

   ...

4. A[utomation] will be developed as far as is conceivable. But what consequences will this development have on the structure of people's brains?[66]

---

65 Horkheimer 1988, 'Kybernetik und Biologie/Theorie der biologischen Information', pp. 466–7, own translation.
66 Horkheimer 1988, 'Notizen zur Automation', p. 253, own translation. See also herein 'Thesen für gemeinsames Arbeiten', where in reference to the book by Robert Jungk, *The Future Has Already Begun*, Horkheimer and Pollock wonder about the 'compensatory' aspects that the robotic transformation underway would lead to.

CHAPTER 5

Critical Theory and Longing for the Other

> Jewry was not a powerful state but the hope for justice at the end of the world. They were a people and its opposite, a rebuke to all peoples. Now, a state claims to be speaking for Jewry, to be Jewry. ...
> HORKHEIMER 1978a, 'The State of Israel'

∴

5.1   The Absent Alterity

From a strictly biographical point of view, it must be said that in Montagnola Horkheimer and Pollock had to deal with old age, illness and finally death in an increasingly radical way. Nonetheless, in 1964, Horkheimer's response to a journalist who wanted to know how he was spending those years of 'retirement' was still imbued with some irony and a touch of irritation:

> Thank you for your letter of the 17th. I'm rushing to respond with a few words in the midst of quite urgent tasks.
> I can't quite apply the expression 'leisure time' to myself. I'm too old-fashioned. In the summer we usually go to the mountains to breathe different air and to rest and relax. During the year I have to satisfy the demands that institutions and people interested in practical matters make on me; otherwise, I'm able to work on something reasonable, write, and formulate ideas. I can't actually talk about this as a hobby, because it's much too strenuous and usually lasts until late at night and not seldom until morning. My remaining time is devoted to the few like-minded people or to the most beloved person I have, my wife. Quite often we talk about everything of interest to us and occasionally play cards, either during work or afterward, that is, even later. Before sleeping I usually read the underappreciated comic strips, not for more profound reasons but because I like them, in a quite naive fashion. We look forward to them from one day to the next. But behind everything, work as well as relaxation, is the thought of threatening reality, the fear of what was and is, and what happens over and over again at every moment.[1]

In short, his (and their) itinerary bears witness to how the thought of 'threatening reality', 'the fear of what was and is, and what happens over and over again', formed the unrestrainable background to his (and their) late reflection. Moreover, it was a background set to become even gloomier, in a movement that seemed to put historical-philosophical vicissitudes *in parallel* with biographical events when, not even three months after the passing of Adorno (who died on 6 August in Visp, Switzerland), Maidon died on 17 October 1969 in Montagnola.

The death of his wife led Horkheimer, then aged 75, to express the intention to put an end to it all. These were his words in a letter from the following month of December:

> My whole life has been so terribly affected that the only reason I'm not giving it up is that SHE would probably not have approved and because I want to act in HER spirit – as long as I can truly function. I'm giving lectures and seminars, am doing radio and television shows, but my innermost being [*mein Inneres*] is not engaged. The significance that everything had only in relationship to HER is now only present in thoughts of the beyond.[2]

In the *Post scriptum* to this letter we can read: 'If it weren't for Fred Pollock, who is helping me immensely, I couldn't even deal with everyday things on my own. I'm grateful to him for more than I can say'.[3]

In another letter sent just after Maidon's death, addressed to the psychologist Fay B. Karpf, author of various studies and married to Maurice Karpf, psychologist, scholar and friend of Horkheimer who had died in 1964, Max writes:

> As you well know, my philosophy is definitely pessimistic and therefore will not give me the courage and strength which I would need in order to go on with my work. I shall try to do so, but my main desire is the longing [*Sehnsucht*] to go wherever SHE might be – probably nowhere.
>
> Yes, it is wonderful that Fred is with me, sharing my pain and helping me in so many things. Yet I think that he too is suffering from the loss so

---

1   Letter from Max Horkheimer to Richard Kirn, 27 November 1964, in Horkheimer 2007, pp. 330–1.
2   Letter from Max Horkheimer to Adolph and Beatrice Lowe, 2 December 1969, in Horkheimer 2007, p. 362.
3   Horkheimer 2007, p. 363.

much that his situation is similar to my own. Maidon was unique, every year, every month, every day more wonderful.

In deep sadness, Max.[4]

In December 1970 Pollock also died in a clinic in Sorengo, close to Lugano, consumed by cancer. On tracing his memories of him in a letter to a correspondent, in January 1971, Horkheimer notes:

> After I had lost my dear colleague Adorno and my beloved wife, a new mortal blow has happened to me, my best friend Fred Pollock died from cancer about a month ago. This means not only a new intellectual pain for me, but also an increase of my daily work. He had helped me in all economic and financial problems, and now my duties become more and more difficult. By the way, he was not only one of the important administrators of the Institute in Germany, Switzerland, the States, and then again Germany, but also one of its members without whom it would probably not exist any more today.[5]

This incredible sequence of losses of people who were dear to him threw Horkheimer into extreme despair. In an emotionally charged letter sent to the famous photographer Germaine Krull, a friend of Max and Fritz since their time as students in Munich, Horkheimer confesses that he really does not know how he will manage to bear the harshness of all those blows.

> Dear Germaine,
>
> Yes, Fred has died of cancer. The only thing medicine could do was to provide him with as many narcotics as possible so that he no longer felt any pain but passed on in his sleep, almost unconscious. You say that he'll come back – this may be, but the HE will no longer be identical with his past I, because the I without memory would not be the same as the previous I. It already breaks down when a person gets drunk, and it will certainly not be preserved when the entire body disintegrates.

---

4 Letter from Max Horkheimer, originally in English, to Fay B. Karpf, 20 November 1969, in Horkheimer 1985–96, vol. 18, p. 746.
5 Letter from Max Horkheimer to Sidney Lipshires, 11 January 1970, in Horkheimer 2007, pp. 365–6.

In any case, after the deaths of Adorno and my Maidon, whom I loved more than anything, Fred's death is a blow from which I don't know if and how I'll be able to recover.[6]

Not only is medical science unable to cope with mortal illness, but neither is philosophy, whose task in this condition increasingly becomes to attest to the longing for the other, *die Sehnsucht nach dem Anderen*. Indeed, philosophy seems forced to give up, it has to face up to its own limits, to the limits of rationality and to those of the historical situation.

A few months before his death, Horkheimer wrote another letter from Montagnola to Herbert Marcuse. Previously in strong disagreement with him owing to their opposing views over the war in Vietnam,[7] he now hoped that he could see his friend again during 1973, despite declaring that he was getting older and 'more stupid' all the time: 'Let us hope we'll finally see each other well again in 1973. I'm already quite old and am getting more and more stupid'. Marcuse's answer from California was memorable: 'No Max – we're not getting more and more stupid, but this world is terrible and is becoming ever more terrible, "beyond our capacity of imagination"'.[8]

For all these reasons too, the problem of the other, also formulated as the longing for the wholly Other, *die Sehnsucht nach dem ganz Anderen*, assumed ever greater importance in Max's research.

Moving between his study and his bedroom, he not only got on with those complex and 'nocturnal' works[9] that go under the title of *Notizen* and *Späne* but, between other conferences, reports and interviews, in Montagnola he also prepared the German edition of *Eclipse of Reason*. Published under this title by Oxford University Press in New York in 1947, while Horkheimer was still living in the United States, the German edition of this important text of his was put together while he lived in Montagnola, coming out under the title *Zur Kritik der instrumentellen Vernunft* [*Critique of Instrumental Reason*] for Fischer Verlag in Frankfurt am Main, in 1967.

---

6   Letter from Max Horkheimer to Germaine Krull, 29 December 1970, in Horkheimer 2007, p. 365. See also the letter of Herta Dembitzer (Horkheimer's secretary in Montagnola) to Hannah Tillich, Montagnola 1973, Horkheimer 1985–96, vol. 18, p. 815 ff.
7   See letter from Herbert Marcuse to Max Horkheimer, 16 May 1967, in Horkheimer 2007, pp. 338–9.
8   Letter from Max Horkheimer to Herbert and Inge Marcuse, in Horkheimer 2007, p. 374.
9   Letter from Herbert Marcuse to Max Horkheimer, January 1973, ibid. Here I borrow the adjective used by Alfred Schmidt in his introduction to the *Notizen*, 'Die geistige Physiognomie Max Horkheimers'. Thematising the influence of Schopenhauer, please see also Horkheimer 1974, pp. xix–lxx.

In the second part of the volume, which was in fact the first German edition of the book, Horkheimer was set on publishing various of his essays and articles documenting the ethic-religious endeavour towards the 'wholly Other' with which he had been increasingly concerned (as also expressed in the interviews with Bettizza and in the Venetian lecture which were dealt with earlier). Texts such as 'Theismus-Atheismus' (1963), 'Religion und Philosophie' (1966) and 'De Anima' (1967), without forgetting numerous aphorisms in the *Notizen* and in particular in *Späne* on the topic, document the progressive explicit appearance of the 'theological' dimension in the later Horkheimer.

Also of importance in this sense is the interview with Horkheimer, made by Helmut Gumnior, on 4 February 1972 in his home in Montagnola and given the suggestive title 'Die Sehnsucht nach dem ganz Anderen'. Moreover, already at the end of 1959, upon specifically dealing with Soviet totalitarianism, Horkheimer had already been forced to write that 'true utopia is sad'.[10]

It is clear that this theological – and more precisely *negative theological* – slant, continuously centred around the Jewish *unrepresentability* of God and his constitutional absence, forms the other face of the critique of instrumental reason. This, in the sphere of 'state capitalism' and the 'totally administered society', seemed to have expanded into *totality*, leading to the exoneration of the individual, the annihilation of personal subjectivity, and a similar loss of sense plus all relevance of the experience of transcendency, the idea of God and theology.[11] But if totality presupposes instrumental-pragmatic rationality and constitutes its supreme expression, what other type of relation, what type of non-instrumental rationality would still be able to weaken, or even break down, totality in order to allow the aspiration to and memory of the non-identical to reappear? Was the relationship with (divine) transcendency, and the relationship with the transcendency-difference of every alterity from the horizon of sameness, *destined* to disappear? What relationship could there be between the endeavour towards the other, the wholly Other, and the advent of that totality of the identical? In their last fragments (*Späne*), Horkheimer and Pollock reformulate the task of critical theory in relation to these same questions:

> Wanting the Other, not making do with instrumental thought: this is where the human being begins. But the positivists indicate this behaviour

---

10 Horkheimer 1991, 'Wahre Utopie ist traurig', p. 312.
11 See Horkheimer 1972c, p. 166.

as a non-binding, private circumstance, an affair of art or religion. Less politely: madness.

But without God there is only instrumental thought. The autonomous subject who does not think in a merely instrumental way, like God, comes to lack function and disappears. Wanting to preserve it is romantic. Tillich sought to save both.

Realising that we have to desire it, but that it cannot be saved, this is *critical theory*.[12]

But how then can we think of the Other from totality? How can we not ruin-withhold its *difference*, without at the same time suffocating the longing for it? This relationship with the Other cannot be defined, and yet it forms the very presupposition for all critical engagement around *truth*; the bond between the same and the Other, which cannot be boiled down to an increase in knowledge. Indeed, it is not a matter of 'knowing more', because in reality 'we do not know enough'. The desire for truth must be recognised in that it cannot be reduced to positive and adequative knowledge, to *Erkenntnis* that tends to grasp its contents by identifying them with the tool of the concept. This knowledge that takes the Other to the conceptual categories of the same does not correspond at all to the search for truth: '*Erkenntnis ist nicht dasselbe wie Wahrheit*'. Parallel to this, 'the truth' must no longer be thought of as a figure or content of the 'will to knowledge'. This *Wille zur Erkenntnis* moves science and is satisfied by sociologists, economists, physicists and positivist 'philosophers'. But 'the truth' does not belong to any of them. It cannot be reduced to the representative intentionality presupposed by their own particular knowledge, each one convinced that to know is to fit the sensitive and fleeting contents of experience in a representation, or to capture them in a conception. But since the search for truth does not fit into the will to knowledge, it will have a different status to the tendentially solipsistic and monological character of representation. Its 'method' will therefore not be that of representation but rather *relation*. The truth engaged in an inappropriable and constant relationship points from the cybernetic laboratories of knowledge-calculation to the secret, noumenal movements of aspiration and desire: 'The truth is like a *Maitresse* who escapes from you if you do not continually devote yourself to her. Even when you have to deal with many other things, the effort around the unconditional [*die Bemühung um das Unbedingte*] must never-

---

12   Horkheimer 1988, 'Instrumentales Denken', p. 340, own translation, italics mine.

theless always remain in the foreground, in every instant'.[13] Besides, all the 'many other things' of the homogenous world of the *extérieur*, as well as all our know-how, feelings and experiences, are conditioned by our sense organs and our possibilities of apperception, as well as by society and the context in which we find ourselves growing. But for this very reason – Horkheimer observes – it would be pointless to note that as a consequence all our expressions are relative. Indeed, when there is something relative, there must also be the *Other*, that which is not relative. Of course, one can still object to this conclusion by stating that the very method of our thought only has a relative validity. 'Even Kant breached his own prohibition, to come out with the concept of the *thing-in-itself*'.[14] This is like saying that the Other, the unconditional, concerns us precisely in that it remains *Other to every phenomenon*, Other to every simple and conditional presence and to every reference we make to the presence of the present (re-presentation). To desire the Other, for this very reason, is *essentially* to feel its absence, to 'long' for it, in the world of the phenomenon and omni-representative will. *Longing*, the lack of presence, the impossibility of co-presence, desire as intentionality without the possibility of filling it, this *longing* is how the Other manifests itself, in an original way that implies a critique of the ontological-gnoseological primacy of presence. Longing, to express which Horkheimer takes up the concept of *Sehnsucht* from romanticism, attests to the departure of the Other, to its not being here with us, to its not being here with the same and as the identical: its undefinability which appeals to us as such, insofar as it is difference. In their *Späne*, or fragments, Horkheimer and Pollock underline this ambivalent condition, in which it becomes 'the very task of philosophy' to express the unconceptualisable undefinability of the Other, or, to use Levinas's words, its 'otherwise than being'. But observing that the Other cannot be defined and that at the same time, in its very difference, it constitutes the presupposition for all commitment to the truth, is like saying that the Other can be thought of with the Cartesian idea of the infinite, the contents of whose *ideatum*, as Levinas would say, exceed the thought of those who think it and hence forever remain *other from every finite being*.[15] With the idea of the infinite, thought enters a relationship with that which at the same time essentially transcends it and exceeds its conceptual-instrumental power, and which hence remains *Other* even in

---

13   Horkheimer 1988, 'Erkenntnis und Wahrheit', p. 249, own translation.
14   Horkheimer 1988, 'Das Andere', p. 370, own translation.
15   Levinas 1969, pp. 48 ff.; but also constantly with Levinas 1981 in mind.

the horizon of the same, where it manages to 'enigmatically', 'longingly' signify its infinite alterity.

Even if they do not take this step with the help of the Cartesian idea of the infinite – as Emmanuel Levinas instead would do – Horkheimer and Pollock repeatedly come face to face, like the French thinker thereafter, with the imbalance and the relationship between the infinite and the finite. Insofar as it expresses a relationship with that which by definition is neither present nor ever has been and hence can only be presented in the manner of a 'longing' characterised by a void, a lack, a distance, the 'longing for the wholly Other' puts across a wholly similar meaning to the one evoked through Levinas and Descartes' idea of the infinite, which speaks of an intentionality that neither is nor can be filled with its *ideatum*. The fragmentary character of Max and Fritz's later reflection, moreover, on no rare occasion seems to testify to the aporia – and in the end, the *aporia* is the logical equivalent to *longing* – outlined between this recognition of alterity, which cannot be reduced to the order of definition and knowledge, and the effort to express its sense without reducing it to the identical. The interruption of systematic and monological thought shows the critical tension prompted by alterity. It exceeds and relativises this thought in the horizon defining the identical, which must in no way be misunderstood as the horizon of truth.

In this sense, their *Späne*, *fragments* or *crumbs*, are such not insofar as they are 'impotent' or 'stuttering' thoughts. Instead, they are testimonies of a saying that tends to continually undo the finiteness of everything said, which, by subtracting and continually reformulating itself and returning, expresses the aporia-longing. The unilateral scientific objectivism, pragmatically aimed at making what is different the same and hence also enclosing it in a complete and systematic form of writing, must be compared with the existence of a non-representative intentionality. This, instead, is similar to what characterises 'works of art', those works of 'new', neither mimetic nor representative art which Horkheimer, on interpreting its secret pact with what is hidden as the critique of every codification-hypostatisation of presence, has always created a relationship with the secret of forms of life. Under the title 'Der Pragmatismus und das Andere' ['Pragmatism and the Other'] we read in a fragment from January 1968:

> The function of the intellect is conditioned by the end. At its highest level, science, it remains purely pragmatic. History is a collection of materials that can perhaps occasionally be used to look back on how human beings behaved in particular situations. Insofar as philosophy is a science, it is equally pragmatic. Logic and dialectic teach the correct way of thinking. All of this nevertheless has nothing to do with the truth.

> The difference between the world image, as it appears when it is seen by a work of art or by a scientist, points to the Other. This Other cannot be defined and nevertheless constitutes the presupposition for every endeavour towards the truth.[16]

In another and even more provocative fragment, entitled 'Anstelle Gottes' ['Instead of God'], we read:

> Instead of God, they worship the WC. The saddest thing about today's situation is that human beings are neither capable of nor have the will to imagine that there is 'the Other' [*dass es 'das Andere' gibt*]. For this very reason, everything that a responsible person thinks and does should be directed towards bringing this 'Other' to expression. What is this 'Other'? It is the task of philosophy to express it. It cannot be said in a couple of sentences, since the truth is the whole. Some words, such as Absolute, Redemption, Reconciliation, allude to this. This is what Schopenhauer thought. The great religions asked the right questions, but they allowed the answers to be bought with the explanation [*Erklärung*] that redemption can be achieved through the rite and that in effect it is already here.[17]

In other words, the original religious question (and *religio* first of all means relation) concerns the Other and the inability to reduce it to a finite answer: religion is the questioning that attests to the constitutional lack-question of the non-identical towards all that is present. Neither a rite, nor a cult, it is rather a *critique*, the delimitation of the arrogant expectations, of every historical determination of the finite. The 'great religions' respond in terms of rituality and theological – or onto-theo-logical – 'systematicity'. Hence they tend to make the infinite immanent, ruining its tension which instead at the outset was critical, and so it must remain, with regard to the claims of every essentially finite presence. In this path, there is no doubt that Horkheimer is also close to what on his part Paul Tillich, Protestant theologian and colleague, interlocutor and friend, indicated concerning the right way to conceive of the relationship between the absolute and the conditional, defining it as 'being on guard against the attempts of the finite and the conditional to rise in thought or in action to the dignity of the absolute'.[18] This theology, as a guardian tasked

---

16   Horkheimer 1988, 'Der Pragmatismus und das Andere', p. 465, own translation.
17   Horkheimer 1988, 'Anstelle Gottes', p. 215, own translation.
18   Tillich 1962, p. 85, own translation.

with defending difference, is expressed in 'the prophetic judgement on religious pride, ecclesiastic arrogance and worldly sufficiency with their respective consequences'. And this is confirmed and repeated 'in the divine and human protest against any absolute claim by a conditioned reality, even if the claim were to be issued by the same Protestant church'.[19] Similarly to the Protestant Tillich towards his own faith, Horkheimer and Pollock's religious contestation of the answers claimed by the 'great religions', as well as their continual being on guard so that no present, no fact and no definitive said should usurp the present absence of the Other, did not spare their own religion, Judaism, either.

This affinity between Tillich's critical and self-critical principle and the Jewish-based critical and self-critical critical theory moreover already appears in *Dialectic of Enlightenment*, where it is said that '[t]he Jewish religion brooks no word which might bring solace to the despair of all mortality. It places all hope in the prohibition on invoking falsity as God, the finite as the infinite, the lie as truth'.[20] In other words, Judaism is meant as the tradition of the Other, upheld through the prohibition against diminishing its difference or providing any representation of it by superimposing categories, images or ontological characters of the same upon it. Thought of in these terms, the *tradition of the Other* is meant as an essentially critical tradition, like the tradition of the critique of the same and its false absolutes. The tradition of the Other is expressed in a critical theory that always essentially remains self-critical too. In the *Notizen* we read:

> The Jewish prohibition against portraying God, or Kant's straying into the noumenal world both recognize the absolute whose determination is impossible. This also applies to Critical Theory when it states that evil, primarily in the social sphere, but also in individuals, can be identified, but that the good cannot. The concept of the negative – be it that of the relative or of evil – contains the positive as its opposite …[21]

And then:

> Any person that clings to the theological tradition in however tenuous a manner should also be sincere enough to admit that there is a contradiction between such loyalty and not just science but any form of thought that sees reality for what it is. … Theology is the opposite of knowledge, it

---

19 Ibid., own translation.
20 Horkheimer and Adorno 2007, p. 17.
21 See Horkheimer 1978a, p. 236, 'On Critical Theory', but see also pp. 232 and 199.

derives from levels of consciousness where perception was complemented by instincts, impulses and emotions which are no longer appropriate to contemporary experience, which is served by machines. Knowledge is ultimately governed by purposes. Theology wants to be free of earthly ends. It is both lower and higher than any form of knowledge.[22]

Taking a closer look, the critique of the superimposition-confusion between the two levels of the finite and the infinite[23] also seems to have implicitly oriented the first and paradigmatic opposition between 'critical theory' and 'traditional theory', meant in particular in its positivistic variant, in its tendency to give infinity to the order of things by dehistoricising and reifying it. This Jewish origin of critical theory subsequently became more and more explicit. It is again in the conference 'La teoria critica ieri e oggi' that Horkheimer on several occasions goes back to indicate the religious dimension. While religion has integrated doubt and given it great space, Horkheimer indicates it as an essential dimension to look towards in order to remove the presumption that the whole order of sense can be constituted through the domination of totality. *Totality* and *infinite* must therefore be recognised as the extreme poles of a critical theory which is confirmed as such, and which is far from somehow being simply reabsorbed in a metaphysical-theological suprahistoricity.

The *longing for the Other* testifies that the Other can now no longer be evoked except in the modality of longing, a modality that also implies suffering for the impossibility of the relationship with its difference, that is, the denunciation of its *banishment* from the current world. Beyond their apparent contrast, neopositivism and fundamental ontology are both an active part of this banishment of the wholly Other from the existent:

> Your mythology is what raises the existent to the one and all, to the one god, outside of whom there must be no others. The way you define science makes the scientist an official of the great dominating organisation. This is why today neopositivism is the characteristic of the reliable elite. The Heideggerian manner fits this situation splendidly. Indeed, it resolves the separation between philosophy and science in the conclusion that, as positivism has it, the latter should restrict itself to the facts. However, that is not all. In this division of labour, the artisan philosopher demands to cultivate the patch of being with the same objectivity with which the

---

22   Horkheimer 1978a, 'Belief and Knowledge', pp. 234–5.
23   See Horkheimer 1988, 'Das Andere', p. 370.

other professors cultivate the different sectors of the entity. But one and the other, both positivism and fundamental ontology – which in the end are the same thing – can get along with tyranny.[24]

Besides, if defined by their absolutist and totalitarian character, the latter no longer seem to know any bounds, and rather express the salient features of the global reality:

> That thought must not oppose the existent with something different, that it cannot look at it from the view of the wholly Other, that therefore theory in its own sense is not recognised, this is valid for Moscow no less than it is for New York.[25]

The recollection and longing for the wholly Other hence also implies a strong criticism of a historical, political and economic condition felt to be increasingly *totalitarian* and not open to difference. The prognosis about the advent of democratic/totalitarian state capitalism, meant in the ambivalence of these variants, constitutes one of the presuppositions of the dialogue of critical theory with the religion of the Other, one of the presuppositions for its critical longing:

> The 'doubt' must be enunciated. The denominations must continue to exist, not as dogmas, but as the expression of a longing [Sehnsucht]. Since we all must be joined by the longing for what is happening in this world – the injustice and the horror – not to be the last moment, for something Other to exist, we ensure this to ourselves in what is called religion. We have to be united in the awareness that we are finite beings. We cannot give up the concept of infinite developed by religion, but we must not make a dogma of it, and we must admit that we preserve certain past customs to keep that longing alive.
>
> There are two religious doctrines that are decisive for current critical theory, albeit in a modified form. The first is the doctrine that a great nonbelieving philosopher [Schopenhauer] called the greatest intuition of all times: the doctrine of original sin ... We all must unite our joy and happiness with sadness; with the awareness of participating in a guilt. This is one of the motifs that are characteristic of our thought. The other is a

---

24   Horkheimer 1991, 'An die Positivisten', pp. 299–300, own translation.
25   Horkheimer 1991, p. 300, own translation.

maxim from the Old Testament: 'You shall make no images of God'. And we understand it as such: 'you cannot say what the absolute good is, you cannot represent it'. ... We can define the evils, but we cannot say what is absolutely right. Those who live with this awareness are akin to critical theory.

The *'Führer'*, whether he is called Stalin or Hitler, presents his nation as the supreme good, he states that he knows what the absolute good is, and the others are the absolute evil. The critique must oppose this because we do not know what the absolute good is and it is certainly not our own or another nation.[26]

Significant in this direction of thought is what Horkheimer writes in a letter addressed to the Jewish theologian Otto O. Herz, as he deals with the funeral arrangements for the death of Theodor Wiesengrund Adorno and seeks to focus on his relationship with Judaism. Only Adorno's father was Jewish, and Theodor had been baptised a Catholic and successively 'confirmed' a Protestant. But beyond these biographical aspects, Horkheimer observes that the critical theory that he drew up together with Adorno without doubt has *its roots in Judaism*, and *derives* from it, and hence, for this reason, as well as his profound identification with the victims, Adorno too could be acknowledged as possessing a sort of *Jewishness*.

> On the other hand, I may say that Critical Theory, which we both developed, has its roots in Judaism. It derives from the idea that thou shalt make no image of God.
> That Adorno identified with the persecuted is proven by his declaration that no poem should be created after what happened in Auschwitz. Had he lived longer, and had we spoken about the funeral before he died, it is not impossible that the funeral would have been conducted in the manner suggested in your letter.[27]

In these observations, it almost seems possible to read an allusion to the fact that the critical theory not only somehow derives from Judaism, but that it also somehow *leads there*, in a movement not also lacking a potentially *self-critical* outcome. As we will see, within this intention to safeguard the difference between infinite and finite, and the undertaking to protest against all

---

26 Horkheimer 1972c, pp. 167–8.
27 Letter from Max Horkheimer to Otto O. Herz, 1 September 1969, in Horkheimer 2007, p. 361.

undue absolutisation-emphaticisation of the historical and finite, Horkheimer and Pollock's dealing with *Judaism* would assume further critical meanings, in particular going to touch on the Zionist interpretation of Judaism.

Before developing this important aspect, it is however appropriate to seek to clarify that the need to relate to religion, that *longing for the wholly Other* surfacing in the later texts, actually originated much earlier, as can also be seen in those texts forming the critical theory. It appears that what Habermas described as the 'conversion of the later Horkheimer in the direction of Benjamin', that is, in the direction of a messianic religiosity, can be seen not so much as a late conversion but as the expression of a relationship with the *tradition of the Other* already in action not only in *Eclipse of Reason*, but also in some previous texts.

5.2 Critique of Instrumental Reason and Religion

Already in *Eclipse of Reason*, the principle of *self-interest*, a foremost aspect of instrumental reason, was grasped as having a particularly penetrating *'intellectual imperialism'*, destructive of every other principle. This imperialism of the subjective form of rationality was in turn criticised as particularly bound to the *industrial era*: 'In the industrial age, the idea of self-interest gradually gained the upper hand and finally suppressed other motives considered fundamental to the functioning of society'. Evidently, in this historical-conceptual process, reason is forced to *'give up its autonomy'* and also to conceive of itself in *operative and productive* terms, and be realised as the *pragmatic coordination of means and ends*, in view of the fulfilment of interests and powers. To carry out this formalistic emptying of the idea of reason, '[t]hought serves any particular endeavor, good or bad. It is a tool of all actions of society, but it must not try to set the patterns of social and individual life, which are assumed to be set by other forces',[28] the hegemonic forces of the authoritarian state.

To highlight the *great change* with respect to the past that the advent of this *instrumental subjective reason* had brought about, Horkheimer underlines how '[t]he philosophical systems of *objective reason* implied the conviction that an all-embracing or fundamental structure of being could be discovered'. If we look at Plato – explicitly mentioned by Horkheimer – noesis left behind the sphere of *doxa* and every empirical contingency, and – '[a]s negativistic as his [Socrates'] teachings may have been' – the work of dialectic, as well as the

---

28 Horkheimer 2004, p. 7 and p. 14.

aesthetic-ethical disposition of those capable of *Eros* '*implied the idea of absolute truth*'.

The expression of 'objective reason', similar to that of *logos*, outlines the effort and capacity to reflect and express the objective order of reality, and as such fundamentally implies the capacity to *listen to it*.

> Everybody is familiar with situations that by their very nature, and quite apart from the interests of the subject, call for a definite line of action – for example, a child or an animal on the verge of drowning, a starving population, or an individual illness. Each of these situations *speaks*, as it were, a *language* of itself.[29]

The relationship with the objective-effective order is thought by adopting the common thread of listening and communication.

This reason 'was intended to achieve more than the mere regulation of the relation between means and end'; in the original sense it was speculative reason, that is, capable of *reflecting-manifesting-revealing* 'the eternal order of things and consequently the line of action that must be followed in the temporal order'. More than once, Horkheimer defines this reason not in a theoretical-intellectualist manner, but by implicitly adopting the common thread of communication, meant in terms of expression-revelation and listening-taking in. This non-instrumental reason not only brings us to encounter situations that speak a language of themselves, but develops through 'intuitions' and notions that presuppose and equate to 'revelations'.

The interpretation that Horkheimer sketches out of Socratism denotes the search for a *practical reason* capable of outlining and orienting human practice in neither subjectivistic-instrumental nor intellectualist terms, but in relational and communicative terms instead. In other words, he seems to lay down an essential and objective interpretation so that it will not be surpassed. He directs the investigation towards a relationship with a reality that seems to reveal itself, forcing the interpretation [*Sinngebung*] of subjectivistic-instrumental reason to flip and be turned into *listening* and relating to an alterity that 'speaks', that can express itself, that has a *face*.

'Socrates held that reason, conceived as universal insight, should determine beliefs, regulate relations between man and man, and between man and nature'; indeed, 'his teachings were put forward as objective intuitions, almost as *revelations*'.

---

29   Horkheimer 2004, pp. 8–9, italics mine.

Now, it appears here that, right from the early 1940s, Horkheimer's critique of the advent of instrumental reason implied his search for a relational form with alterity in which the other was recognised and listened to, and not immediately negated-overlooked as the subject moved towards his or her self-affirmation. Before the advent of the domination of instrumental reason, philosophy had understood truth in similar relational terms, in 'objective' terms, but where objective meant bound to alterity, that is, as manifesting or revealing otherness.

Against this background, it comes as no surprise at all to observe that according to Horkheimer, as a sphere of the manifestation of this objective-revelatory reason, philosophy arose with the aim of *'replac[ing] traditional religion with methodical philosophical thought'*. And in his view, to replace religion does not mean to negate and annihilate it, but instead to reconfigure and confirm it: 'when philosophy began to supplant religion, it did not intend to abolish objective truth, but was attempting only to give it a new rational foundation'.[30]

On this basis, it starts to become clear that the roots of the need to relate to religion, that *longing for the wholly Other* which constantly reappears in the later texts, including those written together with Pollock, actually originated in texts dating a lot further back in time. Horkheimer had dwelt on this in a short but important text from 1935, 'Thoughts on Religion' and in another, longer text from 1936, 'Zu Theodor Haeckers "Der Christ und die Geschichte"' ['On Theodor Haecker's "Christ and History"']. In these texts, it appears that the critique of the 'formalisation' of reason, of its becoming mere 'instrumental reason' set to then overturn and become a 'totally administered world' – a totality without a trace of the infinite and hence without difference, without eschatological endeavour and without sense – has in the end always and structurally implied a discourse on secularisation betrayed as abstract negation. The emancipation of religion – *Enlightenment* – should not have prompted a mere separation from and opposition to the vision of-listening to objective-revelatory truth which did not only belong to religion but also to ancient metaphysics. What it should have caused instead is an *overcoming-salvation*. It should have kept open the space in the relationship between the finite and infinite in order to recognise and welcome the other from oneself. In contrast, the Enlightenment defined itself as the human being's emergence from a state of minority, which otherwise would have weighed down on the intellect in its 'inability' to throw off the 'direction from another'.[31] Yet, without *being directed by another*, the intellect is the intellect of a finiteness which seems able to autocratically become infin-

---

30   Horkheimer 2004, p. 12.
31   Horkheimer and Adorno 2007, p. 63.

ite. However, in so doing, it is upset and turns into reclusion and domination, pathology, or even totalitarian paranoia. As the young Horkheimer writes, it is the intellect that plunges into 'thoughtless optimism' and ends up with 'an inflation of its own knowledge into a new religion'. But abstract negation and cancelling the critical legacy of the tradition of the infinite was not the only practicable route.

The text from 1936 is totally explicit in this sense, openly claiming that in genuine, materialistic anti-bourgeois theory 'the theological motifs are not simply forgotten, but nullified'.[32]

The relationship should have been set out in dialectical terms with regard to Christianity too. While certainly necessary on one hand, criticism of the historicistic-providentialistic implications of Catholic philosophy, which tended to make the non-identical immanent, at the same time should not

> belittle and hide the truth and the bearing of the ideas that are connected to Christianity. On the contrary. With the negation of the ideas of the resurrection of the dead, universal judgement, eternal life as dogmatic constructs, the human need for infinite bliss becomes wholly evident and comes into contrast with evil earthly relations.[33]

The dialectical negation of the dogma brings out its critical meaning, its antagonism towards 'evil earthly relations'.

In line with these assumptions, the harsh criticisms levelled by Horkheimer in *Eclipse of Reason* against the 'religious revival' and in particular neo-Thomism, intend to date back to Saint Thomas and even to Aristotle. They set out to cast light on how, along this path, religion lost its dimension of criticising the existent and its eschatological energy. By becoming formalised, it is reduced to a 'universal panacea', fraught with ideological effects. So Horkheimer says:

> The greatest defect of Thomism is not peculiar to its modern version. It can be traced back to Thomas Aquinas himself, even to Aristotle. This defect lies in its making truth and goodness identical with reality. Both positivists and Thomists seem to feel that the adaptation of man to what they call reality would lead out of the present-day *impasse*.[34]

---

32 Horkheimer 1968a, 'Zu Theodor Haeckers "Der Christ und die Geschichte"', p. 371, own translation.
33 Ibid., own translation.
34 Horkheimer 2004, p. 61.

Along this path, instead of acting as a guardian in defence of difference or as the longing for the wholly Other, it had become the religion of 'conformism' and of the assertion-justification of the existent. Hence, it had been reduced to mirroring what the positivists saw as the subalternity of thought to fact. It had ended up consecrating the inhuman order of the same.

This criticism evidently constituted the other face of a *critical-eschatological* understanding of religion which had already been in action in these texts since a period of the formation of critical theory.

From this point of view, 'Thoughts on Religion' from 1935 possesses a paradigmatic meaning. This is its incipit:

> The concept of God was for a long time the place where the idea was kept alive that there are other norms besides those to which nature and society give expression in their operation. Dissatisfaction with earthly destiny is the strongest motive for acceptance of a transcendental being. If justice resides with God, then it is not to be found in the same measure in the world. Religion is the record of the wishes, desires, and accusations of countless generations.
>
> But the more Christianity brought God's rule into harmony with events in the world, the more the meaning of religion became perverted. In Catholicism God was already regarded as in certain respects the creator of the earthly order, while Protestantism attributed the world's course directly to the will of the Almighty. Not only was the state of affairs on earth at any given moment transfigured with the radiance of divine justice, but the latter was itself brought down to the level of the corrupt relations which mark earthly life. Christianity lost its function of expressing the ideal, to the extent that it became the bedfellow of the state.[35]

And below, instead, are its conclusions. Here, while keeping the gaze fixed on the desire for a rebirth of practical philosophy and a nonconformist way of life, the dialectical nexus between criticism and religion is expressed in the clearest of terms:

> It is a vain hope that contemporary debates in the church would make religion once again the vital reality it was in the beginning. Good will, solidarity with wretchedness, and the struggle for a better world have now thrown off their religious garb. The attitude of today's martyrs is no longer

---

35 Horkheimer 2002b, p. 129.

patience but *action*; their goal is no longer their own immortality in the afterlife but the happiness of men who come after them and for whom they know how to die.

A purely spiritual resistance becomes just a wheel in the machine of the totalitarian state. True discipleship, to which many Christians may once again be called, does not lead men back to religion. ... Mankind loses religion as it moves through history, but the loss leaves its mark behind. Part of the drives and desires which religious belief preserved and kept alive are detached from the inhibiting religious form and become productive forces in social practice. In the process even the immoderation characteristic of shattered illusions acquires a positive form and is truly transformed. In a really free mind the concept of *infinity* is preserved in an awareness of the finality of human life and of the inalterable aloneness of men, and it keeps society from indulging in a thoughtless optimism, an inflation of its own knowledge into a new religion.[36]

5.3   Critical Judaism (beyond Identity, beyond Sovereignty, beyond Zionism)

The mentions of the totally Other that develop during the Montagnola years hence do not appear to be an almost unexpected, even contradictory conversion, but the coherent manifestation of a component that had in fact always been at work in critical theory.

The critique continues to centre around the aspiration towards the Other, towards its unrepresentable truth, different from all identity and presence, the aspiration towards the heterotopic disclosure of its alternative. From this point of view too, the Montagnola years cannot be seen as the period when a however 'stuttering' break was taken from the past path. Instead, it needs to be seen as a period of the expression of a profound characteristic of critical theory: its links to the Jewish tradition, increasingly evoked as the tradition of difference, not only beyond instrumentality but also, tendentially, beyond the theoreticist-cognitive and objectivising primacy of ontology.

Here Judaism is understood and sought as the guardian of difference, as a critical conception ready to touch on every emphatic, authoritarian-absolutist celebration of the historical, political dimension and of the finite in general. With regard to all undue and violent exaltation of the sovereignty of the finite,

---

36   Horkheimer 2002b, pp. 130–1, italics mine.

> [t]he Jews are the enemy because they witness the spiritual God and thus relativize what puffs itself up as the absolute: idol worship, the nation, the leader. The support non-Jews must look for from medicine-men the Jews find elsewhere. This is why their mere existence – the fact that they are "God's people" – becomes a stumbling block. They must be eliminated, and the more absolute a system aspires to be, the more urgent that necessity becomes.[37]

Horkheimer now again draws on the unrepresentability and unpronounceability of God, which he had already claimed to be the source of the negative philosophy of critical theory. He does so in order to *go beyond* the primacy of the representative knowledge that always returns to itself from being other, and to point his research in the direction of moral action, in the direction of acting *for-the-Other without returning to the for-the-self*. The critique of instrumentality demands a return to thinking of *proximity* as the possibility of a *being otherwise*, as the possibility of overcoming the subject's ontological self-preservation as the principle of the sense and conduct of Dasein:

> *Neighborly Love*. In Christianity, the individual was to overcome and sublate himself by devoting and surrendering himself to the neighbor and the lowliest out of love for the Highest. To save egoism by pointing to the 'as thyself' at the end of the commandment is merely a trick of sophistical theologians to ingratiate themselves with the existing order of things. The autonomy of the subject as the gospel understands it is the same as its *negation*.[38]

From the tradition of the Other comes the difficult prospect of a life beyond one's own, beyond the ontological-economic *calculation* aimed at self-affirmation. The critique of instrumental reason and recovery of *noluntas* as the ethic of alterity and solidarity, that is, the Jewish and the Schopenhauerian sources, entwine to give rise to a possibility of being beyond being, that is, also an attempt to respond to *On the Genealogy of Morality*.

And this entwinement between Judaism and Schopenhauerian ethics seems to preannounce the *Otherwise than Being* of Levinas's *Self*. Indeed, the direction of interpretation put forward here can almost act as compensation for the

---

37 Horkheimer 1978a, 'On Anti-Semitism', p. 131.
38 Horkheimer 1978a, 'Neighborly Love', p. 229, italics mine.

missed meeting between Adorno, Benjamin and the young Levinas in Paris in 1936 – the year that Raymond Aron suggested Emmanuel Levinas as a translator for the *Zeitschrift* to Horkheimer, although the proposal did not have any follow-up.[39] The problem of 'critical existentialism', matured starting from the youthful reflection in the 'Memorandums', is confirmed here in the redefinition of the subject, in the attempt to overturn its ontic-ontological closure. Confirmation of this can be seen in the restless and problematic character of aphorism no. 281 of the *Notizen*:

> *Forms of selfishness.* The good reactions of human beings, even those of the differentiated individual, are the fruit of learning, and serve in order to deal with the world to the advantage of the same person. However altruistic they may be, however much they put one's own life in danger and the lives of the others for whom the risk is taken, they are nevertheless borne by the impulse to exalt, to enhance the Self that is negated. Indeed, the more one's own Self is the immanent end, the better the action. The difference with regard to bad reactions lies in the type which is intended for the self. In the bad actions lies a narrow, rigid, tangible and obtuse Self; in the good ones, a Self that has poured itself into a life that has overcome the boundary between itself and the life of others. Reactions are the fruit of learning, and at the same time are the *truth* to which ultimately all learning must refer.[40]

By renouncing the philosophical primacy of ontological theoreticism, the plan of *action*, and in particular of moral action that places love for one's neighbour before one's own self-preservation, to the point of becoming negation, corresponds to the sphere of *truth*. This is the teaching that has to be absorbed, conserved and elaborated starting from the tradition of the Other. *Learning* – which conserves and goes beyond the Torah and Jewish-Christian civilisation to *universal practical-moral truth* – is necessary. Judaism prohibited the representation of God and even writing his name in order to make known that what is fundamental is not what God is like, but what humankind is like,

---

39 See letter from Adorno to Horkheimer, 12 October 1936, in Horkheimer 1985–96, vol. 15, p. 665. Raymond Aron also proposed Alexandre Koyre as a translator. Levinas was a complete unknown to Adorno, who distorted his name and wrote it as Levinasse. In his answer from New York on 22 October 1936, Horkheimer affirms that he thinks that Koyre would not have had sufficient time and added simply: 'I don't know Levinasse', 'Levinasse, kenne ich nicht', in Horkheimer 2007, p. 68.

40 Horkheimer 1991, 'Formen des Egoismus', p. 381, own translation, italics mine.

and how human beings act, that is, by crystallising or, contrarily, overturning their being in view of themselves.

In the words of Horkheimer, here very similar to the Talmud: '*A rabbi can perhaps say: leave my faith in peace, but do what is ordered*'.[41] And it is henceforth from this appeal to do that in his opinion a closeness should be seen between Catholicism and Judaism: 'Catholicism is much closer to Judaism than Protestantism, because in Catholicism action has a much more decisive role than faith'.[42] However, the most crucial thing that must be understood is that starting from these horizons, action is originally thought of as *action for the Other*, the manifestation of a being that is originally for the Other and not for the self, that does not aspire to return to the self. The figure of subjectivity that it gives rise to is hence not guided by Ulysses's cunning but rather by Abraham's heterotopic departure.[43]

In short, these religions seem to offer the outlines for a type of practice that cannot be reduced to the logic of instrumental reason. Nevertheless, what is decisive is that this type of action actually takes place, regardless of its foundation, whether theological or not.

Here the practical-ethical sphere appears as the critical truth of the theological and political:

> That something positive comes to me from this action for the other, from this dedication to the other depends on whether the other gets pleasure from this action of mine. It is the other's positive reactions, the pleasure over my action that makes my life more beautiful. Think of love and friendship. When the other is happy, I am happy too.
>
> So, it is not necessarily the thought of God that determines my action towards the other, that gives it that quality which we call morality. It can simply be the fact that my life, even when I have to sacrifice it for the other, is made more beautiful by the other's reactions.[44]

The pattern of goodness, as that which goes beyond the existent and intervenes there as *dysfunctionality*, is shown in the figures of the Self's distortion of conformist subjection, of *non-assimilation* and of *subtraction*. The infinite that is preserved as such calls the finite towards freedom, resistance, excess,

---

41 Horkheimer 1975, p. 59, own translation.
42 Ibid., own translation.
43 On the difference between Ulysses and Abraham see Levinas 1969. 'In describing liturgy, desire, and the work of art as ruptures of the Economy and the Odyssey, as the impossibility of return to the same, Levinas speaks of an "eschatology without hope for the self and without liberation in my time".' Derrida 1978, p. 95.
44 Horkheimer 1975, pp. 72–3, own translation.

critical negation of any authoritarian crystallisation of the order of the finite. The self-critical freedom of the finite, the radical nonconformism of a self that never returns to itself, is the ethical infinite, that is, its movement of permanent exodus in the face of all will to absolutise the finite. Nonconformist and beyond identity conceived of as a return to the self, the pattern of good is plural, it regards the multitude. Horkheimer is extremely clear on this too:

> Now let us come back to the point in which for me Judaism is so interesting: the identification not with the other, but with the others. I am interested in the destiny of the others, I know that I am a member of humankind, in which I will survive.
>
> When I think of myself, I think of myself as a member of this humankind.
>
> The martyrs, the enlightened of all times have sacrificed themselves so that others could live.
>
> For me at this point it is very important to again clarify the nexus with critical theory. The true social function of philosophy lies in criticising the existent order. This does not mean superficial quibbling over single ideas or situations, as if philosophy were a comical old thing. Nor does it mean that the philosopher deplores this or that situation taken on its own and proposes remedies. The specific task of this criticism is to prevent human beings from losing themselves in those ideas and manners of behaviour that society serves up to them in its current organisation. Human beings must learn to grasp the nexus between their individual activities and what results from them, between their particular existence and the general life of society, between their everyday projects and the great ideas that they recognise.[45]

If the presence of this sense of alterity that is realised as 'unselfish' dedication and *a fortiori* as self-criticism constitutes the Jewish moment of Horkheimer's late philosophy, it has to be added that this very same Jewish moment is also put forward as a strong critical warning against Zionist statolatric temptations.

To remain *Jewish* is not to change into persecutors, but to remain always and everywhere companions of the victims, that is, to see oneself in the universal community of all those who 'fare badly' and to *be engaged* so that in no place or time the horror, the most violent arrogance of a finite that rises to the absolute, may repeat itself. To quote Horkheimer:

---

45   Horkheimer 1975, pp. 82–3, own translation.

> *After Auschwitz*. We Jewish intellectuals who escaped martyrdom under Hitler have a single task: to cooperate so that the horror is not repeated or forgotten – that is, to remain united with those who died under unspeakable tortures. Our thought, our work, belongs to them; the chance by which we escaped it must not make our union with them doubtful but more certain. All of our experiences must remain under the aspect of horror that struck us, like them. Their death is the truth of our lives: we exist to express their despair and their longing.[46]

This community with victims is openly understood by Horkheimer as burdened with an imperative and commitment of *universal* size, where the relation of proximity with the non-identical should rediscover all of its sense and its meaning, which is by no means only formal:

> The Jews that remained Jews – who were made not the persecutors but the fellows of the victims – have evoked an inclination to sympathize with those that fare badly. Quite apart from the satisfaction that lies in being the one that gives, that stands higher, is the more powerful, there is not only unselfishness but also a sense of kinship in such compassion.[47]

As already hinted, the upshot is a tough yet important, and anything but simply depoliticised or resigned Jewish critique of the *State of Israel*. Not without, perhaps, a tragic far-sightedness:

> Through millennia of persecution, the Jews held together for the sake of justice. Their rituals, marriage and circumcision, dietary laws and holy days were moments of cohesion, of continuity. Jewry was not a powerful state but the hope for justice at the end of the world. They were a people and its opposite, a rebuke to all peoples. Now, a state claims to be speaking for Jewry, to be Jewry. The Jewish people in whom the injustice of all peoples has become an accusation, the individuals in whose words and gestures the negative of what is reflected itself, have now become positive themselves. A nation among nations, soldiers, leaders, money-raisers for themselves. Like Christianity once in the Catholic church, but with smaller chances for success, Jewry is now to see the goal in the state of Israel. How profound a resignation in the very triumph of its tem-

---

46   Horkheimer 1991, 'Nach Auschwitz', p. 417 own translation.
47   Horkheimer 1978a, 'Nietzsche and the Jews', p. 200.

poral success. It purchases its survival by paying tribute to the law of the world as it is. Hebrew may be its language, but it is the language of success, not that of the prophets. It has adapted to the state of the world. Let him who is free of guilt cast the first stone. Except ... it is a pity, for what was meant to be preserved through such renunciation disappears from the world as a result of it, as in the victory of Christianity. The good is good, not because it is victorious but because it resists victory. It must be hoped that the national subjection to the law of this world not meet as drastic an end as that of the individuals did [sic] in the Europe of Hitler, Stalin and Franco, and as it may under their overdue successors.[48]

Späne also expresses a wholly similar diagnosis, raising the thought on assimilation to evil to a bitter political reflection. And he places this reflection under the powerful title of 'Israel oder der Verrat', that is, 'Israel or Betrayal': 'In Israel what Christianity did on a large scale is repeated on a smaller one: from a people without power and without a land the Jews became a national state, similarly to how Christianity crumbled into nations, at war with each other'.[49] Judaism betrays itself if it believes that it can resolve the difference between finite and infinite in the form of a nation state, in the affirmation of its sovereignty which is made into an idol. This is the capital betrayal owing to which the same defence of the national territory always risks implying usurpations and annihilations of other people's rights.

Anamnesis of the deadly crisis of practical reason in functional totality therefore does not only generate *longing for the totally Other*, but is translated *ipso facto* into the attempt to critically re-elaborate, to go beyond the concept of the sovereignty of the subject and of the nation. This attempt, it must be underlined, does not only concern individual morality, but, again, in line with the dual reference present in the Torah, the collective and historical-political dimension too.

Religion and Society. In the Torah, the Eternal addresses the people and the individual by the same word. 'Love your neighbor for he is like you' refers both to the collective and the individual. In ascribing an individual soul to every person and thus differentiating it from animals, Christian-

---

48 Horkheimer 1978a, 'The State of Israel', pp. 206–7. On the contradiction between critical Judaism-Zionism also read the aphorism 'End of the Dream', Horkheimer 1978a, p. 221.
49 Horkheimer 1988, 'Israel oder der Verrat', p. 370, own translation; see hereafter also the aphorism 'The State of Israel', pp. 206–7, in Horkheimer 1978a.

ity made the individual the being that counted. Present Judaeo-Christian civilization would have had the task of bringing the two, people and individual, together, *whoever and wherever they might be, to love the other nations and individuals*, and to order the world according to the commandments. Instead, a society that is automatizing itself integrates the individuals as autonomous subjects and makes the collective, the nation first of all, into an idol. The Eternal and His commandments disintegrate.[50]

His last philosophical attempt in short implies the aspiration to relaunch not only a morality of proximity but also a critique of politics starting from proximity, a *politics of proximity*, where

> [t]he line of demarcation runs between respect and contempt for life, not between the so-called left and the so-called right, which is already outdated bourgeois antithesis. Cliques may fight each other where their interests demand it. Their true enemies are individuals that are conscious of themselves.[51]

The politics of respect should imply an essentially *relational* idea of identity characterised by the solidaristic recognition of alterity inside and outside the subject and nation. It should not idolatrise any idea of nation, identity or sovereignty, in a movement that goes beyond all rigid notions of property. The late reflection of Horkheimer, one can say, actually favours the individual moral question over the collective and political one, but while this may seem quantitatively plausible, one has to be aware of the fact that by proceeding as such, Horkheimer ultimately refers – in the wake of the Torah – to the collective sphere too.

Longing for the Other requires and at the same time asks us 'to live with open eyes':

> To be conscious of the untold, horrible physical and psychological pain, and particularly physical torture which is suffered at every moment in penitentiaries, hospitals, slaughter-houses, behind walls and in full view the world over, to see all this means to live with open eyes. Without such awareness, every decision is blind, every sure step a misstep, every happi-

---

50 Horkheimer 1978a, 'Religion and Society', p. 233, italics mine.
51 Horkheimer 1978a, 'The True Conservative', p. 230.

ness untrue. But happiness and truth, like truth and grief, are one. That is what Christianity means where it is not betrayed by its mindless adherents.[52]

As can be read again in *Späne*, Horkheimer hints at a passage between the destruction of the 'personal' experiential sphere and the relationship-solidarity with the persecuted:

> The decisive category is identification. Love is identification with the other, it is solidarity with those who suffer ...
> But with the destruction of the family, love is no longer experienced. Tendentially, the relationship between the genders is reduced to mere sexuality. ...
> In different times and with different peoples and persons, 'I love you' has wholly different meanings. In general, unless it is a piece from a work of art, language is incapable of expressing all these nuances. Here we could talk of the role of music to expand the possibilities of expression.
> The meaning of the myth of original sin should be portrayed. – The guilt of living. – The identification with the persecuted, martyrised, and assassinated, which should resonate in every thought.[53]

But with what language can this identification with the victims still be made to resonate? Language has become a tool at the service of automation, 'small talking', information, calculation, from genetics to cybernetics, homogenisation of every experience of difference.

Art, now music in particular, returns as a model of non-representative intentionality, capable of not erasing the nuances of the human, the possibilities of expression, the relationship with the infinite faces of alterity.

If, as is known, Adorno wondered how it could still be possible to write poems *after* Auschwitz, here we are invited to think that in the space of this *afterwards*, it only has sense to philosophise insofar as *listening* is allowed to take over from *theory*, *dialogue* from monologue, *proximity*, the very condition of writing, its critical truth, from positivistic and reified facticity. 'Objective reason' implies a communicative dimension, it must be seen as a moment of

---

52   Horkheimer 1978a, 'With Open Eyes', p. 222.
53   Horkheimer 1988, 'Stichworte für eine nicht gehaltene Vorlesung über das Leben', p. 319, own translation.

seeking *another kind of discourse*, capable of weaving together the sensitivity of art, intellectual work and the erotic tenderness of the relationship with the other.

On discourse (dialogue versus monologue).
1. Thoughts are not things that are simple to transmit, but they only develop in a dialogue. In order to come to a discourse, initiative is needed which can take the thoughts ahead.
2. A discourse (like thought) can mean:
   a) coin that counts (positivism),
   b) analysis
   c) science (knowledge of domination),
   d) copy of the best and critique of the worst.
3. Distinguishing two genres of discourse: the first aims at dominating nature and humankind. Here it is the right of the interlocutor to exercise an objective critique, to provide proof, to introduce contrary experiences.
   In the other kind of discourse, it is the indemonstrable, the extremely subtle; it originates from the longing for redemption, utopia, or the protest born from utopia against evil society.
4. A similar discourse is only possible on the basis of common suffering and common longing. Discourses between Jews have something similar. In this kind of discourse, there is no place for cheap, that is, unphilosophical objections (incongruency with what had been said before, contrast of the facts).
5. In discourse what is sought is almost always something different from the facts or from the indoctrination on them. If this is what is sought, it is better to follow a lesson or read a book. What should instead be sought is correspondence, a shared position towards the world.
   In the discourse on historical events, it is not only a matter of interpreting the facts, but rather also what we select from the infinite variety of facts and why we choose these ones and not others.
6. What discourse can mean: communication of data; creation of a correspondence of feelings; mutual stimulus and exchange of thoughts, or shared intellectual work, erotic pleasure.[54]

---

54   Horkheimer 1988, 'Über das Gespräch (Dialog versus Monolog)', pp. 291–2, own translation.

The denunciation of the destruction of proximity, also in the form of remembering those lashes to the face of 'the Jewish woman ... when she cursed [the Nazi hireling] as she, as entire swarms were driven into the gas ovens' – as incapable, like 'the devil', of 'lov[ing] the good that is impotent'[55] – is desperately situated in the path of the infinite, and seeks to listen to it in the cracks of a present that tends to rise up to the absolute, to totality of sense, while this same everything is simply false, it remains alone like the paradox of the absolutised finite. 'Das Ganze ist das Unwahre' ['The Whole is the Untrue'] is the name of one of the most celebrated aphorisms put down by Adorno in *Minima Moralia*. The *Sehnsucht nach dem ganz Anderen* from the Montagnola years must be understood against this same gloomy background, whose dramatic continuity with respect to the *annus horribilis* of 1933 Horkheimer still explicitly underlined in his last interview in 1970:

> I'd now like to speak once more of *longing*. You will perhaps understand why I am insisting if I refer you to an article from 1933. Then I tried to outline a world image of which today I have to change almost nothing.
>
> The fight, which extends on a world scale among the large groups of economic power, is conducted at the cost of the atrophy of good human values, of administering lies to the inside and the outside, of diffusing immense hate. Humankind became so rich during the bourgeois period, it avails of such natural and human means, that it could live in harmony and in the pursuit of worthy ends. The necessity to mask this fact of decisive importance determines a whole sphere of hypocrisy, which not only extends to international relations, but also invades private relations; it leads to a reduction in cultural endeavours including science, a brutalisation of public and private life, so that intellectual poverty comes to join the material poverty. Never has the poverty of humankind been in such strident contrast with its possible wealth as in the present, never have all energies been so miserably enchained as in this generation in which children suffer hunger and their fathers' hands handle bombs. The world definitely seems to be heading towards a disaster, or to already be there, a disaster that in the history known to us is only comparable to the

---

55   '*The Devil*. I have made a discovery: that the Nazis kicked the Jews to death, that the hireling who lashed the Jewish woman in the face when she cursed him as she, as entire swarms were driven into the gas ovens has its origin in the perverted longing for the kindness that has power – in the provocativeness of the good. In that lash of the whip lies the inability to love the good that is impotent, the despair that it has no power. The devil'. Horkheimer 1978a, p. 146.

decline of antiquity. The lack of sense in the individual's destiny, which had already been determined earlier by the lack of reason, by the pure naturality of the production process, in the current phase has risen into a characteristic sign of existence. Everyone is abandoned to blind chance. Hence this longing for perfect and consummate justice.[56]

While taking up the legacy of critical thought, it is up to us to ask ourselves whether, since its inception in 1970, this diagnosis – whose genesis and development have been laid out – has been belied or instead radically confirmed.

---

56   Horkheimer 1975, pp. 70–1, own translation.

Appendix: Figures

FIGURE 1   Max Horkheimer and Friedrich Pollock on a path in Italian Switzerland
PRIVATE ARCHIVE

FIGURE 2 The houses of Horkheimer and Pollock in Montagnola (Switzerland): colour painting, signed by architects Peppo Brivio and Rino Tami. The semi-detached layout shown here was not followed in the end
PRIVATE COLLECTION

APPENDIX: FIGURES 229

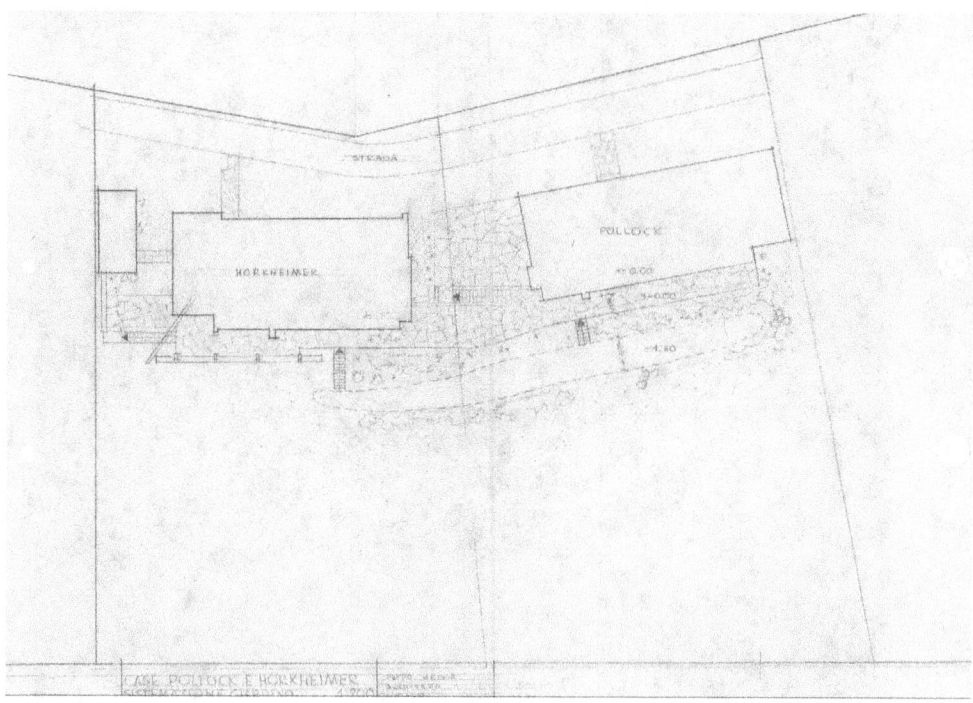

FIGURE 3 The final site plan of the twin houses of Horkheimer and Pollock in Montagnola (Switzerland), architect Peppo Brivio
PRIVATE ARCHIVE

FIGURE 4 Friedrich Pollock and Max Horkheimer, seated
PRIVATE ARCHIVE

FIGURE 5   Carlota Pollock
PRIVATE ARCHIVE

FIGURE 6   Horkheimer's house, photographed from the garden, still preserved in its original state
PHOTO M. PEUCKERT, PRIVATE ARCHIVE

FIGURE 7   Horkheimer's house and Pollock's adjacent house which, alas, has been completely transformed in a neoclassical style. Property speculation has nevertheless not aged to completely devastate the traces of the small utopia, still visible today in extremely proximity of the two hoses, as was originally planned
PHOTO M. PEUCKERT, PRIVATE ARCHIVE

FIGURE 8 Cover of the first English edition of F. Pollock's book, *The Economic and Social Consequences of Automation*, Basil Blackwell, Oxford, 1957

FIGURE 9
Cover of the second German edition of
F. Pollock's book, *Automation. Materialien zur Beurteilung ihrer ökonomischen und sozialen Folgen*, Europäische Verlaganstalt, Frankfurt am Main, 1964

FIGURE 10   Horkheimer's home, Montagnola (Switzerland), interior: Max Horkheimer's study
PHOTO M. PEUCKERT, PRIVATE ARCHIVE

FIGURE 11 Friedrich Pollock and Max Horkheimer
PRIVATE ARCHIVE

APPENDIX: FIGURES

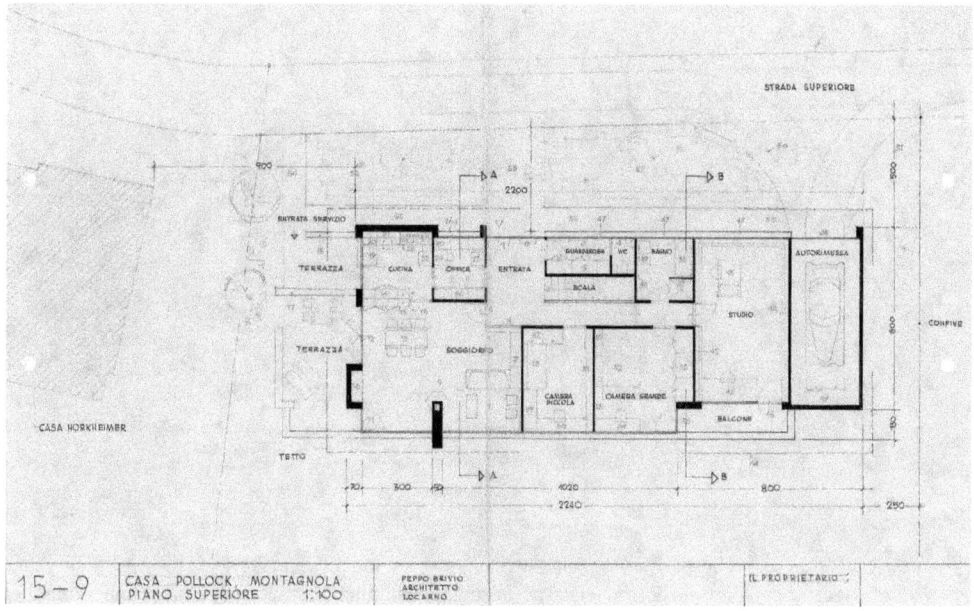

FIGURE 12   Pollock's house, Montagnola (Switzerland), architect Peppo Brivio, first-storey floor plan
PRIVATE ARCHIVE

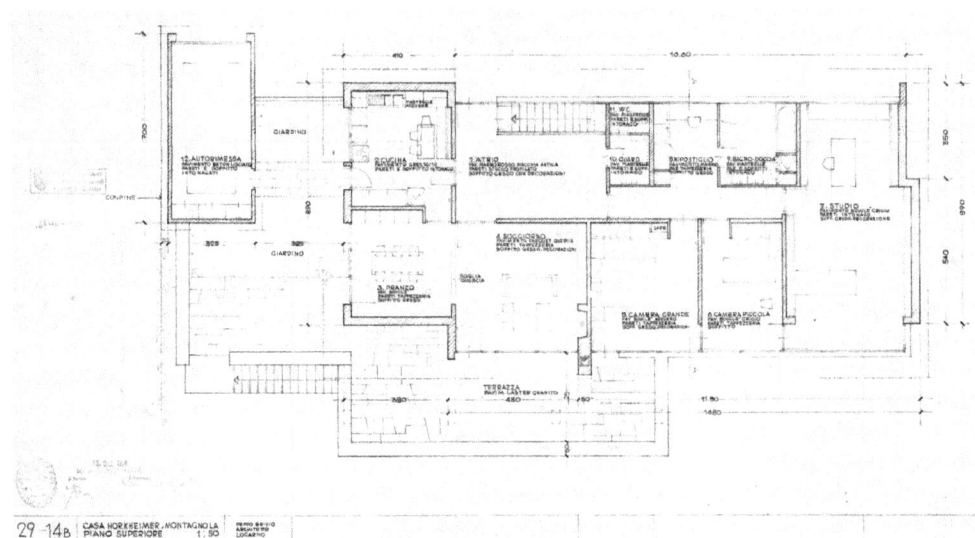

FIGURE 13 Horkheimer's house, Montagnola (Switzerland), architect Peppo Brivio, first-storey floor plan; second and final version, changed according to the indications given by Horkheimer. Note the garage moved to the left, the larger study and the doorway from this room to the small bedroom
PRIVATE ARCHIVE

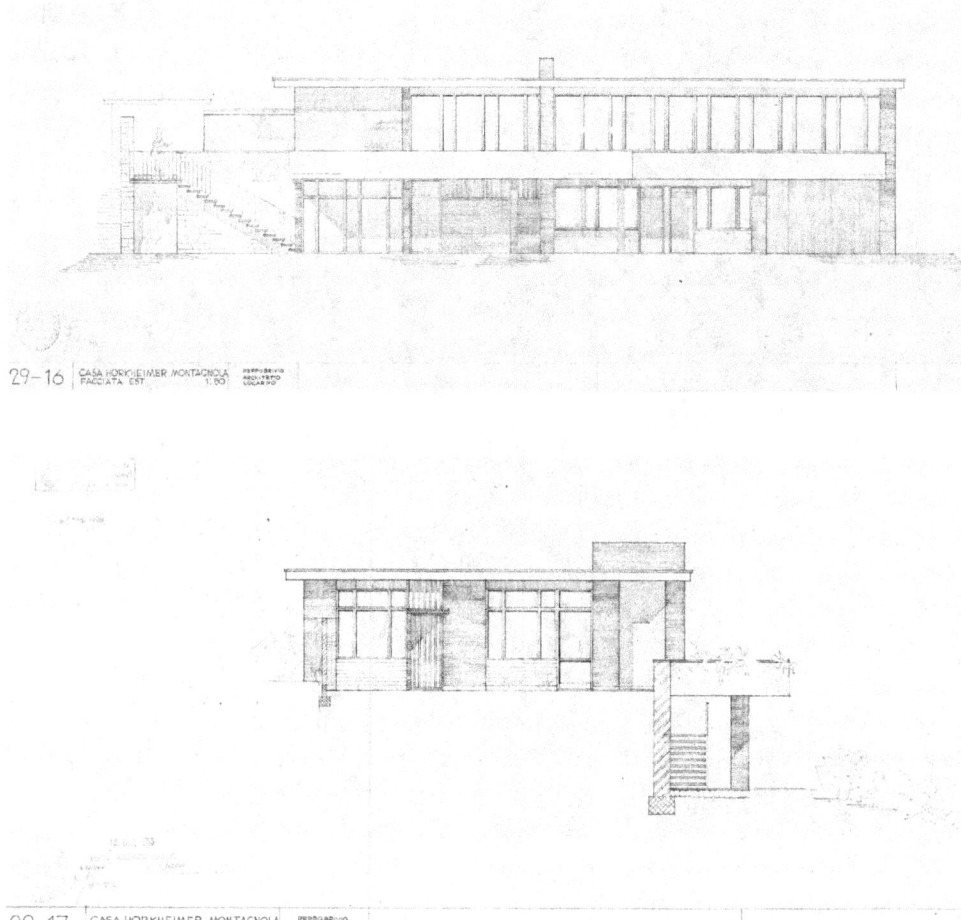

FIGURE 14 Above: Horkheimer's house, Montagnola (Switzerland), eastern aspect. Below: Horkheimer's house, Montagnola (Switzerland), southern aspect
PRIVATE ARCHIVE

FIGURE 15 Max Horkheimer with Carlota Pollock at a folk festival
PRIVATE ARCHIVE

FIGURE 16 Friedrich Pollock and Max Horkheimer at the carnival lunch in Montagnola (Switzerland)
PRIVATE ARCHIVE

Bibliography

Adorno, Theodor W. 1983 [1967], 'Aldous Huxley and Utopia', in *Prisms*, translated by Samuel and Shierry Weber Cambridge, MA: MIT Press.

Adorno, Theodor W. 2005a [1951], *Minima Moralia: Reflections from Damaged Life*, translated by E.F.N. Jephcott, London; New York: Verso.

Adorno, Theodor W. 2005b [1959], 'The Meaning of Working Through the Past', in *Critical Models: Interventions and Catchwords*, translated by Henry W. Pickford, New York: Columbia University Press.

Adorno, Theodor W. 2013 [1970], *Aesthetic Theory*, edited by Gretel Adorno and Rolf Tiedemann, translated by Robert Hullot-Kentor, London: Bloomsbury Academic.

Agamben, Giorgio 1999 [1998], *Remnants of Auschwitz: The Witness and the Archive*, translated by Daniel Heller-Roazen, New York: Zone Books.

Agamben, Giorgio 2016 [2014], *The Use of Bodies*, translated by Adam Kotsko, Stanford, CA: Stanford University Press.

Aly, Götz 2016 [2005], *Hitler's Beneficiaries: Plunder, Racial War, and the Nazi Welfare State*, translated by Jefferson Chase, London; New York: Verso.

Anders, Günther 1956, *Die Antiquiertheit des Menschen, 1: Über die Seele im Zeitalter der zweiten industriellen Revolution*, Munich: Beck.

Arendt, Hannah 2005 [1945], 'Organized Guilt and Universal Responsibility', in *Essays in Understanding, 1930–1954: Formation, Exile, and Totalitarianism*, edited by Jerome Kohn, New York: Schocken Books.

Arendt, Hannah 2006 [1963], *Eichmann in Jerusalem: A Report on the Banality of Evil*, introduction by Amos Elon, New York: Penguin Books.

Baumann, Erich [pseudonym Pollock, Friedrich] 1936, 'Keynes' Revision der liberalistischen Nationalökonomie', *Zeitschrift für Sozialforschung*, 5: 384–403.

Benjamin, Walter 1968 [1942], 'Theses on the Philosophy of History', translated by Harry Zohn, in *Illuminations*, edited by Hannah Arendt, London: Vintage Digital.

Benjamin, Walter 1986 [1919], 'Fate and Character', in *Reflections. Essays, Aphorisms, Autobiographical Writings*, edited by Peter Demetz, New York: Schocken Books.

Benjamin, Walter 1996a [1914], 'Metaphysics of Youth', translated by Rodney Livingstone, in *Walter Benjamin: Selected Writings, Volume 1: Metaphysics of Youth, Writings 1912–1926*, edited by Michael W. Jennings and Marcus Bullock, Cambridge: Harvard University Press.

Benjamin, Walter 1996b [1916], 'On Language as Such and on the Language of Man', translated by Edmund Jephcott, in *Walter Benjamin: Selected Writings, Volume 1: Metaphysics of Youth, Writings 1912–1926*, edited by Michael W. Jennings and Marcus Bullock, Cambridge: Harvard University Press.

Benjamin, Walter 2008 [1935], *The Work of Art in the Age of Mechanical Reproduction*, translated by J.A. Underwood, London: Penguin.

Campani, Carlo 1992, *Pianificazione e teoria critica. L'opera di Friedrich Pollock dal 1923 al 1943*, Naples: Liguori.

Cattaneo, Marino 2003, 'Peppo Brivio' in *Dizionario storico della svizzera*, Volume 11, Locarno: Dadò, https://hls-dhs-dss.ch/it/

Cicero, Marcus Tullius 1777, *Lælius: or, an Essay on Friendship ... With remarks by William Melmoth*, Volume 2, London: J. Dodsley.

Conconi, Piero and Graziella Zannone (eds) 2013, 'Casa Albairone di Peppo Brivio', *Archi. Rivista svizzera di architettura, ingegneria e urbanistica*, 4.

Derrida, Jacques 1978 [1967], 'Violence and Metaphysics: An Essay on the Thought of Emmanuel Levinas', in *Writing and Difference*, translated by Alan Bass, London: Routledge and Kegan Paul.

Dubiel, Helmut 1975, 'Einleitung', in Friedrich Pollock, *Stadien des Kapitalismus*, edited by Helmut Dubiel, Munich: Beck.

Dubiel, Helmut 2001, *Kritische Theorie der Gesellschaft*, Weinheim; Munich: Juventa.

Emery, Nicola 2011, *Distruzione e progetto. L'architettura promessa*, Milan: Mainotti.

Emery, Nicola 2012, 'Memoria e riscatto. Sulla topografia dell'eterogeneo', in *Città Metropoli Territorio*, edited by Luca Taddio, Milan; Udine: Mimesis.

Emery, Nicola 2013, 'Generiert Landschaft Kultur?', *Kunst und Architektur in der Schweiz*, 2: 71–3.

Foucault, Michel 1978 [1976], *The History of Sexuality. Volume 1: An Introduction*, translated by Robert Hurley, New York: Pantheon Books.

Foucault, Michel 2003, *'Society Must Be Defended': Lectures at the Collège de France, 1975–76*, edited by Mauro Bertani and Alessandro Fontana, translated by David Macey, New York: Picador.

Foucault, Michel 2019 [1975], *Discipline and Punish: The Birth of the Prison*, translated by Alan Sheridan, London: Penguin Books.

Frankfurt Institute for Social Research 1973 [1956], *Aspects of Sociology*, translated by John Viertel, preface by Max Horkheimer and Theodor W. Adorno, London: Heinemann Educational.

Freud, Sigmund 2003 [1920], *Beyond the Pleasure Principle*, translated by John Reddick, introduction by Mark Edmundson, London; New York: Penguin Books.

Friedmann, Georges 1955 [1946], *Industrial Society: The Emergence of the Human Problems of Automation*, edited by Harold L. Sheppard, Glencoe, IL: Free Press.

Friedmann, Georges 1978 [1951], *Où va le travail humain?*, Paris: Gallimard.

Fuselli, Enrico (ed.) 2009, *Agra 1914–1918. Il respiro del sanatorio*, Lugano: G. Casagrande Editore.

Galimberti, Umberto 1999, *Psiche e techne*, Milan: Feltrinelli.

Genel, Katia 2013, *Autorité et émancipation. Horkheimer et la theorie critique*, Paris: Payot.

Geninazzi, Luigi 1997, *Horkheimer & C.: gli intellettuali disorganici*, Milan: Jaca Book.

Gentile, Giovanni 1987, *Opere complete*, Volume IV, Florence: Le lettere.
Ginsborg, Paul 2014, *Family Politics: Domestic Life, Devastation and Survival, 1900–1950*, New Haven: Yale University Press.
Goldhagen, Daniel Jonah 1996, *Hitler's Willing Executioners. Ordinary Germans and the Holocaust*, London: Little, Brown and Company.
Grossmann, Henryk 1992 [1929], *The Law of Accumulation and Breakdown of the Capitalist System: Being Also a Theory of Crises*, translated and abridged by Jairus Banaji, preface and introduction by Tony Kennedy, London: Pluto Press.
Gumnior, Helmut and Rudolf Ringguth 1997, *Max Horkheimer*, Reinbeck bei Hamburg: Rowohlt
Habermas, Jürgen 1991, *Texte und Kontexte*, Frankfurt am Main: Suhrkamp.
Hansen, Alvin H. 1953, *A Guide to Keynes*, [s.l.]: McGraw-Hill.
Hegel, Georg Wilhelm Friedrich, 1991 [1820], *Elements of the Philosophy of Right*, edited by Allen W. Wood, translated by H.B. Nisbet, Cambridge: Cambridge University Press.
Heidegger, Martin 1962 [1927], *Being and Time*, translated by John Macquarrie and Edward Robinson, Oxford; Cambridge (MA): Blackwell Publishers.
Hesiod 1932 [c. 700 BC], *Works and Days*, edited by T.A. Sinclair, London: Macmillan and Co.
Honneth, Axel 2009, *Pathologies of Reason: On The Legacy of Critical Theory*, translated by James Ingram and others, New York; Chichester: Columbia University Press.
Horkheimer, Max 1934, *Dämmerung. Notizen in Deutschland*, Zurich: Oprecht & Helbling.
Horkheimer, Max 1950, 'The Lessons of Fascism', in *Tensions That Cause Wars. Common Statement and Individual Papers by a Group of Social Scientists Brought Together by UNESCO*, edited by Hadley Cantril, Urbana: University of Illinois Press.
Horkheimer, Max 1968a, *Kritische Theorie*, Volume 1, edited by Alfred Schmidt, Frankfurt am Main: S. Fischer.
Horkheimer, Max 1968b, *Kritische Theorie*, Volume 2, edited by Alfred Schmidt, Frankfurt am Main: S. Fischer.
Horkheimer, Max 1970, *Verwaltete Welt*, conversation between Horkheimer and Otmar Hersche, Zurich: Die Arche.
Horkheimer, Max 1972a [1968], 'Zur Kritik der gegenwärtigen Gesellschaft', in *Gesellschaft im Übergang*, Frankfurt am Main: Fischer Athenäum.
Horkheimer, Max 1972b [1968], 'Marx Heute', in *Gesellschaft im Übergang*, Frankfurt am Main: Fischer Athenäum.
Horkheimer, Max 1972c [1970], 'Kritische Theorie gestern und heute', in *Gesellschaft im Übergang*, Frankfurt am Main: Fischer Athenäum.
Horkheimer, Max 1974, *Notizen 1950–1969 und Dämmerung. Notizen in Deutschland*, edited by Werner Brede, Frankfurt am Main: S. Fischer Verlag.

Horkheimer, Max 1975, *Die Sehnsucht nach dem ganz Anderen. Ein Interview mit Kommentar von Helmut Gumnior*, Hamburg: Furche-Verlag.

Horkheimer, Max 1978a, *Dawn and Decline: Notes 1926–1931 & 1950–1969*, translated by Michael Shaw, New York: Seabury Press. Partial translation of *Notizen 1950 bis 1969*.

Horkheimer, Max 1978b [1942], 'The Authoritarian State', in *The Essential Frankfurt School Reader*, edited by Andrew Arato and Eike Gebhardt, introduction by Paul Piccone, Oxford: Blackwell.

Horkheimer, Max 1978c [1942], 'The End of Reason', in *The Essential Frankfurt School Reader*, edited by Andrew Arato and Eike Gebhardt, introduction by Paul Piccone, Oxford: Blackwell.

Horkheimer, Max 1985–1996, *Gesammelte Schriften*, 19 volumes, edited by Alfred Schmidt and Gunzelin Schmid Noerr, Frankfurt am Main: Fischer.

Horkheimer, Max 1987 [1914], 'L'île heureuse', in *Gesammelte Schriften*, Volume 11, Frankfurt am Main: Fischer.

Horkheimer, Max 1988 [1950–70], 'Späne. Notizen über Gespräche mit Max Horkheimer', in *Gesammelte Schriften*, Volume 14, Frankfurt am Main: Fischer.

Horkheimer, Max 1991 [1949–69], 'Notizen 1949–1969', in *Gesammelte Schriften*, Volume 6, Frankfurt am Main: Fischer.

Horkheimer, Max 1993a [1931], 'The Present Situation of Social Philosophy and the Tasks of an Institute for Social Research', in *Between Philosophy and Social Science: Selected Early Writings*, translated by G. Frederick Hunter, Matthew S. Kramer and John Torpey, Cambridge, MA: MIT Press.

Horkheimer, Max 1993b [1932], 'History and Psychology', in *Between Philosophy and Social Science: Selected Early Writings*, translated by G. Frederick Hunter, Matthew S. Kramer and John Torpey, Cambridge, MA: MIT Press.

Horkheimer, Max 1993c [1933], 'Materialism and Morality', in *Between Philosophy and Social Science: Selected Early Writings*, translated by G. Frederick Hunter, Matthew S. Kramer and John Torpey, Cambridge, MA: MIT Press.

Horkheimer, Max 1993d [1936], 'Egoism and Freedom Movements: On the Anthropology of the Bourgeois Era', in *Between Philosophy and Social Science: Selected Early Writings*, translated by G. Frederick Hunter, Matthew S. Kramer and John Torpey, Cambridge, MA: MIT Press.

Horkheimer, Max 2002a [1932], 'Notes on Science and the Crisis', in *Critical Theory. Selected Essays*, New York: Continuum.

Horkheimer, Max 2002b [1935], 'Thoughts on Religion', in *Critical Theory: Selected Essays*, New York: Continuum.

Horkheimer, Max 2002c [1936], 'Authority and the Family', in *Critical Theory. Selected Essays*, New York: Continuum.

Horkheimer, Max 2002d [1937], 'Traditional and Critical Theory', in *Critical Theory: Selected Essays*, New York: Continuum.

Horkheimer, Max 2002e [1941], 'Art and Mass Culture', in *Critical Theory. Selected Essays*, New York: Continuum. Essay originally published in English in *Studies in Philosophy and Social Science* 9.

Horkheimer, Max 2004 [1947], *Eclipse of Reason*, London; New York: Continuum.

Horkheimer, Max 2007, *A Life in Letters: Selected Correspondence*, edited, translated and with an introduction by Manfred R. Jacobson and Evelyn M. Jacobson, Lincoln, NE; London: University of Nebraska Press.

Horkheimer, Max and Theodor W. Adorno 2007 [1947], *Dialectic of Enlightenment: Philosophical Fragments*, edited by Gunzelin Schmid Noerr, translated by Edmund Jephcott, Stanford: Stanford University Press.

Horkheimer, Max, Fromm, Erich, Marcuse, Herbert et al. 2005 [1936], *Studien über Autorität und Familie: Fortschungsberichte aus dem Institut für Sozialforschung*, Springe-Völksen: Dietrich zu Klampen Verlag.

Jaeggi, Rahel 2018 [2014], *Critique of Forms of Life*, translated by Ciaran Cronin, Cambridge, MA: The Belknap Press of Harvard University Press.

Jay, Martin 1996 [1973], *The Dialectical Imagination: A History of the Frankfurt School and the Institute of Social Research, 1923–1950*, Berkeley; London: University of California Press.

Judt, Tony 2010, *Ill Fares the Land*, New York: Penguin Press.

Kerenyi, Karl 1963, *Tessiner Schreibtisch: Mythologisches, Unmythologisches*, Stuttgart: Steingrüben Verlag.

Kerenyi, Karl 1972, *Briefwechsel aus der Nähe*, edited by Magda Kerenyi, Munich: Langen-Müller.

Kojève, Alexandre 2014 [1942], *The Notion of Authority: (A Brief Presentation)*, edited and introduced by François Terré, translated by Hager Weslati, London; New York: Verso.

Krull, Germaine 1992, *La Vita Conduce la Danza*, Florence: Filippo Giunti. Unpublished autobiography of Krull in French, *La Vie Mène la Danse*, translated into Italian by Giovanna Chiti.

Levinas, Emmanuel 1969 [1961], *Totality and Infinity*, translated by Alphonso Lingis, Pittsburgh: Duquesne University Press.

Levinas, Emmanuel 1981 [1974], *Otherwise than Being or Beyond Essence*, translated by Alphonso Lingis, The Hague: Martinus Nijhoff Publishers.

Lotringer, Sylvère (ed.) 1989, 'How Much Does It Cost for Reason to Tell the Truth?', in *Foucault Live: Interviews 1966–1984*, translated by Lisa Hochroth and John Johnston, New York: Semiotext(e).

Löwith, Karl 2003 [1993], *Max Weber and Karl Marx*, preface by Bryan S. Turner, edited by Tom Bottomore and William Outhwaite, translated by Hans Fantel, London and New York: Routledge.

Lukács, Georg 1971 [1968], *History and Class Consciousness: Studies in Marxist Dialectics*, translated by Rodney Livingstone, London: Merlin Press.

Marcuse, Herbert 1979 [1977], *The Aesthetic Dimension: Toward a Critique of Marxist Aesthetics*, translated and revised by Herbert Marcuse and Erica Sherover, London: Macmillan.

Marcuse, Herbert 1991 [1964], *One-Dimensional Man: Studies in the Ideology of Advanced Industrial Society*, London: Routledge.

Marcuse, Herbert 1998 [1955], *Eros and Civilization. A Philosophical Inquiry into Freud*, London. Routledge.

Marcuse, Herbert 2009 [1934], 'The Struggle Against Liberalism in the Totalitarian View of the State', in *Negations. Essays in Critical Theory*, translated by Jeremy J. Shapiro, London: Mayfly Books.

Marcuse, Ludwig 1975 [1960], *Mein zwanzigstes Jahrhundert. Auf dem Weg zu einer Autobiographie*, Zurich: Diogenes Verlag.

Marramao, Giacomo 1973, 'Nota sul rapporto di economia politica e teoria critica', in Friedrich Pollock, *Teoria e prassi dell'economia di piano. Antologia degli scritti 1928–1941*, edited by Giacomo Marramao, Naples: De Donato.

Marramao, Giacomo 2013, *Dopo il Leviatano*, Turin: Bollati Boringhieri.

Martinoli, Simona 2011, 'Da Francoforte a Montagnola. La casa del filosofo. Intervista a Nicola Emery', *Kunst+Architektur in der Schweiz*, 2: 34–7.

Marx, Karl, 1976 [1867], *Capital: A Critique of Political Economy*, Volume 1, Book 1, with an introduction by Ernest Mandel, translated by Ben Fowkes, Harmondsworth: Penguin Classics.

Mikhaël, Éphraïm Questa voce va spostata sotto la M 1994, *Poèmes en vers et en prose*, Geneva: Droz.

Neumann Franz L. 1966 [1942], *Behemoth: The Structure and Practice of National Socialism 1933–55*, [s.l.]: Harper & Row.

Petrucciani, Stefano 2000, *Introduzione a T.W. Adorno. Interpretazione dell'Odissea*, Rome: Manifestolibro.

Pfeiffer, Ernst (ed.) 1971, *Friedrich Nietzsche, Paul Rée, Lou von Salomé. Die Dokumente ihrer Begegnung. Auf der Grundlage der einstigen Zusammenarbeit mit Karl Schlechta und Erhart Thierbach*, Frankfurt am Main: Insel Verlag.

Plato 2004 [c. 380 BC], *Gorgias*, introduction and commentary by Chris Emlyn-Jones, translated by Walter Hamilton and Chris Emlyn-Jones; London; New York: Penguin.

Plato 2012 [c. 375 BC], *Republic*, translated and with an introduction by Christopher Rowe, London; New York: Penguin.

Polanyi, Karl 1987, *La libertà in una società complessa*, edited by Alfredo Salsano, Turin: Bollati Boringhieri.

Polanyi, Karl 2001 [1944], 'Freedom in a Complex Society', in *The Great Transformation. The Political and Economic Origins of Our Time*, Boston, MA: Beacon Press.

Pollock, Carlota 1946, *A Program of Art Education*, unpublished typescript.

Pollock, Friedrich 1929, *Die planwirtschaftlichen Versuche in der Sowjetunion 1917–1927*, Leipzig: C.L. Hirschfeld.

Pollock, Friedrich 1941, 'Is National Socialism a New Order?', *Studies in Philosophy and Social Science*, 9 (2): 440–55.

Pollock, Friedrich 1957 [1955], *Automation. A Study of its Economics and Social Consequences*, translated by W.O. Henderson and W.H. Chaloner, New York: Frederick A. Praeger.

Pollock, Friedrich 1958, 'Altwerden als soziologisches Problem', in *Der alte Mensch in unserer Zeit*, edited by Paul Althaus, Kröner: Stuttgart.

Pollock, Friedrich 1964, *Automation. Materialen zur Beurteilung der ökonomischen und sozialen Folgen*, Frankfurt am Main: Europäische Verlagsanstalt.

Pollock, Friedrich 1975, *Stadien des Kapitalismus*, edited and with an introduction by Helmut Dubiel, Munich: C.H. Beck Verlag.

Pollock, Friedrich 1978 [1941], 'State Capitalism: Its Possibilities and Limitations', in *The Essential Frankfurt School Reader*, edited by Andrew Arato and Eike Gebhardt, introduction by Paul Piccone, Oxford: Blackwell.

Ponsetto, Antonio 1981, *Max Horkheimer. Dalla distruzione del mito al mito della destruzione*, Bologna: Il Mulino.

Rapini, Andrea 2012, 'I "cinque giganti" e la genesi del Welfare State in Europa tra le due guerre', *Storicamente*, 8: 1–16.

Ritter, Gerhard Albert 1989, *Der Sozialstaat: Entstehung und Entwicklung im internationalen Vergleich*, Munich: Oldenbourg.

Scafoglio, Luca 2009, *Forme della dialettica. Herbert Marcuse e l'idea di teoria critica*, Rome: Manifestolibri.

Schmidt, Alfred 1974, 'Einleitung. Die geistige Physiognomie Max Horkheimers', in *Max Horkheimer, Notizen 1950–1969 und Dämmerung. Notizen in Deutschland*, edited by Werner Brede, Frankfurt am Main: S. Fischer Verlag.

Schopenhauer, Arthur 2014 [1818], *The World as Will and Representation*, translated and edited by Judith Norman, Alistair Welchman, Christopher Janaway, Cambridge: Cambridge University Press.

Sennett, Richard 2009, *The Craftsman*, London: Penguin.

Thomaneck, J.K.A. and Bill Niven 2001, *Dividing and Uniting Germany*, London: Routledge.

Tillich, Paul 1962 [1928], *Gesammelte Werke*, Volume VII, edited by Renate Albrecht, Stuttgart: Evangelisches Verlagswerk.

United Nations 1948, *Universal Declaration of Human Rights*, https://www.ohchr.org/EN/UDHR/Documents/UDHR_Translations/eng.pdf

van de Moetter, Gerd (ed.) 1990, *Horkheimer und Italien, Dokumente, Texte, Interviews*, Frankfurt am Main: Peter Lang.

Vassort, Patrik (ed.) 2013, *Théorie critique de la crise. Vol. I, École de Francfort. Controverse et interpretation*, *Illusio*, 10/11, Lormont: Le Bord de l'Eau.

Vassort, Patrik (ed.) 2014, *Théorie critique de la crise. Vol. II, Du crepuscule de la pensée à la catastrophe*, *Illusio*, 12/13, Lormont: Le Bord de l'Eau.

Voirol, Oliver 2013, 'L'industrie culturelle comme diagnostic historique', *Théorie critique de la crise. Vol. 1, École de Francfort. Controverse et interpretation, Illusio*, 10/11, Lormont: Le Bord de l'Eau: 139–56.

Wiggershaus, Rolf 1994 [1986], *The Frankfurt School: Its History, Theories, and Significance*, translated by Michael Robertson, Cambridge, MA: MIT Press.

Wiggershaus, Rolf 2013, *Max Horkheimer. Unternehmer in Sachen 'Kritische Theorie'*, Frankfurt: Fischer.

Index

Abraham 228
Adenauer, Konrad 118
Adorno, Theodor W. vii, 6n11, 20–1, 33, 36n90, 45n, 46n130, 52n155–7, 53n158–9, 53n162, 55, 56n169, 57n172, 58n173–5, 59n176, 62n187, 73, 75n221, 77–85, 89–91, 92n35, 97, 101, 110, 111n92, 115, 124n117, 145n58, 146n62, 156n87, 159–61, 181, 194, 198–200, 206n20, 209, 212n31, 217, 223, 225
Agamben, Giorgio 31n78, 124n19
Aly, Götz 87n24, 96n48
Anders, Günther 115n105, 196
Aquinas, Thomas 213
Arendt, Hannah 68n200, 124–6
Aristotle 54, 213
Aron, Raymond 217, 217n39
Atget, Eugène 167

Balestrini, Nanni 139n44
Battista, Fulgencio 128
Baumann, Erich (pseudonym of Pollock) 111n93–4, 112n95–6
Benjamin, Walter 7, 7n19, 8n20, 23, 30n78, 75, 75n221, 132, 134, 145–6, 165n103, 167, 169n113, 186, 210, 217
Berberian, Cathy 139n44
Berio, Luciano 139n44
Bettelheim, Bruno 150, 150n73
Bettizza, Enzo 181–4, 190, 190n51, 201
Beveridge, William H. 94
Bircher-Benner, Max 195
Branca, Vittore 181, 181n27
Brass, Tinto 139n44
Brecht, Bertold 41, 75n221
Brivio, Peppo xi, 130, 138–9n44, 152–5, 158–9, 163–4, 228–9, 237–8
Burckhardt, Jacob 137

Campani, Carlo 23n63, 90n31, 99n54, 101n59, 107n78, 110n90
Cattaneo, Marino 139n44
Chagall, Marc 69, 70n206
Chamberlain, Neville 128
Churchill, Winston 135

Cicero, Marcus Tullius 22
Clairwil 58
Clement, Marcelle 14
Conconi, Piero 139n44

Dembitzer, Herta 200n6
Derrida, Jacques 218n43
Dobb, Maurice 99n54
Driesch, Hans 196
Dubiel, Helmut 42n120, 62n187, 91n34, 104
Duchamp, Marcel 164–5

Eco, Umberto 139n44
Eichmann, Adolf 117, 124–6
Emery, Nicola 139n44, 169n113
Engels, Friedrich 37, 41, 63, 80, 99

Filippini, Enrico 139n44
Fontana, Lucio 139n44
Foucault, Michel 31n78, 54, 61, 61n183, 69, 94n44, 96n48
Freedman, Paul W.H. 149n70
Freud, Sigmund 18–19, 29n76, 42
Friedmann, Georges 177
Fromm, Erich 36, 36n89, 42n120
Fuselli, Enrico 137n41

Galimberti, Umberto 115n105
Gans, Oscar 138n43
Genel, Katia 60n177
Geninazzi, Luigi 99n53
Gentile, Giovanni 66, 66n195
Gerhard, S. 150
Ginsborg, Paul 68n199–200, 70n207, 96n48
Globke, Hans 118
Gobba, Dudu 75n222
Goethe, Johann Wolfgang 73
Goldhagen, Daniel J. 96n48
Gregotti, Vittorio 139n44
Grossmann, Henryk 80, 90, 99, 101, 107–8, 180
Grünberg, Carl 21, 99, 107, 107n78
Gumnior, Helmut 6n15, 33n84, 34n85, 42n120, 140n47, 140n49, 201

INDEX

Häberlin, Heinrich   132, 132n31
Habermas, Jürgen   22n61, 24, 31n78, 32n80, 46n130, 118, 123, 150–1, 185, 210
Haecker, Theodor   212
Hansen, Alvin H.   97, 97n50
Hegel, Georg W.   60, 66, 66n196, 144n57, 156
Heidegger, Martin   8, 24, 26–8, 34–6, 133n34, 167, 169, 207
Hersche, Otmar   191
Herz, Otto O.   209, 209n27
Hesiod   19, 19n50
Hesse, Hermann   136–7, 169
Himmler, Heinrich   124n19
Hitler, Adolf   4, 39, 96, 127–8, 130, 132, 183, 188, 209, 220–1
Honegger, Hans   132–6
Honneth, Axel   22, 46n130
Horkheimer, Moritz   5–6, 9, 13, 34, 69n206, 132, 134, 138–40
Horkheimer, Rose Christine (Maidon)   27n71, 47, 129, 133, 138–40, 148, 152, 154, 158, 163, 163n99, 181, 197–9
Husserl, Edmund   81–2, 89–90
Huxley, Aldous   84, 91

Iofan, Boris   159
Isch, Gertrude   131, 132n31

Jaeggi, Rahel   31n78
Jay, Martin E.   21n56, 99, 101, 107n78–9
Johnson, Lyndon B.   189, 189n46
Johnson, Philip   157
Joyce, James   72–3
Judt, Tony   106n76

Kafka, Franz   81, 84
Kant, Immanuel   10, 26, 32, 36, 41, 43–5, 52, 57–8, 60, 165, 190, 203, 206
Karpf, Fay B.   198, 199n4
Karpf, Maurice J.   198
Kennedy, John F.   189, 189n46
Kerenyi, Karl   169, 169n113
Kerner, Justinus   75
Keynes, John Maynard   80, 96–8, 107, 111–2, 115
Kirn, Richard   198n1
Klee, Paul   69, 70n206
Koepplin, Dieter   70n206
Kojève, Alexandre   60n177

Koyre, Alexandre   217n39
Krull, Germaine   34, 151, 199, 200n6
Khrushchev, Nikita   128

La Mettrie, Jullien O. de   196
Landenberger, Christian A.   69n206
Le Corbusier   162
Levi, Primo   124, 124n19
Levinas, Emmanuel   viii, 203–4, 216–7, 218n43
Lipshires, Sidney   199n5
Loos, Adolf   163
Lotringer, Sylvère   54n165
Lowe, Adolph   81, 198n2
Lowe, Beatrice   198n2
Löwenthal, Leo   129, 129n27, 130, 131n30, 136
Löwenthal, Richard   187n41
Löwith, Karl   48n139
Lukács, Georg   107n79

Malraux, André   162n96
Mann, Katia   135n38
Mann, Thomas   135n38, 140
Marc, Franz   69, 70n206
Marcuse, Herbert   7n16, 16, 55n166, 74, 112, 112n96, 116, 177, 182, 187, 187n40, 200, 200n7–9
Marcuse, Inge   200n8
Marcuse, Ludwig   79n5
Marramao, Giacomo   62n187, 91n34, 107n79–80, 108n81, 111n91–2
Martinoli, Simona   139n44
Marx, Karl (and Marxism)   5, 16, 21, 35, 37, 41, 61, 62n187, 63, 67, 81–2, 84, 99, 105, 107–8, 112, 176, 179–81, 183–6, 189–93
Mattick, Paul   108n81
Mies van der Rohe, Ludwig   157
Mikhaël, Éphraïm   19
More, Thomas   19
Mozart, Wolfgang Amadeus   72

Neumann, Franz   4n6, 80–1, 90, 90n30, 90n32
Niemeyer, Oscar   157
Nietzsche, Friedrich   14, 18, 45, 58, 120, 136, 220n47
Niven, Bill   118n4

Orwell, George   178

Parmenides   156
Pedrazzini, René   139n44
Perilli, Achille   139n44
Petrucciani, Stefano   79n6
Pfeiffer, Ernst   14n35
Picasso, Pablo   69, 70n206, 72, 74, 159
Plato   12, 19, 19n50, 48, 144, 210
Polanyi, Karl   106n77
Pollock Weil, Carlota   47, 47n134, 140, 148, 231, 240
Ponsetto, Antonio   46n130
Ponti, Franco   139n44
Poujade, Pierre   130
Proust, Charles   73

Raphael   72
Rapini, Andrea   94n44
Rée, Paul   14
Reichmann, Eva G.   139n46
Reiniger, Otto   69n206
Ringguth, Rudolf   6n15, 33n84, 34n85, 42n120, 140n47, 140n49
Ritter, Gerhard A.   94n45
Rjazanov, David   99
Roosevelt, Franklin D.   97, 97n51, 105, 128
Ruskin, John   167
Russell, Bertrand   156

Salsano, Alfredo   106n77
Scafoglio, Luca   177n16
Schmidt, Alfred   191n54, 200n9
Schopenhauer, Arthur   viii, 10, 33, 58, 120, 144, 165, 200n9, 205, 208
Schüpbach, Hermann   132, 132n31
Sennett, Richard   164n101
Shakespeare, William   73
Simmel, Georg   31n78
Socrates   48, 210–1
Solti, Georg   78
Speer, Albert   159
Spengler, Oswald   135

Spinoza, Baruch   10
Stalin, Joseph   130
Strasser, Otto   130
Strauss, Richard   78
Suze (Neumeier, Suzanne)   1, 8, 10–3, 11n25, 16–7

Tami, Rino   139n44, 228
Thomaneck, J.K.A.   118n4
Thrasymachus   48
Tillich, Hannah   200n6
Tillich, Paul   202, 205–6
Toynbee, Arnold   175
Tugendhat, Ernst   31n78

Ulysses   218, 218n43

van de Moetter, Gerd   75n222, 120n8, 181n27, 184n33–4, 190n51
Vassort, Patrick   60n177
Voirol, Olivier   60n177
von Haug, Robert   69n206
von Martin, Alfred   136, 137n40
von Ribbentrop, Joachim   130
von Salomé, Lou   14

Walter, Emil J.   173
Warhol, Andy   165
Weber, Max   48–9, 85, 191
Weil, Felix   21, 84, 84n16, 140, 179, 179n22
Weill-Strauss, Eugen   138, 138n43
Weischedel, Wilhelm   152, 152n80
Wiener, Norbert   177
Wiesengrund, Theodor   209
Wiggershaus, Rolf   5n8, 6n15, 10n23, 12n29, 20n54, 36n89, 38n100, 46n130, 47n135, 101n59, 107n78, 118, 122–3, 129n26, 150, 150n72, 187n39
Wilson, Harold   175, 175n9
Wipf, Edwin   137n40
Wittgenstein, Ludwig   31n78

www.ingramcontent.com/pod-product-compliance
Lightning Source LLC
Chambersburg PA
CBHW071233070526
44583CB00017B/2168